# WAR WITHOUT END

# WAR WITHOUT ✦ END ✦

The Story of Michel T. Halbouty's Struggle
for American Energy Security

Jack Donahue

Gulf Publishing Company
Houston, London, Paris, Zurich, Tokyo

# WAR WITHOUT END

By The Same Author—

*Someone To Hate*
*The Confessor*
*Erase My Name*
*Divorce American Style*
*Pray to the Hustlers' God*
*The Lady Loved Too Well*
*Grady Barr* (With Michel T. Halbouty)
*Wildcatter*
*The Finest in the Land*
*Hack Donavon of* The Press

Copyright © 1990 by Gulf Publishing Company, Houston, Texas. All rights reserved. Printed in the United States of America. This book, or parts thereof, may not be reproduced in any form without permission of the publisher.

**Library of Congress Cataloging-in-Publication Data**
Donahue, Jack.
  War without end: Michel T. Halbouty's fight for American energy security/Jack Donahue.
      p.  cm.
  **ISBN 0-87201-921-7**
  1. Petroleum industry and trade—Government policy—United States.  2. Petroleum—Reserves—Government policy—United States.  3. Energy policy—United States.  4. Halbouty, Michel Thomas, 1909-        .
I. Title.
HD9566.D66   1990
338.79′092—dc20                                          89-49209
                                                              CIP

# PREFACE

In 1979 I wrote *Wildcatter (The Story of Michel T. Halbouty and the Search for Oil)*. It was well received, and I was pleased that some critics saw it as more than a personal story, viewing it as a vivid history of the petroleum industry beginning in the 1930s.

I had written what I hoped would be an exciting true story of one of the most active and daring independent oilmen on the petroleum scene. At the same time I got caught up in chronicling his tireless efforts to awaken his fellow Americans and their leaders to the ever-growing danger of the country's over-reliance on foreign oil. Indeed, it was that portion of the book that drew the strongest comments from some critics.

The manuscript of the book you now hold in your hand was delivered to the publisher on June 21, 1987, coincidentally Michel Halbouty's 78th birthday. By 1979 and publication of *Wildcatter*, Halbouty already had won world-wide respect as an earth scientist. In the years following, his advice on petroleum matters was sought by many nations around the globe. For example, it was at his encouragement and insistence that energy officials of the People's Republic of China drilled to greater depths in the remote Northwest Provinces and were successful on their first deep test well.

Meanwhile, Halbouty had continued to wage war against governmental ineptitude, lack of a viable energy policy, and the public apathy that he saw as leading America into the grave danger of becoming a second-rate country.

On this day—his birthday—Halbouty was still going strong, planning more trips to faraway places, more trips to Washington—trying as always to do whatever possible to benefit his country, the petroleum industry, and the professions he represents.

*Jack Donahue*
Houston, Texas

# CHAPTER ONE

Let's set the stage.

The place was the huge convention room of the Ambassador Hotel in Los Angeles where delegates to the annual meeting of the American Association of Petroleum Geologists (AAPG) had gathered.

The time was November 3, 1960.

The speaker was Michel T. Halbouty of Houston, a respected geologist and petroleum engineer who, in years to come, would gain world-wide recognition both as an earth scientist and as a petroleum industry spokesman.

His remarks were sobering, perhaps frightening to those in the packed hall who glimpsed his dark vision of the future. The international oil companies were flooding the United States with foreign oil, Halbouty said, while domestic oil production was dwindling and the search for reserves by exploratory drilling was practically at a stand-still. America was losing the capacity to sustain herself if the necessity arose.

The Suez Crisis, he said, was proof enough that foreign governments, by deliberate action, could deny the U.S. the use of foreign oil. It was obvious to him, he declared, that if the country became dependent on foreign sources, her security and peacetime welfare would be at the mercy of others.

And he issued a warning, with the tongue of prophets:

> I want to end this presentation by making it perfectly clear that, in my opinion, this country is reaching toward a severe economic crisis, as well as an imposition on our national security, by our not doing everything possible to increase our domestic production now.

To continue along the downhill exploratory curve we are now experiencing will surely result in economic chaos. The impact of an energy shortage in this country would be absolutely disastrous.

Unless there is an appreciable and sustained turn-around in our exploratory activities, I can safely predict that between now and 1975 we will have an energy crisis in this country that will cause repercussions throughout the width and breadth of this great nation of ours like a devastating earthquake.

It is appalling to me that the American people can be so apathetic to what is so obvious to some of us in the industry. The people of this country just don't care. They are not experiencing shortages now, and evidently they care less about what will happen in the future.

Some of these days the shortage will catch up with us, and then the people will say, 'The industry is to blame. Why weren't we told?'

Well, I'm telling 'em now!

\*\*\*

Less than two months earlier representatives from five countries responsible for 80% of the world's exports of oil had met in the historic city of Baghdad to form the Organization of Petroleum Exporting Countries, or simply OPEC. The countries were Venezuela, Saudi Arabia, Iran, Iraq, and Kuwait.

The delegates were in a bitter mood. The seven major companies comprising the international oil cartel had cut the pittance they paid the countries for their oil by ten cents per barrel, and without prior discussion. The delegates resolved to fight for restoration of the old price.

They didn't win. The major companies snorted in derision at their effrontery, then proceeded to ignore them. The rest of the world was hardly aware of the organization.

But OPEC didn't wither away as predicted. As time passed it added eight members. And while it remained relatively impotent, it had, by 1971, gained price increases that found their crude bringing $3.30 per barrel.

But in the autumn of 1973, while war raged in the Middle East, Saudi Arabia declared an embargo on all oil to the U.S. and the Netherlands. And while the world was still quaking from this shock,

OPEC ministers met in Teheran and kicked the price of crude to $11.65 per barrel, almost quadrupling the posted price set in April 1971!

The underdogs were now the top dogs—and they had the world's attention!

\*\*\*

In the U.S. the winter of 1973–74 was long and cold and tempers were short and hot. Angry and bewildered Americans waited in long lines to buy gasoline at ever-increasing prices. A short but savage natural gas shortage—never explained to the public's satisfaction—sent utility bills skyrocketing in tandem with gasoline prices.

Meanwhile, newspaper wire service editors had found stories of Michel Halbouty's 1960 prediction in their files, and "up-date" stories were sent across the country to newspapers and radio and television stations. Some of the story headings read:

"GEOLOGIST'S WARNINGS
ARE NOW COMING TRUE"

"ARTICULATE INDEPENDENT
FORECAST ENERGY CRISIS"

"SPEECH 13 YEARS AGO
PREDICTED FUEL CRISIS"

"OIL CRISIS FORESEEN"

"HALBOUTY CAN NOW SAY:
'I TOLD YOU SO IN '60' "

The Michel Halbouty who had addressed the AAPG convention back in 1960 was no stranger to the podium. He was a formidable orator with a commanding presence and a voice as resonant as a cathedral organ. And because he generally was deeply concerned with his subject, his speeches were charged with a passionate conviction. "He may not always be right," said an admiring oilman, "but he's never in doubt." Said another, "I'd walk across a hot pavement barefooted just to hear the son of a bitch describe a handshake."

He was a slender, handsome man with glossy black hair and eyebrows and moustache to match. He was sharp-featured. His bold black eyes gleamed, and his perpetual tan was an inheritance from his Lebanese ancestors. He was as comfortable in a fashionable suit as he was in oilfield boots and khakis.

Halbouty came to a modest fame early. After a brilliant scholastic career at Texas A&M University, he was credited with discovering the High Island, Texas oilfield only six weeks after his graduation. It was the beginning of a rewarding career as a wildcatter and producer—an independent oilman.

As he became more successful in finding oil, he grew in demand as a speaker before geological and petroleum engineering groups. He was, in fact, a lecturer, sharing the excitement of discovery with his listeners, offering bold new theories, exciting their interest in their professions. And because he believed that the wildcatters and "creekologists" of the past were more colorful, and more American, than the cowboy of the Old West, his talks were loaded with high adventure and love of the land they all had studied.

But something occurred in the late 1950s that caused a decided change in the thrust of his speeches and, indeed, in the course of his life. Halbouty and Pan American Petroleum Corporation had discovered and were beginning to exploit a rich gas and condensate field in the Port Acres area in Jefferson County, Texas. Word of their success brought a flock of promoters and oilmen on the run. They immediately began leasing up town lots in Port Acres whether the lot was vacant or held some kind of structure.

Some of the town lots were as small as two-tenths of an acre. Those who leased them went to the Texas Railroad Commission, the regulatory agency overseeing the state's oil and gas industry, for "exceptions" to Rule 37, which prohibited the drilling of a well within 300 feet of a completed well or one being drilled, and within 350 feet of a property line.

In every instance, the Commission granted the exceptions.

Now, the Commission earlier had fixed 160 acres as the size of producing units in the field—one well per 160 acres. With the granting of the exceptions, it was breaking its own rule. Every town lot operator, it was saying, could drill a well on his town lot whatever its size.

It was obvious that the town lots, comprising only 5% of the field, would be producing as much as 40% of the gas and condensate! It was equally obvious that such over-drilling could result in the loss forever of millions of barrels of rich condensate.

Halbouty asked the Commission to re-think its position. And he asked whether recycling of the gas to promote better recovery of the condensate should be conducted.

The Commission refused to halt drilling of the town lots. It refused to demand recycling. And it refused to change its allocation formula for the field, as Halbouty had recommended.

Halbouty sued the Commission, knowing that if he won he would lose millions of dollars in the re-allocation of reserves. The court upheld the Commission, saying it could not deprive an owner of his vested right to recover the oil and gas under his land.

Halbouty appealed; the appellate court said the lower court had made the correct decision. By now 22 wells had been drilled on 21.3 surface acres, and there were 500 town lots waiting for the drill.

Halbouty took his case to the Texas Supreme Court, and to the people. He spoke everywhere he could get an audience—before oil groups, PTAs, Lions, Rotarians, Elks, Chambers of Commerce. He offered what he considered an ideal formula for the field and suggestions he said would bring about "total conservation" of the state's petroleum resources.

By an 8-1 margin, the Supreme Court upheld Halbouty. It said the Port Acres allocation formula was invalid in that it "does not afford an opportunity for all parties to produce and save their fair share of the minerals or their equivalent." The town lot operators had drilled at their own risk, said the Court, but they should be allowed to recoup their expenses and make a reasonable profit.

The Commission bent to the Court's judgment.

Halbouty's "ideal formula" for producing the field—accepted and installed by the Commission—cost Halbouty an estimated $2.3 million in lost reserves. "That's a lot of money to pay for a principle," said Judge Frank P. Culvert, who wrote the Court's 8-1 decision.

Most of the town lot operators quickly pooled their holdings into 160-acre drilling units, with one well doing the job of many. Field pressure was thus maintained. The remaining few got back their investments and a small profit.

The Commission overhauled the improved field regulations statewide. The Texas Legislature then enacted statutes making pooling mandatory.

These measures did not provide "total conservation," but they were steps toward it. Halbouty's successful fight against unnecessary drilling had enhanced the cause of conservation and helped save the state's oil and gas reserves—and revenues.

\*\*\*

Halbouty had seen much waste of oil and gas in fields as he had traveled the state during the "Battle of Port Acres." This was on his mind as he prepared the speech he was to deliver before the AAPG convention in Los Angeles on November 3, 1960. After his talks and lawsuit, the Railroad Commission had moved to eliminate much of the waste. Perhaps now he could talk the American people into looking into the future with him, he thought. Perhaps the terrible situation he foresaw could be avoided if he could awaken them. He was determined to try.

We know now that he went unheeded. But he had traversed the country during the 13 years between his Los Angeles speech and the Arab embargo, preaching his sermon to anyone who listened, spending his time and his money in the effort.

But he had too much imagination, too much intellectual curiosity, and too much love for his profession to be completely absorbed by his crusade. So he spoke on other subjects, tried to find new fields.

He became fascinated with Alaska. There were few geological references on the vast territory, but he studied them all. He hired a bush pilot in Anchorage and was flown over the entire territory, leaning out the cockpit to photograph every phase that interested him. He returned home convinced that a treasure trove of oil and gas lay beneath the rugged terrain.

Halbouty spoke before interested groups, telling them of the wonders he had seen and touting Alaska as the next great petroleum province. And he put his money where his mouth was by forming a company, Halbouty Alaska Oil Company (Halasko), and vowing to be the first independent to test the land.

While he was readying his effort, Richfield Oil Company, with the only oil drilling rig in Alaska, discovered the Swanson River field on the Kenai Peninsula at Cook Inlet. Halbouty was right behind Richfield, setting up his rig (he personally supervised its shipment from Long Beach, California to Alaska) on his own leased acreage 4½ miles from the Richfield discovery well.

He got a dry hole; he was less than one quarter mile outside the limits of the field, later development showed.

After drilling more dry holes in the Kenai region, he leased his rig to other companies and one, Union Oil Company of California, used it to discover the great Kenai gas field.

Halbouty would not give up. He had lost most of his acreage, but he moved the rig to a lease at West Fork, about 7 miles from the Swanson River field. He proceeded to drill the deepest well drilled in Alaska to this point, a 14,000-foot bore-hole with a gas producing sand just below 5,000 feet.

Eighteen years would pass before the rising price of gas would make the well an economic asset. But during those years he returned to Alaska time after time. Those who followed him—the major companies—uncovered the riches he had sought. In 1968 Arco found the tremendous deposits on the North Slope at Prudhoe Bay. The field became the greatest on the North American continent, and Alaska was on the road to being the shining petroleum province of Halbouty's predictions.

***

Halbouty was born in Beaumont, Texas just 8½ years after the nearby Spindletop gusher shot 100,000 barrels of oil per day toward a cloudy sky. He grew up on its legends. He worked as a roustabout in the great field during his high school and college vacations. Halbouty was imbued with the thrill of discovery.

In his speeches he often returned to the events that had made petroleum history. It was not so much that he was in love with the past but that he believed the past was a beacon for the future. He saw nothing wrong with idolizing the giants of yesteryear. He spoke of them reverently, in a modern idiom.

The speech that follows was made at the National Engineers Week Banquet in Beaumont on February 22, 1973, only months *before* the Arab oil embargo. The American people and their political leaders were still unaware of the disaster ahead. So once again Halbouty tried to alert them to the danger, but he spoke warmly of the oil pioneers before he waved the red flags.

The speech was titled, "Petroleum—Its Meaning to America."

> Americans are amazingly uninformed about the petroleum industry. Yet, it is their industry. It was conceived, born, and brought up here. It sprang from our soil and spread around the world. It is our only native American industry. It is loaded with the ingredients of the great American story—ambition, frustration, opportunity, drama, romance, color, excitement, adventure, struggle, success, and failure.
>
> I defy you to read about the men who pioneered this industry and not be completely fascinated. They were almost all men of humble beginnings who were hungry for success.
>
> They were men like Rockefeller, who was a poorly paid clerk, or Sinclair, the son of a small town druggist; like Phillips, who was a barber, or Carter, who was a soldier with the Medal of Honor; like Benedum and Skelly, both of whom started their own small oil companies at the age of 16.
>
> This is an industry with which all Americans can easily relate. The lives of the men I have mentioned, and hundreds of others in the same category, are inspiring stories of individuals who made great contributions to your way of life and mine. They saw a way to chase a pot of gold to the end of a rainbow. A way to use our system of competition and freedom to find success.
>
> Most of these men became wealthy. I believe it is also a part of our national character to ignore or forget a vastly larger army of oilmen who went broke. But they, too, made their contributions.
>
> As a young graduate of Texas A&M University with advanced degrees in geology and petroleum engineering, I chose to enter the

petroleum industry although I had offers in other categories in geology and in engineering.

It was only natural that I became involved in petroleum if for no other reason than the great oil discovery known as Spindletop was a home-town institution; I worked there as a water-boy and did odd jobs during the second boom in 1925 when I was still in high school.

Further, I had read or heard of the success of so many men who started out no higher up the financial ladder than I was at the time, which was flat broke and in debt to the Former Students Association at Texas A&M to pay back money I borrowed to finish my education.

Also I felt strongly that, as far as an industry was concerned, petroleum was really the life blood of this nation, and I deeply wanted to be a part of it.

I firmly believed that America's destiny was directly related to the oil industry as borne out by the three most important events in the history of domestic petroleum. They were participated in by men who were certainly unlikely oil pioneers.

The first was a railroad conductor on sick leave whose name was Edwin Laurentine Drake. He was persuaded to go to Titusville, Pennsylvania to drill the first well ever drilled for the express purpose of finding oil. The chief reason Drake was selected was because he had a railroad pass that would take him to and from the proposed drillsite.

The well he drilled on the banks of Oil Creek was a total freak. The oil came from a stray sand or small crevice at $69\frac{1}{2}$ feet below the surface. Although that well opened the oil industry, no other successful well was ever drilled near the site of the Drake well. You would want to believe that divine guidance had a hand in that fortuitous discovery.

That well gave birth to oil's Illumination and Lubrication Era. It provided the kerosene for lamps at a price anyone could afford at a time when whale oil was petering out and was so expensive that only the wealthy could buy it. It opened a new world of light for the hours after sundown, enabling people to work and study after they left the field or the shop. Oil, therefore, was a boon to education. But it also provided the lubrication to give drive and force to the embryonic machine age.

The next great well in history, the one that opened the Liquid Fuel Age, was the Lucas Gusher located just a few miles from where this auditorium stands. Anthony Francis Lucas was an ensign in the Austrian navy and an engineering graduate from the Polytechnic Institute of Gratz when he emigrated to this country.

The man who attracted him to Beaumont was Pattillo Higgins, who had lost an arm in a sawmill accident. Higgins tried to promote oil at Spindletop, a marshy area near Beaumont when every expert in the country scoffed at the idea that oil could be found in the unconsolidated sands of the Texas Gulf Coast. All of Higgins' efforts were failures. When he ran out of money, he talked Lucas into taking up the search.

Lucas believed with the experts that there was no oil at Spindletop, but he thought he could find sulfur.

I think it is interesting that although both were mature men, neither had ever had a minute's experience in the oil industry.

Lucas' first well was a mechanical failure, but to his surprise he encountered oil at a very shallow depth and was able to save enough of it to put in a jar to show to the skeptics. Later, with the help of the oil firm of Guffey and Galey and money from the Mellons, both from Pittsburgh, he brought in the gusher that changed the world. The date was January 10, 1901—the dawn of a new century.

Before Spindletop oil was not a fuel. Its supply was too limited for it to replace coal or wood. But the Lucas gusher came in flowing an estimated 100,000 barrels a day. That was more oil than most wells made in a lifetime prior to that.

It was such an impressive well that it was capable of producing as much oil as 37,000 eastern region wells; twice as much as Pennsylvania, the leading oil state at the time; six times as much as California produced; or half as much as the entire United States output. With five such wells, Spindletop would have been able to produce more oil than all of the other wells of the world combined. The field toppled Russia from the rank as the leading oil producing country and put this country in that spot.

It was not, therefore, surprising that the world believed this magnificent well represented an inexhaustible supply of cheap oil that could be used as a fuel. It was the first time there was sufficient oil to justify an industrial conversion of boilers from coal to oil. It was truly the beginning of the Liquid Fuel Age.

Oil was a fuel available immediately for railroad engines, boilers in sugar cane mills, laundries, breweries, ships, and for domestic use in millions of homes.

No one envisioned the day of the automobile or the airplane. In fact, that very year of 1901, a leading magazine, the old *Literary Digest*, had said the automobile would never become as popular as the bicycle. It was the same magazine, incidentally, that predicted 32 years later that Landon would beat Roosevelt.

In 1902, Henry Ford organized his company. In 1903, the Wright Brothers made their famous flight at Kittyhawk. Chances are neither would have been practical without Spindletop.

Following the discovery of Spindletop, wildcatters began drilling everywhere, making great discoveries in California, Oklahoma, Kansas, and Louisiana.

Spindletop crushed Standard Oil's monopoly far more effectively than the courts did a decade later. It also destroyed almost all monopolies in all fields of endeavor. It even routed the slow growth toward socialism which had been taking hold in the land.

In its first months, Spindletop also provided the low-priced fuel to enable Herman Frasch to put his remarkable hot-water sulfur mining process to work and make America the leading sulfur-producing country in the world.

For the next 30 years, the oil industry was characterized by spasms of boom and bust, feast and famine, shortage and surplus. The price of crude oil fluctuated with each new discovery or great new market. There was no stability.

Roving wildcatters, eager to fill the biggest new orders, wantonly drilled wells where they were not needed, gutted precious reservoirs, and filled the land with the stench of oil going to waste.

But most of all, these conditions led to surpluses and shortages and no assurance that oil would be available in emergencies.

It was the norm for most fields to come in with wells gushing, only to go to the pump in a few months, and soon thereafter to salt water, leaving from 80–90% of the oil in place unrecoverable.

In spite of this waste, there was a steady climb toward the better life for all Americans. Farms moved toward mechanization. Workers were able to overcome the drudgery of toil. Machines eliminated child labor. No business or industry was without the benefit of liquid fuel energy.

The American way of life became the envy of the world.

Experts would warn that we had only a few years' supply. Then someone would bring in another Signal Hill, or an El Dorado, or

Glenn Pool. Then the same experts would cry that we had too much oil.

In spite of these wasteful years, the United States became a world power. Productivity in this country, due to a combination of industrial genius, resourceful labor, and cheap energy fuel, put America in the forefront of nations in industrial power, progress, and prosperity.

But something had to be done about avoidable waste. There were numerous efforts toward petroleum conservation, but none of them were effective for a variety of reasons, including ignorance, politics, and selfishness.

Then came the last oil boom in this country. There has been nothing like it since and probably never will be.

In 1930, Columbus Marion Joiner was an experienced oilman, but he was a most unlikely prospector. He was more than 70 years old, in ill health and drilling on a shoestring in an area where almost every major company in the business had tried to find oil at one time or another without success. In fact, some of the best scientific minds of that day condemned the area; they flatly stated that no oil would be found there. This included both geologists and geophysicists.

Dad Joiner got the money to drill his wells largely from peanut farmers, small merchants in East Texas, and widows in Dallas. He was a failure as an oilman but a very persuasive promoter.

He raised his money on a so-called geological report written by a man educated as a veterinarian. The report was contradictory to all geological knowledge. Nothing in it was remotely accurate; it was really a figment of imagination.

However, Joiner used the report to raise money and raise money he did. And though the report was inaccurate as a scientific document, it proved to be accurate even to within ten feet of where Doc Lloyd, the veterinarian, stated that Joiner would hit the Woodbine sand.

So all Dad Joiner did was discover a field containing 6 billion barrels of oil!

It was the largest oil field in the world at the time. It was the greatest treasure ever found in America.

But East Texas brought chaos to the industry. For months drilling activities in almost every other oil field east of the Rockies came to a halt. The flow of oil from thousands of wells in the field was uncontrolled. The governor of Texas declared martial law, but the courts overruled him.

Eventually proration was put into effect, but that, too, was declared illegal. Then the field was shut down to test the decreasing bottom-hole pressures, but still the drilling continued. Oil dropped to a nickel a barrel, and lower.

There was serious talk of federal control over the entire industry. The situation was chaotic. In 1930, no one really needed any more oil. There was a domestic surplus, a depression was just getting a full head of steam, and imports of oil from Venezuela and Mexico were flooding the country.

As a result of this tremendous overproduction of oil, workable conservation laws were passed. Those laws required proration of Texas production with well allowables based on market demand.

California and several other states thought that they had fairly good conservation laws even before the East Texas field came in, and refused to join a federally sponsored Interstate Oil and Gas Compact Commission.

The basis of conservation was prevention of waste. This meant waste of gas as well as oil, both below and above ground. And since it could not be wasted by venting it into the air, there was suddenly a tremendous amount of gas available. This led to the development of the natural gas industry as we know it today.

As a commercial product, natural gas has a much longer history than oil, but it was never an important fuel until after conservation laws were passed. Immediately after World War II, the natural gas industry came into its own. Trillions of cubic feet of gas were available with no market.

So, smart men such as Paul Kyser of El Paso Gas Company, Gardiner Symonds of Tenneco, and a dozen others started organizing natural gas transmission companies to take gas to the markets in the east, the north, the mid-west, and the west coast.

Another beneficial result of conservation and the saving of natural gas was the full development of the petrochemical and liquid natural gas industries. All of these now compete with the oil industry in importance, yet they all stem from the oil industry.

Another important step in the petroleum industry was the development of offshore drilling, which started in the late 1890s at Summerland, California. There wells were drilled directionally or off piers into the Santa Barbara Channel. Now the channel is regarded as the most important potential oil reserve on the west coast. More than $600 million was paid in bonuses alone for federal leases in channel waters in 1968.

Starting with nothing except an idea, backed by a small investment, the Drake well gave birth to an industry that has produced more than 120 billion barrels of oil and untold trillions of cubic feet of gas. These products have been the difference between the living standard in America and the rest of the world. They have made us strong, progressive, and prosperous beyond the wildest dreams of our founding fathers.

Oil reduced the average working man's day from 70 to 40 hours a week. And in doing so, it enabled one man working 40 hours to produce as much as three men did in 70 hours in the last century. It provided the average citizen with goods and services on a workingman's salary that only the wealthy could afford in the old world.

Drake's well was drilled to a total depth of $69\frac{1}{2}$ feet to find the first oil. In comparison, some months ago a well was drilled to a record depth of 30,050 feet in Beckham County, Oklahoma, at a cost of $5\frac{1}{2}$ million. It was, incidentally, a dry hole.

And the kerosene that helped light American homes a century or so ago, mixed with liquid oxygen, was the propellant that lifted the giant Saturn 5 rocket into space in 1967. This fuel lifted the 36-story-high rocket 38 miles in $1\frac{1}{2}$ minutes. The rocket consumed 2,300 tons of propellant which, as I figure it, is something over 600,000 gallons. Just think what has happened to our space program since 1967. Without petroleum the whole space program would not have existed.

Besides its use as a fuel, we all come into contact with some product of oil or natural gas many times daily, either as medicine, cosmetic, building material, clothing, rubber, toys, plastics, or in 2,500 other different forms. You ladies in this room—the lipstick you are wearing came from a drop of oil.

With only 7% of the world's population we consume 35% of the world's oil and about 90% of the natural gas.

The United States exported its great industry to the four corners of the world, first the product and then the techniques and tools for exploring, drilling, producing, transporting, and marketing oil. Starting with oil for the lamps of China, the industry spread many benefits to most countries of the world.

In this country we respect individual and property rights. In other countries all minerals belong to the state. In those countries you don't have to bother with the rights of landowners, titles, royalties, or rights-of-way and the like. You simply do all that at one time through the government. That means you don't have to drill wells that are not needed to accommodate the correlative rights of all landowners concerned.

Thus, on the average, an American oil well produces about 12 or 13 barrels of oil a day compared with a well in the Middle East that produces 10,000 barrels of oil a day. I believe the economics are obvious.

Balancing this apparent inequity is that in America the benefits of oil go to the people. Elsewhere, the benefits of oil go to the state, and the state decides what the people get.

The most obvious characteristic of the American petroleum industry is competition. There are more than 5,000 producing companies in this country and no one corporation controls more than 10% of them. There are 148 refining companies and the largest of these controls 10% of the business. There are more than 1,000 transportation companies, some 12,000 wholesale distributors of oil products, and more than 200,000 retail outlets. If you don't think that is competition, compare it with any other major industry—steel, automobiles, coal, railroads, airlines, or others.

Yet, today this industry—your oil industry and mine—is in serious trouble. At this moment drilling and exploration are at the lowest point in more than a quarter of a century, even though we are facing almost incredible demand growth in just the next decade or two. New reserves are not keeping pace with consumption.

We are gradually dipping lower into the cracker barrel and eventually, and soon, unless we do something about it, we will plumb run out of crackers.

It is unthinkable that our nation, which depends on the oil and gas for three-quarters of our energy requirements, and which has been the greatest oil developer around the world, should ever be faced with an oil shortage. But we are surely headed in that direction, and fast!

Some people say we should get what we need from the prolific Middle East. This would be suicide. We found the oil *in* the Arab countries, *for* the Arab countries, but there are few indications that we have really developed mutual understanding with the Arabs.

This vast source of oil is unreliable, as we have already twice seen. No free nation can ever depend on it, despite its size.

It is really ironic that we helped develop an area in the shadow of the Soviet Union that contains 60% of the world's oil reserves that the Communists want to eventually control.

We must realize that our domestic petroleum is the only available dependable supply. Other sources are subject to nationalization, expropriation, confiscation by exorbitant taxation, the caprice of foreign sovereigns, wars, and other emergency disconnections.

When the Arabs cut off production to the western nations in the 1967 Arab-Israeli war, included was some 200,000 barrels daily to Allied combat forces in Vietnam. Germany, the United Kingdom, and other western powers friendly to the United States were also denied oil until the Arabs felt the pinch of the economic loss. We met the crisis by pulling on our own reserves and from those of South America.

It is contended that Middle East oil costs only pennies a barrel to find and produce. This is an illusion.

This does not include the costs of our fleets in Mediterranean waters to protect these interests. It does not include the hospitals and schools and highways and untold other facilities that we have to build for these countries.

It does not include the international accommodations that are costly to our taxpayers and have to be made at every turn. It does not include the cost of the tremendous damage to our domestic industry which has seen exploration virtually limited to offshore areas, which has seen the disappearance of thousands of independent domestic operators, and which has seen experienced and needed drilling contractors fold their rigs and move out of the picture.

I contend that oil from the Middle East is the most costly commodity we have in the world today.

I am not opposed to an intelligent handling of this serious import problem based on a balanced import-domestic relationship which, to date, we have not had. I believe the people of the United States had better examine the subject before the matter gets out of hand and we are left at the mercy of foreign powers.

So I will reiterate; unless there are some changes soon, we are going to be in a lot bigger trouble than we can imagine.

When you consider our economic dependence on energy, it might amaze you to learn that there has not been an increase in crude oil prices in five or six years despite growing inflation, higher costs for labor, materials, and services. Gasoline prices are about the same as they were in the '20s—or more than 50 years ago. Natural gas prices are even lower.

In the absence of incentives to drill more exploratory wells, or the rapid development of synthetics such as shale oil or gasoline from coal, we are in mortal economic danger that could lead to serious social change.

If the Soviets ever control Middle East oil, and that is their prime goal in world politics, they will be able to first woo our allies in western Europe and Japan with cheap oil, gear their economics to energy, and then move in for the kill by simply threatening to turn off the valve.

In the meantime, unless there is a change of political climate and attitude in this country, the trend toward a weakened domestic oil and gas industry will continue.

Today the government nullifies the law of supply and demand with threats to increase imports or open the valves on federal offshore oil at the slightest mention of price increases demanded by rising costs.

Furthermore, our industry has been harassed and abused in many ways by continuous, ill-conceived government regulations and restrictions. Frankly, it is remarkable, and to its credit, that the industry has not wilted under the constant harassment by the bureaucrats in Washington.

More, it is inconceivable to me that the people of this nation would sit idly by and permit a few hard-nosed, hysterical environmentalists to shut down a most vital project, the Alaskan pipeline.

The Alaskan pipeline is one of the most engineered projects in the history of man. The tremendous studies made by the petroleum industry on this line have reduced the environmental and ecological risks to minimum. Those who have prepared for the discovery, development, and transportation of this great source of energy found in our Arctic region have left nothing to guesswork in making the pipeline route, the refinery site, the docks, the gathering lines, and the shipping lanes as free from danger as anything could possibly be. Almost every intelligent suggestion made by environmentalists has been considered with reason and worked out in detail into the entire system.

Today we have 8 years' supply of oil in known reserves. This is the lowest supply we have ever had. We have 12 years' supply of natural gas, the lowest since we entered the modern phase of the gas business. Both of these figures are based on present rates of consumption.

Due to anticipated population increases, marked growth in per capita consumption, and similar considerations, demand for energy in this country by 1980 will be 50% higher than it is today. Unless there is a big breakthrough in synthetics, oil and gas will have to continue to carry the major burden of meeting this demand. We probably could meet it easily with imports, but this nation cannot afford to become dependent on foreign sources, even disregarding the Soviet threat.

*If you are afraid of higher prices, you haven't seen anything until this country starts to depend on oil from foreign countries.*

Can you imagine what will happen to our balance of payments situation if we should ever be forced into that trap? What would our recourse be? Ask yourselves these questions. The answer you will get is simple and to the point—disaster!

The wolf is at our door, and he will remain at our door, and he will knock the door down, and he will eat us up, if the situation is not alleviated.

I will go so far as to bow my neck and predict that shortly, in the very near future, within eighteen months, we will have rationing in all categories in the use of petroleum, starting first with the amount of gasoline that you and I will be able to put in our cars, followed with the number of hours you may use your air-conditioning and heat, and your electric lights.

The storage capacity of petroleum in the United States is virtually zero as compared with 60 days for Europe and approximately 15 days for Japan.

Actually, storage is only an insignificant safeguard, a back-up, for an unexpected decrease of domestic production, and certainly more of a back-up for an unexpected cut-off from foreign sources.

The great concern of the have-not countries that depend on a large amount of imports—and certainly the United States can be now considered to be a have-not nation—is the unpredictable politically-inspired cut-off. The United States is particularly vulnerable to a Middle East cut-off because of its partiality to Israel.

It is interesting that all Arab cut-backs so far have been aimed against Israel's friends—in 1956, over the Suez Crisis, and in 1967, over the Six-Day War.

One inescapable conclusion is that in order for this nation of ours to maintain its rate of progress and to preserve the American way of life, the United States cannot afford to be on bad terms with the whole Arab membership of OPEC. This truism holds no matter how much the individual Arab country in question may differ politically or ideologically within the Arab league. In other words, in the long run the Arabs are sticking together.

Those in the White House may well ask the question, "Can we still import our tremendous requirement in the 1980s if there is no resolution of the Arab-Israeli dispute by then?"

Frankly, it is a risk that this nation cannot afford to take. So far the Arabs have not exercised outright "political blackmail" on the United States, but we all know that the possibility is always present and can be used unexpectedly and be as sharp as the edge of the guillotine.

The Russians are fully aware of this and it is no secret that they are continuously prodding the Arabs to use their most powerful weapon, oil, to punish the United States and other world powers friendly to the Israelis.

Because of this and other unstable international activities in the field of petroleum, the western world is indeed in great jeopardy. It will require strategic and expert diplomacy of the first magnitude to alleviate the serious situation which prevails.

At this moment the western nations and our own government and citizens have their heads in the sand. At this moment I am hoping that all of us will recognize the dangers that threaten the most important industry in the history of world progress and our way of life.

Fearful though I am, I also am an optimist, as all wildcatters must be. So today I express my faith that Americans will protect America, that they will meet the challenge of finding the energy requirements of the future right here in this country.

The oil and gas are here, locked beneath our soil.

We must unlock them at once!

\*\*\*

Halbouty was relentless in his efforts to stir his government and his people to find the key to unlock the energy beneath the American soil, and he was back in July 1973 to spread his message at the 50th Annual Golden Anniversary meeting of the International Oil Scouts Association of Houston. The title of the address was strange and curiously attractive. Following is much of what he had to say:

> I have chosen an odd title for my talk today. It is "What This Nation Needs Is More Dry Holes." This could explain why I was escorted to the door of this meeting room by two gentlemen in white coats. They released my strait-jacket just to allow me to make this speech.
>
> I am thoroughly convinced, however, that this nation does need more dry holes. Dry holes constitute about 90% of our exploratory effort. There can be no doubt that exploration can be the answer to our energy supply problems in the next couple of decades, or longer. Today we, in this industry, are being called on to provide 78% of the energy Americans use. An increasing amount of this 78% is coming from foreign countries and this can lead only to more problems, even larger than the ones we have at this time.
>
> Including development wells, the records show that 40% of all wells drilled in this country are dry. So we need dry holes for field development as well as wildcat exploration.
>
> Therefore, I am undertaking a campaign for dry holes since the more dry holes we drill in this country, the more successful discovery wells and development wells we are going to bring in.
>
> I wish I had thought of this earlier. It is possible that a campaign for more dry holes starting 10 or 12 years ago could have prevented the energy shortages we are facing today.
>
> No dry hole has ever been a total loss. You know as well as I that every dry hole provides us with geological and even engineering ideas that help us define the subsurface, or how to penetrate the earth better and understand the challenge it constantly offers.
>
> In addition to learning the secrets of the composition of the subsurface strata, we also learn the structural attitude of significant formations, the porosity and permeability of potential reservoir beds, the environmental setting, and the possible nearby presence of hydrocarbons through shows in the cuttings, cores, logs, and more sophisticated geophysical techniques.
>
> In the history of petroleum most fields have required from two to a dozen or more dry holes before discovery. There have been a few exceptions such as the Lucas gusher at Spindletop, but even in that case the Mellon brothers had budgeted for six tests in order to

find what the great wildcatter, John Galey, was convinced would ultimately be found here.

I have friends who have drilled scores of dry holes before ever finding a successful wildcat. One wildcatter who lives here in Houston says he drilled about 120 dry holes before his first producer. D. Harold Byrd of Dallas drilled 56 and acquired the name of "Dry Hole" Byrd before his first success—and then brought in a gusher to lose his amateur standing.

Even statistically, dry holes are important. Each represents one less to be drilled before the next producer will be completed. But dry holes are also important because each one is a potential producer and is essential to future discoveries. All of us are familiar with some abandoned holes that have been taken over by others and deepened to find important oil or gas fields.

Each dry hole is based on an idea and each is capable of providing more ideas. Victor Hugo once said that "greater than the tread of mighty armies is an idea whose hour has come."

So, dry holes are necessary because each one provides some new bit of information or stimulates someone's imagination, and the result often is a suggestion of a new place to drill or a new depth to drill, or even an idea for something that has been passed up on the way to the target. Each leads to structural and stratigraphic control of an area and supplies varying degrees of clues toward the generation of new prospects or the evaluation of adjacent areas for future drilling. Or, maybe, they guide the explorationist to the sound idea that there must be far better hunting grounds somewhere else.

You know and I know, and I wish those in Congress knew, that geologic ideas can be confirmed only by drilling. Most of the reserves we have in this country today were discovered as a result of information provided by abandoned dry holes.

Annual statistics support a close correlation between the total wells drilled and the reserves added in this country, or at least, the addition of new oil and gas. For instance in the past 20 years there has never been a year in which fewer than 12% of all wildcats have found oil or gas, and there has never been a year in which more than 20% of the exploratory wells have found oil or gas. And there is an equally near-constant figure relative to all wells which hovers right around 40% dry, ranging from between 36 and 42%. Therefore, it is obvious that the greater number of dry holes equates almost constantly to the greater number of discoveries.

Naturally, we would all like to see the dry holes eliminated, in spite of the remark on the Senate floor by the late Senator Douglas of Illinois that if dry holes were the reason tax incentives were needed by the oil industry, then the industry should stop drilling dry holes. No one has come up with a way to eliminate or even reduce the ratio of dry holes. The senator, as smart as he was, couldn't suggest a way to do it.

Another famous remark about oil occurred in the '30s when the great Harrison and Abercrombie well was blowing out of control at Conroe. One day Colonel Ernest O. Thompson, chairman of the Texas Railroad Commission, received a telegram from Oil Czar and Secretary of Interior, Harold L. Ickes, of New Deal fame, demanding that the blowout be controlled immediately. The colonel showed the telegram to Sam Harrison, a partner in the blowing well, who suggested an answer.

The colonel sent it to Ickes. It said simply: "I have read your telegram *to the well* and it is still blowing. Stop. Please advise what to do now. Signed. Thompson."

These are simply two of the outstanding examples of the type of help the industry and the consumers of petroleum products in this country get from Washington.

***

In this speech Halbouty once again found reason to lambaste those he characterized as "the hysterical and uninformed self-styled protectors of the earth," the fanatical environmentalists. At one point he said:

Let's take a took at some of the history of the contamination of the environment in this country. It came from many sources.

Before oil was known to exist in commercial quantities in this country, parts of this country were subjected to many seeps of oil on land and in water. Indians found lakes of oil and rivers were constantly covered with it. The Indians and early oil pioneers skimmed the oil and used it for various purposes.

In 1543, Spanish explorers found great seeps at Sabine Pass near what is now Port Arthur. Oil extended far into the sea and covered the beaches. Spanish ships were caulked with the tars from the heavy asphalts that accumulated.

Seeps dumped oil into Lake Superior and other inland waters of the nation. In 1543, the Spanish reported pools of pitch in the Pacific off Carpenteria. Captain James Cook, the great English mariner and explorer, reported that Santa Barbara Channel was covered with a thick layer of oil from one end to the other and extending far out to sea.

Burning rivers of oil existed in the early history of the nation. They were caused by natural seeps as well as oil leaks from water wells. When these rivers ignited from the oil, the flames skipped majestically down most of the important waterways of this nation. People were entertained but not frightened or ever concerned by these fiery displays.

In 1864, Professor Benjamin Silliman, distinguished Yale chemist, reported that oil was struggling to the surface at every available point in many areas off California and running down rivers for miles. All these natural seeps were pouring oil into the Pacific Ocean at dozens of points.

During the early oil booms the valleys and waters of western Pennsylvania, and West Virginia, Ohio, Indiana, and New York were covered with oil from leaking wells, blowouts, and barges of oil en route to market. Waste oil from the famous Glenn Pool in Oklahoma spread over the entire length of the Arkansas River and down the Mississippi to New Orleans.

There was no outcry. People understood the hazards and welcomed the promise of new industry. These spills were gradually cleaned up and the industry, as it grew in stature and knowledge, began to learn how to control the waste.

And on the subject of pollution, horses provided the greatest menace in history up to and including the present. For instance, in 1908, there were 120,000 horses in New York City alone—and tons of manure were deposited daily. The horse was called an economic burden, an affront to cleanliness, and a terrible tax on human life. Each deposited from fifteen to thirty pounds of manure daily on the streets, amounting to from two to three million pounds in New York alone. Other large cities had similar problems all over the nation.

This horrid smelling dung spread cholera, malaria, typhoid, infant diarrhea, and a variety of serious intestinal diseases, and all infectious diseases, such as smallpox, were rampant.

The streets were worked constantly by prisoners, those on charity, children, and the poor. Dumping of horse manure in neighborhoods was commonplace, causing clouds of flies to spread disease. When it rained, the streets were cesspools of liquefied manure. During droughts, the dried manure filled the air as sand in a desert. Horses died on the streets and were left there to decay and spread more disease.

What ended all of this? It was the horseless carriage powered by liquid fuel known as gasoline, the same instrument of our economy that is now blamed for pollution from coast to coast.

Long before there was oil or gas to burn and pollute the air, the forests of the nation were being stripped of wood. This was happening all over the world. Then, the same type of environmental intellectuals were blaming agriculture for the sin of destroying the precious land of its beauty and fertility and creating deserts. It was suggested that agricultural activities be curbed, controlled, or discontinued altogether.

You know what stopped this rape of the forests? Fossil fuels known as coal and oil.

There are thousands of true stories which, if presented to the public with the same fervor with which the side of the highly emotional environmentalists is presented, would prove that our industry has done more to terminate pollution than it will ever do to impair the environment.

Now, in view of the great strides in environmental protection, do you know who is doing most to rid this nation and even itself of damage to the environment? It is your industry and mine.

As far back as I can recall the oil industry in this country has been fighting pollution of the environment, especially that for which it is responsible.

But do you know that for the seven years from 1966 through 1972 that the oil industry alone spent $4.4 billion for environmental protection in all forms for which the industry could be blamed. Percentagewise, 49.4% of this was spent on air pollution abatement, 44.2% on water pollution and the remaining 6.4% on land and other pollution. Thus, the industry is spending approximately $700 million per year to protect the environment.

Can any other industry match this record? I doubt it. The environmental extremists do little except complain and misrepresent facts to a gullible public. They are fighting to the death the one industry which is doing most to end pollution in this nation.

I bring this point up to illustrate the nature of the emotional activity that is doing the most to deny the public full access to an abundant supply of fuel in this country. The industry is being totally blamed, but the hysterical environmentalists, and the ignorant, weak-kneed, flannel-mouthed, office-seeking politicians who stand in awesome fear of them, especially in Washington, but also at other levels of government from city, to county, to state, are the real culprits.

I believe in protecting the environment as much as any man, or woman, in this country. I take my hat off to the sincere and dedicated environmentalists who are entitled to great credit, but I have nothing but contempt for the unscrupulous environmentalists who undermine not only American industry and the consumers of this nation, but also the honest efforts of the balanced, devoted, and sincere environmentalists who are trying to eliminate danger by cooperative effort with all industries, to not only this country, but the world.

***

In this speech Halbouty touched on other matters he considered of great importance, but he always returned to the original theme—the drilling of more dry holes meant the drilling of more successful wells. And the drilling of more and more productive wells, he declared over and over, was vital to the nation's welfare.

So, he had spoken often, and to the point. But the key to unlock the oil and gas was not used in time. Three months after the "dry hole" speech, the Arab embargo was imposed. Halbouty's prediction had come true.

Had his warnings been heeded thirteen years earlier, in 1960, the embargo may have had little impact, or it may not have occurred at all. And America's energy well-being may not have been continually dependent on the political and economic whims of others.

# CHAPTER TWO

In the early days of his career, before World War II, Halbouty had discovered oil in abundance for others, and he had won respect—and financial rewards—for his work as a consultant. And he had become noted as a writer, not only for oil trade publications but for scientific journals as well.

During the war, he was transferred out of the infantry and ordered to serve on the Army-Navy Petroleum Board; his job was to use his talents as an earth scientist and engineer to increase production wherever the Allies were producing oil for the war effort. He journeyed widely, and he did his job well. Because of his military training at Texas A&M University and the refresher courses he took over the years, he entered the army as a captain. He was discharged as a lieutenant colonel.

With the war over, Halbouty determined to strike out for himself as a wildcatter. Amazingly, he discovered the Ashland field in Natchitoches Parish, Louisiana on January 1, 1946 and, four months later to the day, discovered the Lake End field in an adjoining parish! The odds were 53 to 1 against finding a small commercial field in the United States with a wildcat well. He had found two in four months!

By the time of the landmark speech in Los Angeles in 1960 he was firmly established as a highly successful wildcatter-producer with an interest in 32 fields.

***

During the 13 years from his first warning speech in 1960 to his final one before the embargo in 1973, Halbouty had been honored by his peers and others with coveted awards. In 1965, for example, he received the Distinguished Service Award from the Texas Mid-Continent Oil & Gas Association. In 1968 he was named Engineer of the Year by the Texas Society of Professional Engineers and the Engineers Council of Houston; and Texas A&M University granted him the Distinguished Alumni Award. (Back in the mid-1940s, after his first wildcat successes, he had established a postgraduate fellowship in geology in his name at A&M, the first of many benefactions directed toward his alma mater and her students.)

He was given an Honorary Life Membership in AAPG in 1969, and in 1970 he received an Honorary Life Membership in the Houston Geological Society. The following year the Society of Petroleum Engineers of AIME awarded him the DeGolyer Distinguished Service Medal, and in the next he was given an Honorary Membership in the Spindletop Section of the Society of Petroleum Engineers. In 1973, the year of the embargo, he was granted an Honorary Membership in the American Institute of Mining, Metallurgical and Petroleum Engineers.

In years to come he would win many more awards and serve as ranking officer in organizations that had honored him. He would be cited for his contributions to civic betterment in Houston, in Texas, and in the country he loved so well.

\*\*\*

Halbouty's professional life appears to have been divided by the energy crisis of 1973–74. Before the Arab embargo, he had devoted his own energies to finding oil and trying to warn his countrymen about the impending disaster. Afterward, he was doggedly determined to exercise his talents on a global basis, hoping he could help ensure petroleum supplies for every country in the world.

In the late 1960s he had become concerned with the almost total lack of geological information on the land areas encircling the Pacific Ocean. At the time he was a member of the executive committee of the division of earth sciences of the National Academy of Sciences. He was not satisfied to wonder why the information was so sparse; he set out to rectify the situation.

In 1972 he got several geologists to meet with him at the U.S. Geological Survey office in Menlo Park, California. The group set up the Circum-Pacific Council for Energy and Mineral Resources. The men were aware that most of the countries in the region had information about their own lands but didn't relate it to the geology of their neighbors and the region as a whole. Halbouty dreamed of pulling all that information together. In that way, he hoped to advance the exploration and development "of the total energy and mineral resources of the Circum-Pacific area. . . ."

The first conference was held in Honolulu in August 1974 while the taste of the embargo was still strong in Halbouty's throat. The meeting was designed, of course, for representatives from countries bounding the Pacific, but countries removed from the ocean also sent their delegates. More than a thousand delegates from 67 countries attended. Plans were made for representatives to convene every four years. As general chairman of the conference, Halbouty was at his diplomatic best in promoting the free exchange of ideas.

A committee was set up to develop a series of geological maps of the huge area, a formidable task that would require thousands of hours of labor by scores of scientists, including Russian and Chinese experts. Halbouty was to continue to serve as chairman and president of the Council, but he would make sure the Council's work was not an American project. Council directors would include scientists from the Soviet Union, China, Australia, Canada, New Zealand, Japan, Chile, Mexico, Peru and the Philippines.

It would be said in Washington diplomatic circles that the Circum-Pacific Council created a rapport between the participating countries that the U.S. State Department could not have accomplished.

The Council also gave Halbouty an opportunity to practice what he preached—the free flow of scientific information among the nations of the world. His work for the Council took him from remote villages to major cities where, as he transmitted knowledge, he picked it up like a blue serge suit gathers lint.

(The original map project would grow to an integrated series of 51 maps by 1986 with work yet to be done. "The plate tectonics map is now used by every geologist involved in this area," Halbouty would tell an interviewer. "You can't work this area without this map. Millions of people in this area will benefit from what this

Council has done. Half of the present population of the world will benefit. Every country bordering the Pacific has benefited. . . ." He would say later in life that he regarded creation of the Council as his greatest achievement.)

\*\*\*

Shortly before the first Circum-Pacific Council meeting in 1974, Halbouty went north to lecture the Canadians. It was a time of strong anti-American feeling there. Halbouty spoke his mind before a joint meeting of the Independent Petroleum Association of Canada, the Alberta Association of Petroleum Landmen, Canadian Society of Petroleum Geologists, and the Calgary Chamber of Commerce. His speech was titled, "Don't Make The Same Mistakes We Did."

Here is a shortened version:

> When I first read of strong anti-American feelings in Canada, I was shocked. How could the United States and Canada possibly have ill feelings of any kind towards one another?
>
> All of my life I have considered our countries almost as one—not one sovereign country—but one people. We look alike, talk alike, think alike, love freedom alike, and act alike in most respects. Our people are so much alike that the outside world lumps us together as North Americans. And we are as close as any two nations in the world have ever been.
>
> Almost five years ago, in a speech in Los Angeles, I extolled the virtues of Canada and its people. I stated then, and I repeat now, that I am mystified that Canada and the United States did not long ago reach a firm international energy policy. On that occasion I denounced the President's action in limiting Canadian oil exports to thiting Canadian oil exports
> to the United States.
>
> Now, I am just as critical of Canada limiting and overtaxing such exports to the United States.
>
> Before I get too far along in this speech, I want it understood that I did not come here to tell Canada how to run its petroleum industry. If I had that power, I would use it better at home.
>
> That doesn't mean I don't intend to discuss your petroleum industry here tonight. I discuss ours at home. I don't get very far, but I certainly raise a lot of smoke and a little fire at times. Probably

I won't get very far with my discussion of your policies here tonight. But I surely will tell you what I think of them.

Canadian politicians have been quite frank in their utterances about our petroleum relations, and they have been very frank about their feelings toward the United States. I hope you will forgive me tonight if I also am frank. It is my way.

Recently, Congress voted for legislation to roll back producer prices of crude oil in the interest of the gasoline consumer. Fortunately, this was vetoed by the President, and his veto was upheld by the Senate. Such action, if it had passed, would have reduced domestic crude supply, which is the cheapest supply available, and would have increased dependence on foreign crude, which is the most expensive crude available.

One of our congressmen called attention to the many completed oil and gas wells in the Gulf of Mexico that are shut in. He demanded that they at once be connected and start producing. That was a show for the sake of his constituents.

This man knew it was impossible to start producing those wells because the operators have been trying unsuccessfully for several years to get Federal Power Commission approval to build the pipelines to move the oil and gas. The pipelines have not yet been approved and the oil and gas remains shut-in—all because of bureaucratic stupidity.

When you get right down to it, I guess in our country we have to place a considerable amount of blame for the energy crisis on the consumers. Some of the blame has to be placed on the oil industry. And some has to be placed on many of our stupid congressmen who repeatedly labeled as self-serving scare tactics the honest, serious warnings voiced by responsible individuals who foresaw the inevitable consequences of our government's insouciant energy policies.

A few years ago we had a chance to provide—to gain—energy self-sufficiency for our country. Now the United States is leaving an energy era of "cheap and plenty" and entering the era of "high costs and scarcities."

We are now depending on outside sources for oil in the United States, and the price of foreign oil—as you know—is out of sight.

Even Canadian oil is far in excess of the cost of American domestic oil since your new export tax of $6.40 has been applied.

Today we are only 65% self-sufficient, compared with Canada's self-sufficiency of at least 98%.

Today we have a vast energy producing potential in our country that should be explored and produced. But we are blocked by an aggressive cadre of political wreckers.

Don't let that happen to Canada.

As a geologist, I can safely say to you that your country has only scratched the surface of its energy potential, but it may never be developed if restrictions are forced on those who want to develop it by politicians who are ignorant and oblivious of the consequences of their acts.

You and your organizations should go to the people now. Open a constructive line of communication. And don't depend on a soliloquy as we did. Listen to the people. Hear their attitudes and their viewpoints. Answer their questions fully, completely, and frankly. I believe that is the only way that the Canadian petroleum industry can overcome the confusion that politicians can heap on the people.

Don't do what the United States did. We adopted an energy policy that made us dependent on foreign oil and turned right around and adopted a foreign policy that took even that oil away from us.

From the beginning of the petroleum industry in Canada, Americans have been eager to invest in your country's exploration, production, refining, marketing, and transportation businesses. Billions of American dollars have enhanced every segment of Canada's petroleum industry to the benefit of your people and your country.

Now, just recently, Canadian Energy Minister Donald Mc-Donald declared that the government would propose a National Petroleum Corporation that would be empowered to take over all existing oil companies. Threats of this kind do not win foreign investments. Also, such threats certainly do not win the friendship of domestic and foreign independents and companies that have already invested billions of dollars increasing the wealth and energy potential of Canada.

Threats of such magnitude strain and worsen U.S.-Canadian relations and there might be no further appreciable investment of United States capital in Canada until such a threat is resolved one way or the other.

While the past has been good, the future, in light of Washington-Ottawa bickering and the growing nationalism of some Canadians, and the confused political output from the national and provincial parliaments, has a sort of unhappy outlook, one marked by anti-Americanism, protectionism, and the diminution of United States-Canadian trade.

Under the protection of Canadian policy in the past, Americans were happy to invest money and know-how in this country. A huge share of this investment went into hydrocarbons, and there have been estimates that 90% of Canada's petroleum industry involves large American interests. Also, this industry's output is on lands leased on acreage 84% owned by the Canadian Federal Government and 16% by the provinces and private Canadian companies and individuals.

The returns on American investment, across the board—not only oil—have been good. Some $2 billion to Americans alone in 1971 is the figure, I believe. And, incidentally, half of that amount was re-invested in Canadian enterprises.

The returns to the Canadian investors on enterprises largely American are relatively no less substantial than to the Americans. There have been, of course, the wage packets, foreign earnings, direct private income, and tangible national resources development which all accrued to Canadians.

Lease payments, for example, had brought the Canadian government alone more than $2 billion by the end of 1971. This figure, of course, would be much more substantial now. Even today, however, American cross-border transactions involve something like $40 billion a year!

I believe this has been a good arrangement for Americans, as well as Canadians, and I know that both of us have profited from it. But this fruitful policy is now threatened with collapse. Disagreements have existed over the years, but all of it—Washington bumbling, truculence in Canadian provincial circles, general political uncertainties between the two countries—now pose serious problems.

This has all been highlighted by the energy crisis. Further, my country's handling of this situation and its internal uncertainties have been shameful, as I'll point out.

Probably the Washington-Ottawa confrontations began in earnest in the summer of 1971. It was then that Washington devalued our currency officially; halted gold purchases, and adopted a hard-line trade push that could only upset Canadians.

The subsequent general deterioration of United States-Canadian relations—at the public level—hit some sort of low with the preemptory cutoff of fuel supplies by Canada to the state of Maine's paper mills at the end of 1973, and the state's retaliatory threats to stop crude oil flow through Maine to Canadian refineries. What was involved was panic reaction by both sides to the fuel crisis, and it was quickly resolved, but it was unnecessary. It just created more mistrust and hard feelings.

United States-Canadian airlines bickered over fueling rights, and Canadians apparently were refused gasoline in New England towns. This was all pretty silly, but it is symptomatic.

One more bit of bickering involved British Columbia and other authorities who bitterly objected to shipments of United States oil by tankers through the Juan de Fuca Straits between the state of Washington and Vancouver because of oil spills. But Canadian oil goes that way now, enroute along the West Coast of the United States through the Panama Canal, to the East Coast of Canada.

I don't know what the objection was to the United States oil shipments along the same route now used by Canada, but I am certain that something could have been done to resolve the misunderstanding by proper across-the-table discussions of both parties.

Then I think that most of you recall in autumn of last year when the Canadian "Labor Day National Oil Policy" was enunciated in Ottawa. Terms of the policy included a crude oil price freeze, an export tax, a two-tier pricing system—one for Canadians and a higher one for American users of Canadian-produced oil and oil products—and specific proposals for construction of the Sarnia-Montreal pipeline.

I believe that the discriminatory tax will hamper the financing of energy exploration and development in Canada, which could result in energy shortages and higher energy costs for you in the future.

I have already mentioned the threat of Canadian nationalization and confiscation of the entire petroleum industry. Then there are the rumors suggesting screening of existing and future possible foreign corporate citizens.

Also, the demagoguery displayed when the petroleum industry was castigated and the oil companies referred to as "Corporate Welfare Bums." It is ironic that such a demeaning tag would be placed on the oil companies that are responsible for billions of dollars of taxes and income paid to the governments and the people of Canada.

And there is the continuous, unresolved politicking with key issues between Ottawa and the provinces. It does not warm the hearts of proposed investors. In fact, it chills them to the bone!

Indeed, the climate is so unfavorable at the moment that it prompted the prestigious *World Oil* magazine in January of this year to headline a gloomy article with the words, "Should the U.S. Depend on Oil from Canada? Probably Not."

I'll have to admit that as an American this worries me a great deal. But I believe there is no way that Canada can provide the United States with very much oil in the future unless exploration is stepped up considerably.

Now let's look at Canada's potential as an oil and gas producing nation. The Geological Survey of Canada estimates that there are 99.2 billion barrels of oil and 783 trillion cubic feet of gas potentially available in this country.

I don't want to smother you with figures, but a few more might be useful. For example, the Canadian Petroleum Association estimates that a sustained exploration off Canada's East Coast could find in the nature of 32 billion barrels of oil and 115 trillion cubic feet of gas, which is almost three times the amount of oil and just under twice the amount of gas estimated as potential in the North Sea, where, incidentally, more and more Canadian money and know-how is going for better profits.

All of this oil and gas recovery is going to cost a lot of money. The East Coast offshore work alone can come to more than $780 million by 1978. It is indicated that some $20 billion a year will be spent on your hydrocarbon resources through 1980. And if guesses are correct about the cost of extracting and handling Athabaska tar sand reserves at a billion dollars per plant—perhaps 20 plants—then cash demands are going to be astronomical.

For all of this activity foreign investment in Canada seems to me to be absolutely vital as, indeed, it has been in the past.

I would like to cite the areas of interference and obstruction that stunted the United States' effort to attain economic self-sufficiency in energy supplies:

1. Ignoring repeated industry—and expert—assertions of the pressing need for sound, national energy policies.
2. Delayed lease sales of Federal Offshore Tracts and then leasing too little acreage, and on an irregular and infrequent basis.
3. Moratorium on Santa Barbara Channel leases already sold, delay in exploration and production on 35 tracts for about 4 years, and then delay in production at Santa Inez.

4. The imposition, for more than 20 years, of artificially low prices on natural gas in interstate commerce, a measure that drove investment out of new-field exploration and investment generally.
5. Raising the oil industries tax burden of more than $500 million a year by the simple expedient by reducing the percentage of depletion 5½%. This $500 million a year is roughly the cost of drilling 5,000 wells, when an increase in drilling, not a decrease, was so vital. Presently, there is a proposal in Congress to eliminate percentage depletion altogether. This, then, would add the cost of another 25,000 wells which is about all of the wells that are drilled in the United States now. There is no way that this can do anything in our country except to tremendously increase the price of oil, gasoline, and other products—and cause another and more severe energy crisis.
6. A 5-year delay in approval of the Alaska pipeline at the critical time of impending shortage. And, incidentally, it hasn't been approved so far by the Alaska state government, which is an example of national and state differences similar to your national and provincial differences.
7. The effective loss of some 380 thousand barrels of oil a day for 365 days a year in gasoline by the imposition of ill-considered emission controls.
8. Asinine delays to promote discovery of new petroleum reserves.
9. Bureaucratic red tape in approving research and development of our many other sources of energy.
10. Constant government harassment of the petroleum industry by a constant flow of restrictions and orders hampering exploring, developing, producing, refining, and transporting petroleum.

And, if I had time, I would name you 40 more deterrent items.

Any of these sound familiar to what's going on here in Canada?

Politicians affect the public, and this is the one fact that the Canadian petroleum industry must watch and counteract. You should start at once to remind the people of the importance of what you produce for them.

Right now Canada is walking in the same footsteps my country so firmly planted.

You gentlemen must start a campaign of informing the people. You must not be afraid to talk back and fight the politicians who attempt to hamper you.

Take your tails from between your legs and fight back with all of your might! You are not fighting for yourselves, you are fighting for the people of this great nation. Your failure becomes the people's failure, and the nation's as well.

Before closing there are two blunt questions which need answering by the national and provincial governments of Canada:

First, is Canada interested in continuing United States investment of money and know-how, or isn't it?

Second, is Canada interested in permitting America to share its vast hydrocarbon potential, or isn't it?

If the answers to these questions are "no"—or anything approaching it—then let us know! Be frank with us and quit threatening us with political innuendos and insinuations!

We have $1 trillion 350 billion to spend as a minimum through 1985 developing a respectful energy sufficiency for ourselves. If Canada does not want us to spend some of this amount in its borders, we would like to know so we can plan on spending this vast amount in our own country or elsewhere.

Canada is not in an energy crisis as we are in my country, but it can surely get there in a very short period of time.

All Canada has to do is to be as stupid as we were!

*** 

Halbouty's advice to the Canadians was not heeded—and the Canadian government led its people down the sorry path the Americans had so clearly marked.

# CHAPTER THREE

In early 1975, Halbouty received the Anthony F. Lucas Gold Medal from the Society of Petroleum Engineers. It will be recalled that the Society had given him the DeGolyer Distinguished Service Award in 1971, but it appeared that the Lucas Gold Medal held a special meaning for him. Lucas was a hero in Halbouty's eyes, suffering one heartbreak after another before bringing in the great Spindletop Gusher in 1901 near Halbouty's hometown of Beaumont. It is likely that Halbouty had no trouble in identifying with Lucas.

In Washington in 1977, Halbouty received the highest honor the American Association of Petroleum Geologists could bestow. It was the Sidney Powers Memorial Medal, named for an early-day earth scientist who had devoted much of his life to the building of AAPG.

Halbouty, then, had received the three highest honors from the American Institute of Mining, Metallurgical and Petroleum Engineers (AIME) and the American Association of Petroleum Geologists (AAPG) and was the only earth scientist to have been so singularly honored by the two professional societies.

Also in 1977, he was given the William T. Percora Award by the National Aeronautical and Space Administration and the Department of the Interior. Dr. Percora, while director of the U.S. Geological Survey and undersecretary of the Interior Department, had urged the use of satellites to study the earth's resources from space. He and Halbouty were good friends. The oilman became an ardent advocate of such a program. He spoke on the subject at every opportunity, and his paper, "Application of Landsat Imagery to Petroleum and Mineral Exploration," delivered at the 1976 AAPG annual meeting, became a classic in the field.

His cup overflowed, however, when his old school, which had presented him with the Distinguished Alumni Award, named the campus geoscience building "The Michel T. Halbouty Geoscience Building." He was an "Aggie" to the marrow of his bones. There was little doubt that the naming of the building in his honor swelled him with a proper pride.

He was equally proud when he was asked to deliver the commencement address for the graduating class of 1979. It was a simple, straightforward advisory, devoid of the harsh criticisms and oratorical flourishes that characterized most of his public utterances. It went like this:

> President Miller, members of the faculty, members of the graduating class of 1979, honored guests, ladies, and gentlemen: Before I undertake to deliver to you my words of wisdom, which, of course, is expected from a commencement speaker, I would like to make an observation:
>
> I am embarrassed at the speed with which I accepted the offer of your good president to be your speaker. The reason is that in the past I have openly stated that commencement speeches should definitely be eliminated. I am sure that you graduates are wholly in agreement with this view. Unfortunately, it seems that no one in higher authority shares that feeling.
>
> The basic fact is that it is difficult to listen to commencement speeches. Sometimes a speech is good and even warrants attention, but most everyone is thinking of other and more important things.
>
> In other words, the psychology of the occasion is not proper for listening. I am sure that it would be much better to have the speech printed and a copy attached with the diploma. In this manner, someday, perhaps when the excitement of the moment has died away, the graduate might read the speech and possibly obtain some guidance from it.
>
> I must confess to you that just a few minutes after receiving my diploma, many years ago in old Guion Hall, I did not remember the name of the speaker who delivered the commencement address. I do recall, however, that as we all mingled outside the auditorium, I agreed with everyone that it was a terrific speech, but could not agree with anyone that I remembered a thing the speaker said.

Therefore, after this ceremony breaks up, it won't hurt my feelings to think that you may have no idea of *who* spoke to you on this occasion. But it *does* concern me that my appearing here might be a complete waste of your time.

Since your time is most valuable, I decided that instead of blistering you for an hour or more that I would rather make you a sporting proposition: if you'll promise to listen, I'll promise to stop in ten minutes—and maybe I can leave just one thought with you which may be of some real value in your future endeavors.

We live today in a volatile world. Many world-wide and domestic problems that drastically affect our lives are political. These problems, whether small or large, will be resolved by politicians who are either controlled by the people in a democracy or dictated to by totalitarian rulers.

Political events that shape our lives do not just accidentally occur. They are maneuvered and regulated by those who participate in political activities.

Consequently, many political events occur from time to time that leave us with a sense of dismay that such "things" can happen, and we begin to wonder how these ever began and why they were not stopped before it was too late.

As individuals, we complain of the results of these events, but in the final analysis we can only blame ourselves because we have participated too little in proper political affairs. We let the "other fellow" do the thinking for us, and this "other fellow" usually belongs to a group organized for the sole purpose of gaining a selfish objective.

These selfish-interest groups are assassins without guns; they poison uninformed minds, connive to obtain their selfish purposes, and slowly achieve the assassin's results by killing what is right through propaganda and demagogic procedures. Those who believe differently do very little, if anything at all, to initiate countermeasures.

The answer lies in one basic philosophy: to participate more in public and political affairs.

Unfortunately, professionals of all types have created a destructive vacuum by their ivory-tower attitude toward public affairs. That vacuum has been filled by "ward-heelers," special interest groups, minorities within the minority groups, political hacks, and others who have in mind their own particular interests, as opposed to the public and nation's interests.

Occasionally, professionals do step out and express themselves, but they usually wait until only a crash program of public relations or participation can forestall a disaster that has been building for years right under their noses.

Obviously you would not bother with taking the time and effort to be politically active in a total monarchy. The king and his ministers take care of all political decisions in such countries.

It would be suicidal, unless you were part of the governing clique, to participate in public affairs in a dictatorship.

However, it is especially important for you to be active in public affairs in a democracy such as ours.

The United States has a people's government based on the freedom of the individual. Our way of life will exist *only* as long as the people participate in political action which, in turn, ensures that our government at all levels will perform its role efficiently and effectively for the welfare of the people.

Yet, although we have a people's democracy, this country is crying for leadership at all levels of government, but many who are highly educated and possess leadership qualities are either too timid, too smug, or too reserved to become active.

You owe it to the public and the nation to use your stature, intelligence, and prestige to participate in political activities. You must have the courage to speak out and to act decisively without equivocation and without fear.

In particular, the people would welcome the viewpoints and the expressions of experts and specialists on matters affecting the public and the nation's welfare.

Also, to become politically active affords the opportunity to guard against the destruction of the free enterprise system which is the foundation of this nation. If this freedom is ever lost, the spirit that made this country grow and prosper would die and individuality would be smothered. There would be no regard for personal achievement.

Stifling government controls would become rampant and would strangle our industrial and economic strength. This, in turn, would lead to greater restraints on the people, which would lessen their personal liberties and the desire to live and produce with a free will.

This would surely result in a different form of government. We would no longer have a government "of the people, by the people and for the people." What we would have is a government in regulation of the people!

This truism was ably stated by Thomas Jefferson when he said, "Were we directed from Washington when to sow and when to reap, we should soon want bread."

Nearly a century and a half later, Woodrow Wilson said it more eloquently when he remarked that "The history of liberty is a history of the limitation of governmental power, not the increase of it, because concentration of power is what always precedes the destruction of human liberties."

So, you must always remember that in a free society freedom of the people depends on their participation in the power of government. Without an active participation in this governing power, there is a gradual erosion of the people's freedoms.

Many of the freedoms upon which this country prospered have disappeared during the past ten years. Federalism in the industrial and social complexes of the nation are growing with each administration. The greatest economic growth in this country has always occurred when there were fewer federal agencies.

In the last decade, however, new agencies increased over 400% and put the federal government deeper and unalterably into the affairs of society and the economy. Currently, there is no corner of the nation in which the government does not intrude and confuse.

These new agencies seem to operate the new regulations without regard for the economic health of the industries or for the welfare of the people and the nation. Their only aim appears to be the perpetuation of the agency and extending the monstrous arm of the bureaucracy.

The real effect of all of this has been the gradual, but certain erosion of our constitutional rights to exercise our freedom to trade, freedom to build, freedom to expand, all of which spring from natural human wants and needs.

If we do not stop the disintegration of our freedoms, many of us will live to see a complete domination by Washington of every business, every industry, every facet of an individual's way of life, and the resultant loss of every one of our cherished freedoms!

Therefore, your activity in public and political affairs could easily be the difference in whether this country will cease to exist under its founding ideals and principles.

Never, never, ever forget for a moment that the law was made for the people, and not the people for the law.

Because of this doctrine it was decreed that the government would not be ruler of the people, but that the government would be the servant of the people.

About 2,400 years ago, Pericles told the citizens of Athens:

"An Athenian citizen does not neglect the state because he takes care of his own household. We alone regard the man who takes no interest in public affairs, not as a harmless, but as a useless character."

Under Pericles, Athens rose to her highest glory. Indeed, that period has never been equaled in many respects before or since. Yet, when Athens began to ignore this basic philosophy, she was destroyed by Sparta, which was no more than a police state.

So, you must not ever underestimate the influence of an individual or a single organization in public affairs. It is your duty to speak out whenever you think the welfare of your industry, your profession, or the public is at stake.

You then will be doing a service to your company, your community, your state, and your nation.

You will also assist in preserving the future and assuring the security of a healthy, growing, and a strong democratic government.

By preserving these ideals and principles you will ensure yourself a productive career, and a better life for you, for your families, and for America's future generations.

Most importantly, you will also ensure that our government remains a government "of the people, by the people, and for the people."

And in closing, God be with you in all your endeavors, and may your future contributions make this world and its people much better than they are on this graduation day.

***

The seniors had clapped and whistled with good humor during Halbouty's early remarks, particularly when he promised to limit his speech to ten minutes. But they had grown quiet, caught up in his oratory, after that.

At the end they stood as one. There was no whistling, just a solid wave of sound from clapping hands. There was a solemnity in it, and Halbouty quickly turned his face to hide the tears that had come into eyes.

Years later a regent told Halbouty that as far as he knew no other commencement speaker had received a standing ovation before or since that address.

\*\*\*

The graduation scholarship program Halbouty established in 1946 from the fruits of his first wildcat ventures had, through 1987, provided funds for 76 geoscientists and petroleum engineers scattered around the world.

From time to time Halbouty hears from them; they bring him up to date on their lives and work. They refer to themselves as "Halbouty's Scholars." He calls them "My young geologists and engineers."

\*\*\*

The year 1977 also produced one of the greatest surprises in Halbouty's life—and a thrilling surprise at that. OPEC, the cartel he had denounced from a dozen platforms, asked him to be the lead-off speaker at a three-day seminar at its headquarters in Vienna!

The theme of the seminar was "Present and Future Roles of National Oil Companies." (It will be recalled that Halbouty detested the thought of nationalization of the oil industry and had fought against it strenuously in the U.S.) Halbouty was invited to deliver a paper with the title "Future Trends in Exploration to Discover New Hydrocarbon Reserves throughout the World, and the Role to be Played by OPEC Member Countries' National Oil Companies."

The most powerful non-military organization on earth was seeking his advice in his own field. The invitation itself suggested that he had reached the peak of his profession.

He gave OPEC what it asked for—and a whole lot more.

It became obvious immediately that the OPEC leadership was in an aggressive mood. The welcoming speaker, Ali Jaidah, Secretary General of OPEC, was critical of the international oil companies that had once controlled OPEC countries' production, and he was critical of the consuming nations. OPEC, he said, had taken over the setting of oil prices. Now, he said, OPEC intended to participate in every phase of the industry. So far, he said, the oil industry had not been helpful.

"We have been buying technology at exorbitant prices while turn-key projects have proved to be tied to the suppliers of technology for patents, spare parts, operations, research, and so forth.

"The present terms of transfer of technology are a source of deep concern to us, not only because they are of a grudging nature, but also because we are denied access to the markets for the products in the developed countries."

OPEC countries, he continued, commanded only 6% of the world's refining capacity, 3.2% of the petrochemical industry, and less than 3% of the shipping of OPEC production.

"Gentlemen," he said, "I must say, in all seriousness, that unless greater progress is made in redressing the imbalances in this area, our member countries will have no recourse but to adopt collective strategies to achieve their aims. . . ."

Halbouty had been asked to tell the 300 delegates—and some major oil company representatives who had been invited to attend—where the new hydrocarbons would be found, and how they would be found. He had prepared his speech in Houston, and he did not deviate from his text in Vienna. Still, many of those present felt that Halbouty had "answered" Jaidah's challenging remarks.

And, unintentionally, perhaps he had. For while he picked up his listeners with his eloquence and took them on a world tour of the basins his careful studies had convinced him contained hydrocarbons, while he explained his conclusions and suggested how the hydrocarbons might be recovered, he had other things on his mind as well.

He was looking into the future as he had always done. There was presently an oil glut, he said, but it would not last forever. Despite conservation in some countries, global demand for oil would rise to unprecedented heights. And no one, he said, was preparing for that eventuality by exploring for new reserves.

"Finding as much oil and gas as possible stand out as a very high global priority," he said. "All of us, whether in the government sector or the private sector, whether in a market-controlled economy or a centrally planned economy, must do our utmost to accelerate the discovery of new oil and gas in order to provide a smooth transition into the post-oil era. If we fail, a world catastrophe is a not improbable outcome. All of us will be losers."

He chided the OPEC countries for not exploring on its own or joining with the major companies in a world-wide search.

"I strongly emphasize that there should be coordinated and effective joint ventures between government companies and private companies in the exploration, development, and production effort—and by this I mean a true, a real true, profitable partnership—for the new petroleum supplies of the future," he said.

The world couldn't wait for OPEC to do it on its own, nor could it wait for the transfer of technology from the private companies to OPEC. "Your philosophy may be to hang tough in the hope that the private companies will eventually come to heel, but I wouldn't bet on it if I were you," he warned.

His remarks were made on foreign soil before powerful strangers, but his theme was a familiar one. Just as he had warned Americans about the domestic shortage, now he was warning the world of a world shortage in the future.

And he was pleading for world cooperation in postponing the day when all the wells would run dry.

In the late 1980s those who had heard him speak at that OPEC meeting still talked about his knowledge of world energy potential, needs, and problems.

# CHAPTER FOUR

Almost as strong as his devotion to Texas A&M University was Halbouty's dedication to the Republican Party. He was part of the first Republican group that met and vowed to change Texas from a Democratic stronghold into a two-party state. He supported the party financially and with expenditures of his amazing energy. But his love went unrequited; his hopes always exceeded the political results he longed for.

The GOP was not a factor in Texas politics, however, until the election of Dwight Eisenhower as President in 1952. Texas conservative Democrats and independents swarmed to the polls in support of Ike, and many would remain in the Republican fold thereafter. Halbouty was among the first to speak out for Ike.

But Eisenhower proved to be a disappointment to Halbouty and other independent oilmen. Several ploys he initiated failed to reduce the flow of foreign oil. Even worse to the industry, he vetoed a bill that would have freed natural gas from federal regulation, and gas regulation to the independents was a despised restriction and an insult to the free enterprise system.

The next Republican in the White House, Richard Nixon, was so embroiled in the criminal wrongdoings of Watergate that he had little time for oil industry concerns, though some in the industry had supported him financially to the point of criminality. He didn't fight strongly enough on their behalf, the oilmen thought, when Congress reduced the Depletion Allowance, and he placed price controls on the industry, complete with controls on the wholesale price of gasoline. Some contended that he helped precipitate the Arab embargo with what they saw as diplomatic ineptitude. When Libya unilaterally hiked the price of crude, and threatened to cut off all exports to the U.S. if Washington continued to support Israel, Nixon responded by threatening a buyer's boycott.

Nixon's threat was an idle one on the face of it. By now the U.S. needed foreign oil and could not afford to ban it. And the threat infuriated the other Arab states, already angered by American support of Israel, and the embargo quickly followed.

Gerald Ford, Nixon's hand-picked successor, perhaps was the biggest disappointment of all to independents, and certainly to Halbouty. Congress passed an energy bill, "a compromise package," that contained provisions for continuing Nixon's oil and gas controls and rolling back domestic oil prices. As House Minority Leader, Ford had been an industry friend and would have loathed the bill. President Ford, on the other hand, could feel Contender Ronald Reagan breathing on his neck, and he was convinced that signing the bill would greatly improve his chances to retain the presidency.

Texas Senator John Tower and Peter O'Donnell, former Texas GOP chairman, urged Halbouty to join them in Washington to plead for a Ford veto of the bill. Tower told Ford that he had taken an unofficial poll; Halbouty was the man to explain the industry's opposition to the bill. Tower already had told Ford there were enough votes in the Senate to sustain a veto.

Halbouty went to Washington. For 45 minutes in the Oval Office he did his eloquent best to explain why a veto was in the best interest not only of the industry but of the country. He returned to Houston believing he had fulfilled his mission.

Four days later Ford signed the bill.

Halbouty told reporters, "I feel the President has caved in to the pressure of radical members of Congress. As an American in search of leadership, and a Republican who has stood with his party through thick and thin, I am disgusted!"

He threw his support to Ronald Reagan, working vigorously on his behalf. Ford won the nomination from Reagan, but lost the ensuing election to Jimmy Carter.

\*\*\*

Years earlier, in 1968, Texas GOP movers and shakers had beseeched Halbouty to run for governor. He had made an appearance on national television. He had always approached the medium with a fine mixture of force and finesse, and after this appearance he received a telephone call from George Bush, then a Texas congressman. "You were great, Mike," Bush said. "You really project on television. I seriously think you should be a Republican candidate for governor, and I urge you to consider it."

Halbouty was pleased, but his interest was not piqued.

Several hours later Senator John Tower called him. He was more urgent than Bush. The party needed Halbouty; he should run; he could win, Tower told him. Halbouty thanked Tower for the kind words, but said he wasn't interested.

Then Peter O'Donnell, then chairman of the state GOP, called from Dallas. George Bush had called him, he said. "We've got to talk, Mike," O'Donnell said, "and I mean right away." He asked Halbouty to meet him the next morning in the Petroleum Club of Houston. Halbouty said he would.

It was a Saturday and the splendid club was almost empty of members on that morning. O'Donnell was most persuasive. He promised that adequate campaign funds would be made available. "Whatever it takes, Mike!" He played on Halbouty's party loyalty. "With a great chance to win, you owe it to the party to run!"

Halbouty demurred.

There wasn't much time for pondering, O'Donnell said. There would be a party caucus in Austin in two weeks.

"Let me think about it," Halbouty said.

It seemed likely that Preston Smith would be the Democratic nominee. Smith had been a state representative from 1944 to 1950, a state senator from 1957 to 1963, and at present was serving as lieutenant governor. He was an experienced politician but no more charismatic than a "bodark" stump.

Democrat Lyndon Johnson was retiring from Washington, leaving his party in disarray with little hope of finding a candidate to successfully challenge Richard Nixon, who was having a second shot at the Presidency. It seemed like a propitious time for a Republican to gain the governor's chair in Austin.

Halbouty went to Chicago to deliver a speech. Once the speech was made he secluded himself in his suite at the Palmer House, remaining incommunicado to all save his office. For ten days he paced the floor while the battle raged within him.

He would awaken with an intention of making the run for governor. By 10 a.m. he would have changed his mind. By 2 p.m., yes. By bedtime, no. Ten days of yes, no; yes, no.

He finally decided no, he would not run. He detested compromising, and compromise was the soul of politics. He could not bear to think that he would have to relinquish convictions or cede positions he had long held inviolate. Compromise meant looking for an average; as a wildcatter he couldn't abide that.

He went home. At his office he received a call from Paul Eggers, a Wichita Falls attorney and former Wichita County GOP chairman. Eggers wanted to know what Halbouty was going to do. Halbouty told him he was going to call Peter O'Donnell in the afternoon to announce his decision. "If you don't run, I'd like to make the race myself," Eggers said. Halbouty told Eggers he would call him after he talked with O'Donnell.

Halbouty called O'Donnell. Firmly, but perhaps a bit regretfully, he said he would not make the race. He repeated that decision in a call to Eggers.

Eggers ran, and lost to Preston Smith by a narrow margin, leaving Halbouty convinced that he could have beaten Smith handily.

Several years later Halbouty stepped into Cafe Lasserre, the fine Parisian restaurant at 17 Franklin D. Roosevelt Boulevard. Peter O'Donnell jumped up from a table and grasped Halbouty's shoulder. Swinging wide his arm, O'Donnell announced to his friends, "This is the man who should have been the first Republican governor of Texas!"

Halbouty bowed at the introduction, but if there had been any lingering doubts about his decision, they by now had dissipated.

***

Jimmy Carter's turbulent tenure of office found him in constant conflict with the oil industry. He showed little regard for whatever virtues the industry claimed, and the industry looked on him as an enemy from the moment he took office.

He preached conservation to the American people as a way to combat OPEC, encouraging them to cut back on use of gasoline, natural gas, fuel oil, and other petroleum products. Some in the industry publicly praised him for his stand, but few believed conservation would have an impact of significance on energy problems.

By executive order, Carter created the Department of Energy to implement his policies, and named James R. Schlesinger the first secretary. Schlesinger had held other ranking government and quasi-government posts, but was generally regarded by the industry as an "egghead," not a complimentary appellation, and the Department of Energy was seen as just another load of wearying red tape and binding restrictions.

At Carter's urging, Congress passed the Fuel Use Act which was intended to reduce the use of gas and oil as boiler fuel in industrial plants and promote the use of desulfurized coal.

Oilmen frothed.

The "compromise" energy bill signed by Ford had called for continuation of oil and gas controls until 1979. Newly-discovered oil brought a price competitive with OPEC's $12.08 per barrel, but "old oil" brought an average of only $5.03 per barrel. Independents insisted that all domestic crude should be priced as one, and competitive with OPEC's price.

And they still cried out for deregulation of natural gas.

A sharp OPEC price increase helped bring action from the White House. The Natural Gas Act of 1978 totally deregulated "deep gas"—gas found below 15,000 feet. Restrictions on gas from "tight sands," more costly to produce, were modified. "Old gas" was permitted to increase in price in accordance with the rate of inflation. Along with these concessions came a great number of confusing provisions that seemed destined to proliferate.

Oil and gas prices were rising. Oil was due to decontrol in 1979, but Carter called for "phased decontrol" of oil prices beginning June 1, 1979, and ending with total decontrol on September 30, 1981.

Oilmen further frothed.

And Carter also called for a "windfall profits tax" to "prevent unearned, excessive profits which the oil companies would receive as a result of decontrol and possible future OPEC price increases. . . ."

Oilmen cried out in protest. They marched on Washington demanding that Congress vote against the Carter proposal. It was not a "windfall profits tax" Carter was calling for but a plain and simple excise tax, the oilmen argued, the taking of capital from the producers and handing it over to the government. Without that capital, they said, the industry could not drill the wells necessary for an American revival.

Among other things, Halbouty called the proposed tax "punitive."

As the debate grew hotter, the Shah of Iran was driven out of his country by revolutionaries, Americans were seized as hostages, and Iranian oil ceased to flow to the U.S. and other western nations. Imported oil prices rose again, and so did domestic prices. And again there were long lines of angry, impatient motorists at service stations across America.

Halbouty, like many other independents, called on all of his resources to fight imposition of the tax. He spoke out at public meetings. He buttonholed Congressmen. He wrote hundreds of letters and sat through scores of interviews. But Carter was not to be denied. The tax became effective.

But Carter had little time to savor his victory, if victory he deemed it. The Republicans selected Ronald Reagan to contest him in the 1980 election, and it quickly became apparent that Reagan's charisma, if nothing else, would defeat a President who had lost the public's confidence.

\*\*\*

Despite the oil industry's disaffection with Carter, his administration coincided with the wildest boom since the discovery of the giant East Texas field. The rising oil and gas prices prompted increased drilling, some of it even in the boondocks.

Practicing what he had been preaching since 1960, Halbouty went west to drill three rank wildcats, one in Idaho, one in western

Nevada, one in eastern Oregon. He had claimed for years that oil and gas could be found in Idaho, Nevada, Oregon, Washington, and northern California. And he believed strongly that great pools lay in what was called the Utah-Idaho-Wyoming "thrust belt," a swath of twisted, tortured formations paralleling the eastern edge of the Rocky Mountains.

Halbouty got three dusters for his efforts, but Amoco drilled the discovery well of the Ryckman field in the "thrust belt," and seven other fields in that region quickly followed. Drilling spread to other areas.

By mid-1980—at the time of the Democratic and Republican national conventions—new oil was bringing $30 per barrel and "deep gas" more than $9 per mcf! Even "old gas" was bringing as much as $5 per mcf! Every individual and company that could lay hands on a drilling rig sallied forth to get rich or richer!

But the oil industry wanted total decontrol of oil and gas and other incentives Carter had denied it. Oilmen believed that Ronald Reagan would treat them differently.

***

Halbouty was a Reagan delegate at the Republican convention of 1976. Reagan lost that nomination to Ford who lost the election to Carter. Halbouty and Reagan never lost touch with each other after the initial contact. From time to time Reagan called for Halbouty's advice on energy matters.

It did not take long for the news media to begin referring to Halbouty as "Reagan's Energy Guru."

On visits with Reagan at his home in Pasadena and elsewhere Halbouty hammered home the points the oil industry had for so many years advocated—total decontrol of oil, deregulation of natural gas, a revamping of offshore leasing practices, and access to public lands for energy exploitation. There were, of course, new concerns—the "windfall profits tax" and the Fuel Use Act, both products of the Carter administration.

Further, and not the least in importance, Halbouty urged the abolition of the Department of Energy, commonly called DOE. Every time they met, Halbouty would tell Reagan, "DOE is no good!" It became a solemn joke between them, with Reagan echoing Halbouty, "DOE is no good." At the June 1980 Republican Convention, Reagan told the giddy throng in his acceptance speech that DOE would be dismantled. And during the campaign against Carter, he made it clear that he favored all the other changes the oil industry was crying for.

Halbouty's ardent support of Reagan had drawn some occasional fire in the past. As the 1978 AAPG convention in Oklahoma City drew near, the executive committee was seeking a speaker of prominence. More than 5,000 delegates would be in attendance. As a former president of the organization and an honored member, Halbouty was asked for a suggestion.

"Why not Ronald Reagan?" Halbouty asked.

"Can you get him, Mike?"

"I can try," said Halbouty.

He called Reagan in California. Said Reagan: "You've done a lot for me, Mike. Certainly I can do something for you."

Halbouty went for Reagan in his personal jet. On the flight from Los Angeles to Oklahoma City they ran into a terrible storm. It was frightening, but the pilot managed to fly around the turbulence and they entered the Oklahoma City airport from the east. As the plane landed, the storm struck Oklahoma City, deluging the area. That night Halbouty gave a party honoring Reagan that was limited to 50 people. Reagan spoke briefly to the group.

At the convention meeting the next day the audience was swollen to more than 6,000 by outsiders who wanted to hear Reagan. Halbouty concluded his introduction of Reagan by declaring, "Ladies and gentlemen, it gives me great pleasure to introduce to you the next President of the United States."

Reagan's speech was soundly applauded, but a short time later some AAPG members criticized Halbouty's reference to "the next President" remarks, saying he was putting AAPG in the political arena. Halbouty accepted the rebuke with unaccustomed placidity, and the mild furor died. But after the 1980 election, Halbouty remarked, "I told 'em Reagan was going to be the next President of the United States, and by God I was right!"

***

Halbouty had initially been attracted to Reagan by what he considered to be Reagan's strong patriotic stance, his denunciation of appeasers of all stripes, and certainly the Reagan thesis that the least government is the best government. Halbouty saw in the California governor-Presidential candidate a man of honest views with the eloquence to gain nation-wide support of them.

Halbouty was a delegate-at-large to the 1976 GOP convention where Reagan lost the party nomination and at the 1980 convention where he won. Occasionally, Halbouty accompanied the candidate on the campaign trail throughout the summer. After a stumping in Houston, Reagan asked Halbouty to travel with him to San Antonio aboard the campaign aircraft.

During the flight, Martin Anderson of the Hoover Institution, a member of Reagan's inner circle, told Halbouty, "Mike, the governor is going to ask you to be chairman of an energy task force, so be prepared."

Halbouty was prepared, and his answer to Reagan was yes. "Well, you and Marty get this thing organized," Reagan said.

On August 2, 1980, Halbouty received a letter formalizing his appointment as chairman of the candidate's Energy Policy Advisory Group. The letter said:

> "Dear Michel, I just want you to know how much I appreciate having you to serve as Chairman of my Energy Policy Advisory Group. It is extremely important that individuals with your expertise have an opportunity to focus on the critical issues that a new administration must face.
>
> "I look forward to reviewing the Committee's recommendations after the fall election. Sincerely, Ron."

All over the country outstanding citizens were being asked to serve on similar advisory groups in other governmental areas. Halbouty and Anderson went to work to find men they believed would bring brains and dedication to the energy group. Selected were 16 men to work under Halbouty's direction:

Pter Beckman, Electrical Engineering Department, University of Colorado; John Bookout, president of Shell Oil Company; W. J. Bowen, president of Transcontinental Pipe Line Company; W. Kenneth Davis, vice-president of Bechtel Power Company; H. J. Haynes, board chairman of Standard Oil Company of California; Hollis Hedberg, professor emeritus (geology) of Princeton University; Edward G. Jefferson, president of E. I. du Pont de Nemours & Company; George O. G. Lof of the Solar Energy Applications Laboratory; John J. McKetta, E. P. Schoch Professor of Chemical Engineering at the University of Texas; Edward J. Mitchell, professor of Business Economics, Graduate School of Business at the University of Michigan; Thomas G. Moore, Director of Domestic Studies of Hoover Institution; Bernard J. O'Keefe, board chairman of EG&G; Robert H. Quenon, president of Peabody Coal Company; Joseph R. Rensch, president of Pacific Lighting Corporation; Philip K. Verleger, Jr., Senior Research Scholar of the School of Organization and Management at Yale University; and Fred J. Russell, former undersecretary of the Interior and deputy director of the Office of Emergency Preparedness.

Each member contributed ideas and beliefs, and the group would meet from time to time in Washington to solidify a consensus.

During the long weeks when the advisory group was shaping its thoughts and reaching decisions, Halbouty was sought out by the news media not only for progress reports but for his personal views. There were no progress reports; Halbouty declared he would not preempt the group and the job to which it was committed. As for his personal views, they were reported from coast to coast. The key to energy sufficiency, he reiterated, was to "produce, produce, produce!" He had other remarks to make, of course, but they dealt with *how* the industry, with the proper incentives, *could* "produce, produce, produce!"

Reagan overwhelmed Carter at the November 4, 1980 election, and the very next day Halbouty personally delivered the group's report to the President-elect. He and Verleger had composed the final draft, which was submitted to the other members for final input and approval.

### The Policy Theme

It is our great fortune to be one of the richest energy nations in the world. Yet, judging by our current economic condition, who would know it? Shortages of gasoline and fuel recur and are widely feared; unemployment is widespread; inflation is rampant; and the dollar continues to fall against the strong currencies of the world. In this land of energy plenty, why have we fallen with the energy poor, rather than prospering with the energy rich?

It is not because energy has been ignored. President Carter has proposed several energy programs and the Democratic Congress has acted on hundreds of energy bills in the last four years. Much has been done. But what has been done is to impede production and curtail consumption. The government has acted on the principle that the way to deal with energy is to do away with it. Instead of unleashing the resources of a wealthy nation, we have, in the name of saving energy for some unspecified future time, tucked energy away like a rare bottle of wine.

But energy in this nation is not rare or scarce. The U.S. has the potential to produce as much oil and gas in the future as we have produced in our entire history. We have sixty times more coal than oil and forty times more coal than natural gas. There is more oil in shale in one single area, twenty-five miles in radius, than has been discovered in the whole Middle East. And, the United States is the world leader in most energy technology, especially petroleum.

The policies expressed in these pages value energy as a commodity to be used, not to be revered on the mantlepiece. By undoing the restrictive legislation of the past four years, we expect to create an open and competitive energy market that will meet the demands of our economy and the needs of our society. For, if the national economic pie does not grow—and it cannot grow without energy—those at the bottom of the economic ladder cannot rise without pulling someone down from the top. The price of energy failure is not just economic stagnation, but social upheaval.

We reject the notion that the energy dilemma can be solved only by halting the use of energy. Conservation, properly understood, does not mean non-use; it means optimal use over time. Energy resources are valuable only if they are produced and consumed. They will be used at the proper time only if producers and consumers see the correct signs of their value at each point in time. No mechanism has yet been devised to order the use of resources over time better than the free market.

The keystone of our energy policy must be the use of the market system to decide who produces what, where, and for whom. To substitute instead the fads of government bureaucrats is to condemn us to economic waste on a grand scale. In the world of changing tastes, technologies, and resource discoveries, the fanciful goals of so many barrels per day of this or that in such and such a year are the stuff of dreams, not reality. We do not know today which energy sources will prove cheapest or cleanest in 1995. We do know how to find out. Let the producers compete in a free and open market, and let the consumers choose the winners.

Our policy is to remove the onerous constraints on the production and use of energy in the form of price controls, licensing requirements, use controls, taxes, and subsidies that do not permit the best and cheapest to win out in the marketplace. Specifically, we call for decontrol of oil and gas, opening up public lands for exploration and development, placing environmental policy on a scientific cost-benefit basis, encouraging research and development of new energy technologies, building a substantial emergency petroleum reserve, and encouraging the production of energy throughout the world.

**Oil and Gas**

Over seventy percent of the energy used in the United States comes from oil and natural gas. Thus, the nation's standard of living, the continued functioning of our economy, and, indeed, our national security, depend vitally upon an adequate supply of these fuels.

The outlook will not change much in the next decade. Despite all the nation can do to conserve energy, increase the use of coal and nuclear power, and develop new energy resources, oil and natural gas will still be called on to supply at least sixty percent of our energy wants in 1990.

In place of the hostility and antagonism toward the petroleum industry which now exist, government must adopt a more positive, or at least, objective role. One key to a new attitude is utilizing personnel with experience in the oil and gas and other energy industries in the government's energy agencies. The technical knowledge and experience of people from the energy industries should be utilized by government in developing and implementing our national energy policy.

The national energy interest of the United States extends far beyond our borders. Other nations can make an enormous contribution to energy security in the United States, as well as in their home markets. We must encourage the development of oil and natural gas resources throughout the world and especially in the case of more reliable economic partners. Federal policy should recognize the contribution that reasonable amounts of LNG imports can make in meeting our essential energy needs. We must encourage U.S. petroleum companies to make use of their technological superiority abroad by granting them tax status at least equivalent to their foreign competition. We must develop a clear and consistent foreign policy to stabilize and improve relations with oil exporting nations.

*Petroleum Decontrol*

The most important step the federal government can take toward developing greater domestic energy supplies is the removal of all price and allocation controls on crude oil and natural gas. With this one action, market forces will efficiently allocate available supply, and provide an impetus for conservation and a major stimulus for domestic exploration and production of oil and gas and the development of alternate energy sources.

We should continue the orderly phase-out of all price and allocation controls on crude oil and petroleum products to completion on September 30, 1981, as scheduled.

Some special groups enjoy artificial competitive advantages from price controls and allocations. Their efforts to block decontrol or to substitute protective legislation for themselves should be restricted. Subsidies and advantageous allocations of raw materials that promote the continued operation of uneconomical facilities, which are non-competitive in a free market, should be terminated.

We must begin phased price decontrol of all natural gas prices. Control of most natural gas prices, notwithstanding present "decontrol" legislation, keeps the price of gas to some customers considerably below equivalent fuel oil prices. This encourages wasteful uses of gas, and discourages conservation and desirable conversion to alternate fuels. Under the Natural Gas Policy Act, most intrastate gas prices will be decontrolled by 1985, as will some interstate gas prices. However, "vintage" interstate gas (i.e., gas from wells drilled prior to February 1977, and gas from most offshore wells on federal property leased prior to 1977) will *not* be decontrolled.

Natural gas prices should begin phased decontrol over a short time period so that all gas prices are decontrolled as soon as possible.

*Public Lands*

Our public lands offer an enormous petroleum potential, but nowhere is the threat of excessive environmentalism to the nation's energy development felt more keenly than in the area of access to and development of these lands, both onshore and offshore. As an example, Congress is favorably considering a bill to lock up over 100 million acres of federal land in the state of Alaska for timely development, including exploration for oil and gas. This is being done against the wishes of the people of Alaska, and the land in question contains some of the most promising remaining potential hydrocarbon-yielding acreage in the nation. Years of experience in the United States and abroad have demonstrated the industry's capability to find and produce oil and gas with little or no significant damage to the environment. Absolute prohibitions on exploration and production in promising areas are a luxury we can no longer afford. Rather, careful development of productive areas is a national necessity.

We must return to the nation's historic policy of multiple-use for most federal lands. The policy of multiple-use for most federal lands served our nation well for most of its history, and federal lands have been an important resource in our economic development. Withdrawal of land for a single-use (e.g., recreation) should be limited to those scenic or other areas that are truly unique, and such withdrawal should be legislated, with a periodic reassessment provision. Single-use designation precludes all exploration and evaluation of such lands, to the detriment of the public. Furthermore, classification of lands for single-use often denies needed access through these areas for purposes of transportation to and from multiple-use public lands.

We must stop designating public lands as instant wildernesses without a thorough evaluation of the natural resources they may contain. At a time when the public itself has become increasingly aware of the nation's need to develop natural resources and to continue to explore to such resources, it is inconsistent and wasteful to lock up potential resource reserves without first providing for exploration and inventorying. Specifically:

- The National Petroleum Reserve—Alaska and the William O. Douglas Arctic Wildlife Range should be opened for exploration and development by private industry, with appropriate provisions to protect the environment.
- A high priority should be placed on resolving the debate between state and federal governments (the so-called Sagebrush Rebellion) on how much federal land should be set aside for non-development and, more basically, on who makes the decision.

We should adopt a "leasing on demand" policy for the Outer Continental Shelf lands. Because of its size, geology, and relative lack of development, the Outer Continental Shelf is outstanding among the many areas within the country for its potential to add to our petroleum reserves. There is no legitimate national purpose served by delaying exploration and development of lands believed to have economically recoverable resources. The OCS Lands Act Amendments of 1978, the Endangered Species Act, NEPA, the Marine Protection, Research and Sanctuaries Act, etc., and all of their implementing regulations should be reviewed to ensure that their provisions are compatible with the need to increase oil and gas production from the OCS and other areas.

In general, we should retain the types of leases and leasing terms which have worked well for areas explored in the past, onshore and offshore. Cash bonus bidding for these kinds of areas has proven successful for both government and industry over many years and should not be replaced by variable royalty or net profits schemes which may result in leaving valuable recoverable reserves in the ground. However, in order to meet future petroleum needs, it is recommended that in unusually costly remote deep-water or otherwise difficult harsh environmental areas, consideration should be given to adopting a new leasing procedure which would permit the granting of much larger regional tracts to consortiums of companies to explore in joint efforts.

*Environmental Restrictions*

Programs involving environmental protection and energy resource development are often unnecessarily posed in conflict. The resulting delays mean losses to society in both areas. A balance must be struck. A thorough analysis of the social and economic costs of specific types of environmental protection should form the basis for all environmental regulations. An immediate review of the regulations "implementing" environmental legislation is necessary, as there are many instances where these regulations clearly exceed the intent of Congress. We should (1) revise existing laws in order to remove oil and gas development impediments which do not yield commensurate environmental benefits; and (2) enact effective fast-track legislation to accelerate and place time limits on the permitting process for energy projects.

*Conservation*

Conservation must play an important role in achieving a balance between the supply and demand for oil and natural gas. The basic guideline in establishing effective conservation programs should be to rely as much as possible on voluntary actions by the private sector, and to keep mandates to a minimum. We accept the principle that competitive market pricing will be the chief reliance for encouraging conservation and the efficient use of oil and gas, as well as other fuels. Market pricing is the most effective way to bring about energy conservation throughout our economic system. It stimulates capital investment in energy-saving applications and directs available supplies of energy to the uses that have the highest value.

We must remove unnecessary regulatory barriers to converting large-volume oil and gas consumers, such as utilities, to coal. It is inequitable (and useless) for the Department of Energy to mandate utility conversion to coal as long as the Environmental Protection Agency maintains unrealistic coal-burning emission standards. Full price decontrol of oil and natural gas will quickly encourage widespread conversion if such impediments are removed.

An absolute ban on the utility use of gas is unwise. Natural gas distribution companies often need a boiler fuel market as a place to sell the gas supplies they have contracted for to serve homes and other high priority users when warm weather reduces that demand. Further, while boiler fuel is not a high value for natural gas, it can replace fuel oil in some instances, effectively cutting our dependence on foreign oil imports. Finally, limited gas use can significantly increase our ability to burn coal with less air pollution.

*Emergency Preparedness*

Despite the nation's best efforts to achieve more domestic energy production, the United States will continue to depend for many years on foreign supply sources for a significant proportion of its petroleum needs. Workable and equitable standby federal emergency supply procedures which rely as much as possible on the private sector for implementation should be in place in order to deal with possible shortages promptly and effectively.

We should fill the Strategic Petroleum Reserve as soon as practicable. Government and industry should work together to plan for utilizing the SPR in an emergency and dispensing the available crude oil. Plans should be developed in as much detail as possible, and as soon as possible, to permit effective advance planning by both industry and government.

Recognition should be given to the fact that companies involved in natural gas supply and distribution also monitor a sizable "strategic reserve" of natural gas in their seasonal storage. Thus, in an emergency, gas can displace oil in some stationary uses, thereby freeing up oil for transportation use.

We should review existing legislation establishing standby authority for government action during emergency supply interruptions and prepare a workable emergency contingency plan for our nation's security to be implemented quickly in the event that a major interruption should occur in the supply of foreign oil. Much legislation is already in place (EPAA, EPCA, EECA, etc.) dealing with government's authority in this area after the September 30, 1981, decontrol deadline. However, recent studies by the General Accounting Office, the National Petroleum Council and others have questioned its appropriateness and adequacy. An impartial Executive Branch audit of this area is necessary to assure that the necessary legislation is in place to provide for needed, but not excessive, federal authority in an emergency.

We should establish a specific triggering mechanism to engage and disengage any system of emergency controls. Triggers, set to a significant and specified degree of shortage, should discourage the use of controls except in real emergencies. This will facilitate planning by government and the private sector by setting forth clear criteria for invoking emergency procedures.

*Windfall Profits Tax*

The Windfall Profits Tax, which is really an excise tax on oil production, is designed to reduce oil industry income after federal income taxes by at least $227 billion over the next decade.

The Windfall Profits Tax applies to a conventional new oil development. It does not apply to alternative supply sources, such as synthetics, shale oil, and imports. Thus, it discriminates against the domestic development of conventional petroleum resources. This will lead to misallocation of the nation's resources, resulting in lower future domestic oil production and higher costs to consumers.

Economic use of our nation's resources dictates that we should eliminate the Windfall Profits Tax. If this is not practical immediately, then the Tax must be restructured and phased-out on an accelerated basis. Improvements must be made to reward success in finding new reserves and in maintaining and increasing oil production. These should include provisions to:

- Eliminate the Windfall Profits Tax on newly discovered oil, heavy oil, incremental oil, and stripper oil.
- If the Windfall Profits Tax on newly discovered oil can not be eliminated, it is recommended that a plowback provision mechanism be established to encourage exploration in undeveloped "wildcat" areas.
- The Windfall Profits Tax on all other oil production must be phased-out at an accelerated rate.

*Divestiture Proposal*

We must recognize that attempts to break up petroleum companies or prevent them from going into other areas of energy or other businesses are anti-competitive, counterproductive to energy development, and should be rejected.

More domestic energy production of every kind will be urgently needed for decades. It makes no sense to exclude any industry from joining in efforts to produce it. Attempts to require divestiture of the oil companies, for example, distract the nation from the serious task of energy production.

**Coal**

Coal is the most abundant yet least utilized of our domestic energy resources. It represents seventy-two percent of our known remaining fossil fuel supplies, but accounts for only nineteen percent of our current energy consumption. In terms of proven reserves, we have sixty times more coal than oil on an energy equivalent basis and over forty times more coal than natural gas.

More important, coal is cheaper than the other two fossil fuels for large stationary energy sources such as electric power generating stations. In May, 1980, the average delivered price paid by utilities for coal came to $1.33 per million Btu; the comparable average prices paid for oil and gas were $4.03 and $2.12, respectively.

Expanded use of coal can play a major role in alleviating the severe national security problem created by our dependence on imported oil. Oil and natural gas consumption by the utility sector alone still accounts for approximately three million barrels of oil equivalent per day. This, in turn, represents about forty percent of all United States oil imports.

Coal can be mined, transported and used safely and without significantly degrading the environment. The technological and procedural know-how to achieve these objectives has clearly been demonstrated, and sufficient legislative authority already exists to ensure that these tools are utilized in an effective manner.

In addition to easing our balance of payments problem by replacing oil in many applications and thereby reducing our need for imports, coal can make a positive contribution to becoming a major export.

Most experts agree that coal will be one of the basic ingredients for providing the synthetic gas and liquid fuels of the future. But for coal to fulfill its proper role in the energy market, we need to remove the unnecessarily restrictive regulatory burdens that have been retarding its use. Air quality regulations currently in effect or proposed represent the area that is most in need of reform.

The Environmental Protection Agency's current review of National Ambient Air Quality Standards (NAAQS) should be based upon an evaluation by an *independent* body of scientific experts of all research conducted to date on the potential linkage of sulfur dioxide, nitrogen oxide, carbon monoxide, and particulates to human health and welfare. The results of this evaluation should be used to revise the existing standards for these pollutants as appropriate.

The current rigid system that establishes relatively inflexible emission limitations for new units regardless of air quality should be discarded. A new process that permits consideration of existing and projected loadings should be adopted in its place. Specifically, the current New Source Performance Standards requirement that a seventy to ninety percent reduction in sulfur dioxide emissions be achieved for all new electric power generating stations should be modified to permit the use of cost-benefit analysis in determining the degree of control required.

All regulations should permit flexibility with regard to the accomplishment of the mandated results. Federal coal development should not become the land-use of last resort; it must be given high priority along with other energy-related federal land-uses.

In recognition of the competitive nature of the coal market and the extensive use of long-term contracts, federal coal leasing should be expanded to provide ample supplies to satisfy any reasonable market conditions.

The procedures for developing and processing Environmental Impact Statements should be streamlined and the process accelerated.

Emphasis should be shifted from an across-the-board enforcement effort on safety to one that focuses on coal mines with poor accident records.

Permitting and siting procedures should be consolidated and simplified to reduce the time required to obtain federal approvals associated with the mining and burning of coal.

**Nuclear and Electric Power**

An expanding and healthy economy requires increasing electric supply capability. In addition, obsolete and oil and gas fired capacities will need to be replaced. Only coal and nuclear plants can fill this need and they are highly capital intensive.

The most serious problem the utility industry faces is achieving adequate revenues to be able to finance new facilities. Federal leadership can be helpful in achieving favorable action by state regulatory agencies including inclusion of the cost of construction work in progress in the rate base, the retention by the utilities of the intended benefits of accelerated depreciation and investment tax credits, as well as satisfactory rate structures.

Revitalization of the essential nuclear power program requires top-level national leadership which itself can substantially strengthen public support and facilitate necessary legislative changes.

The Carter Administration's policy of benign neglect toward nuclear power has left the Nuclear Regulatory Commission (NRC) adrift without support or guidance from the White House. This situation has contributed directly to the current nuclear plant licensing quagmire. It currently takes up to twelve to fifteen years to license and construct a nuclear power plant. It is absolutely essential that NRC licensing procedures be streamlined to reduce the time between the application for a construction permit and commercial operation. Expediting the licensing process would force all regulators to separate the important from the unimportant and thus direct sufficient attention to safety matters which have currently become smothered in a morass of detail. In this process, the government must take all steps necessary to assure that the lessons learned from Three Mile Island have been implemented and that the public health and safety continues to be the primary concern. Reducing the licensing time for nuclear power plants by focusing on substantive issues only will enhance safety—not compromise it—and speed the time of United States energy security.

In addition to nuclear plant licensing, licensing requirements are currently being developed for facilities important to the balance of the nuclear fuel cycle, such as away-from-reactor spent-fuel storage facilities and commercial radioactive waste repositories. Licensing procedures for these facilities as well as spent-fuel reprocessing plants must be equally expeditious.

To the current time, the federal government's nuclear waste disposal program has been characterized by sudden and arbitrary changes in direction, emphasis and objectives and an unwillingness to fund and begin an adequate demonstration program. The result has been the mistaken perception by the general public that technologically feasible solutions to the waste disposal issue are not within our grasp. The fact is that the difficulty has been political and institutional rather than technical. Several technologically sound waste disposal techniques are available for utilization now. To accommodate the transition period between now and the time when the nuclear fuel cycle is closed, we need rapid construction of away-from-reactor spent fuel storage facilities.

Effective policies with respect to proliferation of nuclear weapons are essential. Those of the Carter Administration have not only been counterproductive by increasing the risk but also have seriously damaged the United States' domestic and export nuclear program. An immediate review of these policies needs to be carried out especially as they affect international leadership cooperation and institutions as well as the domestic program including nuclear fuel reprocessing and development of the breeder reactor.

Federal "fast-track" legislation is needed that avoids infringement on substantive state and local prerogatives, yet provides an effective mechanism for coordinating and expediting decisions on high priority major energy projects, including specifically coal-fired and nuclear power plants. Such legislation will also provide for expeditious judicial review of such decisions so that we, as a nation, can be about the business of building the energy security we desperately need.

We believe that electrical energy generated with our vast indigenous coal and uranium resources can make a major contribution to reducing the national security threat created by our dependence on imported petroleum and ensure that an adequate reserve of electrical energy is available to support future United States economic growth.

**Synthetic Fuels**

The conversion of solids and near-solids to liquids and gases is expensive and technologically difficult. As the cost of foreign liquids and gases rises, however, converted solids become more competitive.

Private industry has the wherewithal to continue to develop the required technologies. However, a great deal of technology which is not currently being properly utilized exists in our government-sponsored laboratories. A strong program encouraging technological transfer from government laboratories to private sector is sorely needed.

A major issue confronting the new Administration is the Synthetic Fuels Corporation. Immediately after the election, a special task force should be appointed to study the desirability of its continuation.

*Coal Gasification, Liquefaction, and Oil Shale*

Coal gasification, liquefaction, and oil shale are crucial elements of any synthetic hydrocarbon program. Coal gasification represents a basic step in the conversion of coal to both gases and liquids. Gas made from coal can displace oil in most stationary uses, thereby making more oil available for transport use. Coal liquefaction directly addresses a critical energy problem for the United States: a sufficient supply of liquid hydrocarbons for transport fuel use and other uses where substitution is difficult, costly, or time-consuming.

To accelerate the commercial development of these important technologies in a cost-effective manner, government energy policy should provide an economic framework to encourage private sector competition and resource allocation.

Specifically, during the formative period of development and demonstration, government policy should:

- Place maximum reliance on the private sector.
- Allow accelerated depreciation of investment costs, as contained in proposals such as 10-5-3, and other incentives to attract private capital.
- Provide a "fast-track" mechanism to coordinate and expedite federal, state, and local actions and judicial review to accelerate decision on key energy projects.
- Support governmental synthetic fuels research and development efforts with strong emphasis on the need for technology transfer to the private sector.

Oil shale presents a very different set of technological and environmental conditions than coal. The potential is enormous. There is more oil in one single area, twenty-five miles in radius, than has been discovered in the whole Middle East. The advantage of shale oil is that it can be extracted in liquid form. The problems of residue disposal and process water are large in the scenic and arid regions where oil shale is located. Properly handled, these difficulties can be overcome. Federal policy should emphasize the following:

- Recognize that the benefits of oil shale development are long-term while the costs are short-term. Design federal policies to recognize the short-term problems and to assist state and local governments in the transition period.
- Water resources in shale-rich areas can be as valuable as hydrocarbons. Public policy must be designed to develop hydrocarbon resources and water resources concurrently. Emphasis must be given to mechanisms to coordinate federal regulations of the two types of resources.
- Timely and responsible permitting, eliminating time-consuming challenges and later changes in ground rules, will be particularly

necessary in developing shale oil resources because of the long lead times and immense amounts of capital required.

*Tar Sands*

The United States tar sand resource and its total contribution to future energy supply is likely to be small. However, as the price of energy increases, it may be feasible to develop certain tar sand deposits through mining or through in-situ heating techniques.

The same policy of timely and responsible permitting necessary for oil shale development is required for tar sands as well.

*Ethanol and Methanol*

It is practical to extend gasoline supplies for motor vehicle use by mixing the gasoline with five to fifteen percent alcohol. The mixture is commonly termed "gasohol." Two types of alcohol can be used, ethanol and methanol. Ethanol from grain is currently used almost exclusively since it requires no engine modifications. However, ethanol production from grain using oil for fuel is energy inefficient using more petroleum than it displaces, and presently very uneconomical. Methanol, on the other hand, can be produced from coal and may be more efficient even though some engine modifications will be required. Government policy should recognize the differences and adopt separate policies.

**Renewable Energy Sources**

Solar radiation is the primary source of several forms of renewable energy available for practical use. The principal forms of these energies are hydropower, wind power, biomass, and solar energy itself. Ocean waves caused by wind, and seawater heated by the sun are secondary renewable forms produced by solar energy.

To the extent that these renewable energy sources can be substituted for imported oil, they can increase the security of the nation and benefit its economy. With the exception of hydropower and biomass for fuel wood, these sources represent an insignificant fraction of national consumption. Approximately 3 quads of hydroelectric energy are produced per year, and it is estimated that fuel wood, mainly as industrial waste wood, provides 1 to 2 quads. Geothermal steam is supplying about 0.1 quad and solar heat to buildings about 0.01 quad.

Although the present contribution of renewable energies to the total annual demand of 80 quads is less than five percent, the potential of these sources is substantial.

Government policy should include the following strategic elements:

- Provide reliable information to the public on the costs/benefits of using renewable energy sources.
- Provide financial support for further research and development in technical areas not yet fully commercial and where the benefits of federal funds can be maximized.
- In adopting these policies, the type and level of government financial support for solar energy research and development should be justified by cost/benefit analysis. The "glamour" of solar energy should not lead to government financial support beyond levels commensurate with economic and strategic national energy requirements.
- Government standards for funding the development of solar systems should provide for the amount of actual payment to be related to performance. Much government funding now goes to systems that are patently inefficient, and do not live up to promised performance.
- All qualified individuals and companies who wish to participate in developing solar resources should have equal opportunity to enter the industry and equal access to government incentives.
- Federal codes and local ordinances should be examined to be sure they do not discriminate against the construction of solar facilities.
- More government lands with geothermal potential should be opened up for development. Present leasing practices keep many potential lands off-limits.
- Utilities should be encouraged to take geothermal resources at competitive values where available. Efforts should be made to overcome any reluctance which may arise because of the remote location and limited amounts of power generated at individual sites.
- Environmental rules on emissions to air and reinjection of "used" fluids into the ground should be reasonable. Restrictions should be limited to those really required to protect the environment.

**Energy Transportation**

Efficient and timely development of energy fuels requires a transportation network that can be counted on to deliver these fuels to market economically. Indeed, some resources such as western coal will depend heavily for their development upon transportation. We, therefore, recommend that:

- The deregulation of all rail transportation should be completed subject to the imposition of appropriate safeguards to protect "captive shippers" from excessive rate increases or deteriorating service.

- A coal slurry pipeline bill, without restrictions on owners-shippers, should be enacted and implemented authorizing the use of eminent domain.

- Oil pipelines be removed from regulation by the Federal Energy Regulatory Commission (FERC). Oil pipelines had been regulated for decades by the Interstate Commerce Commission in a manner allowing rapid development of pipelines and flexibility of rate-making. The recent shift to FERC regulation threatens the continued viability of the industry since FERC (mostly the old Federal Power Commission) appears to be treating oil pipelines, a risky and competitive industry, as if they were natural gas pipelines, a relatively low risk public utility-type industry. Although a change in regulatory approach, back to the ICC method, would probably be satisfactory, total decontrol would be more in keeping with the nature of the industry.

- Cargo preference legislation, i.e., legislation requiring that a certain percentage of our oil imports be carried in United States flag tankers, should be rejected. The much higher cost of U.S. tankers would result in added costs to U.S. consumers without bringing benefit to the nation as a whole.

- Only one port capable of receiving deep-draft Very Large Crude Carriers (VLCC) is under construction in the United States. This is the Louisiana Offshore Oil Port, which will begin operation in early 1981. To secure the impressive economies of scale which exist in tankers, the federal government should work toward removing the barriers of environmental regulation and obstructionism which stand in the way of the development of additional deep-draft ports.

- The federal government should cooperate with United States industry as well as potential foreign governments and purchasers to facilitate the shipment of coal overseas. These efforts should include the expeditious handling of export licenses and the construction of deepwater ports along the East, West and Gulf Coasts.

**Petrochemicals**

Over ninety-five percent of the total oil and gas consumed in the United States is burned as a fuel. The remaining four and one half to five percent of U.S oil and natural gas consumption is used as a hydrocarbon source in the manufacture of petrochemical products. These products are used throughout society in a great variety of ways. Almost eighty percent of total rubber products and over fifty percent of our nation's fibers are man-made based on petroleum. In addition, thousands of useful products are produced from petrochemicals.

In terms of total sales, the petrochemical industry is significantly larger than such basic industries as steel, aluminum, and pulp and paper manufacturing. Over 310,000 persons are employed directly in the petrochemical industry. The industry invested $4.6 billion in new plants and equipment in 1978—which was over ten percent of the new capital invested by all United States manufacturers during the year. Perhaps even more important, almost every industry purchases some petrochemicals and, therefore, is dependent upon petrochemicals to some degree. Clearly, petrochemical products have made a significant contribution to modern society and are major factors in the nation's effort to achieve greater energy efficiency.

Government energy regulations distort the energy market and jeopardize the petrochemical industry's access to feedstock materials. In general, petrochemical industry concerns, relative to government energy regulation, fall into two broad categories:

- Government regulation, by its very nature, results in some dislocation and diversion of energy resources.
- Government regulations create competitive disadvantages within the petrochemical industry and opposite foreign competition.

Therefore, this task force recognizes that the petrochemical industry plays a vital role in our economy and recommend that we, as a country, maintain a viable and robust petrochemical industry, i.e., one that can function without unreasonable regulatory constraints. Because of the relationship between the oil and chemical industries, it is imperative that any government energy policy provide ample supplies of petrochemical feedstocks.

A government policy that treats all energy fuels and users equally in a free and open market will place the petrochemical industry and other major industrial users on an equal competitive basis in the United States and world markets. If during periods of severe energy disruption some form of government intervention is required, any controls should not disadvantage petrochemicals in competing for available supplies.

### Law of the Sea

An advisory U.S. Technical Marine Boundary Commission should promptly be established to advise and inform U.S. officials and political delegates to the Law of the Sea hearings on geological and other technical considerations with respect to the drawing of political boundaries in the oceans. This Commission should be composed largely of marine geologists, geographers, biologists, engineers, and other technical personnel. The United States should not approve the Law of the Sea Treaty without consideration of the recommendations of such U.S. Technical Marine Boundary Commission. In the meantime, the United States should claim and retain jurisdiction over resources underlying its continental shelf and slope out to the seaward edge of the continental margin (base of the continent) without regard to water depth; also, restricted seas, such as the Gulf of Mexico and the Bering Sea, should be divided equitably in their entirely between the United States and the other bordering countries.

### The Department of Energy

The Department of Energy has become a large and unmanageable institution with a variety of programs ranging from essential to useless. Some of its functions, such as the petroleum price and allocation controls, are unnecessary and counterproductive. Other functions such as in the entire military and nuclear areas may belong under a separate entity. Still other functions such as the Strategic Petroleum Reserve should probably be located in a newly created entity. In view of the serious organizational questions surrounding the existing DOE, an immediate task force should be created to review, in detail, its various functions and to recommend restructuring the organization.

***

Reagan later would call the report "excellent," complimenting the group several times on the report's "contents and usefulness."

# CHAPTER FIVE

Like other Presidents before them, Jimmy Carter and Ronald Reagan arranged for a peaceful transfer of power. Reagan chose Edward Meese, a member of the inner circle—the "kitchen cabinet"—to head up transition teams that would study every administrative section of the government. The Carter administration was to maintain control of government until January 20, Inauguration Day, and cabinet officers and their employees were expected to ease the transition by cooperating with Reagan's men.

Reagan wanted Halbouty to chair the energy transition team, and the word was given to Halbouty by Meese, Martin Anderson, and Richard Fairbanks, another inner circle member. Halbouty said he would take the job. He moved to Washington. He lived at the Capitol-Hilton and Fairbanks arranged for offices at DOE headquarters in the Forrestal Building. He was given a 16-person staff. He didn't know a single one of them, and none of them was in the oil business. The majority was under 40 years old.

Fortunately for Halbouty, however, they were bright and energetic and, most importantly, the majority had proven track records in the corridors of power. They understood the task at hand much better than did Halbouty. So it was a splendid wedding: the oilman gave the team strong leadership while being educated in the mysterious workings of bureaucracy by its knowledgeable members. A camaraderie was established, based on mutual affection and regard.

Halbouty's deputy was James B. Atkin of the prestigious San Francisco law firm of Pillsbury, Madison, and Sutro, and for five years before joining the transition team Atkin had been retained as project director for a committee formulated by the petroleum industry to resist divestiture legislation.

Danny J. Boggs also was an attorney, being of counsel with the Washington, D.C. firm of Bushnell, Gage, Reizen, and Byington. He had been deputy minority counsel to the Senate Energy Committee, assistant to the chairman of the Federal Power Commission, and assistant to the U.S. Solicitor General. (In 1986, he was U.S. circuit court judge for the Sixth Circuit Court of Appeals in Cincinnati.)

John Busterud was president of RESOLVE, Center for Environmental Conflict Resolution, Palo Alto, California. He had been special adviser on environment as Aspen Institute for Humanistic Studies, chairman of a presidential council on environmental quality, and deputy assistant secretary of defense for environmental quality. (In 1986, he was senior counselor to Ecology and Environment, Inc.)

Randall A. Davis was associate minority counsel for the House Interstate and Foreign Commerce Committee, and had served as minority staff associate of the Energy and Power Subcommittee. (In 1986, he was associate director of the Office of Management and Budget.)

Joseph P. Kearney was director of Energy Programs for System Development Corporation. He had been with the Office of Management and Budget where he was responsible for DOE's non-regulatory programs, and had been assistant to the chief scientist at Combustion Engineering. (In 1986, he was with ANR Pipeline Company in Detroit.)

Charles King Mallory III was a partner in Hunton and Williams, a Washington, D.C. law firm. He had been assistant secretary of Interior for energy and minerals, deputy assistant secretary for Power Resources and Regulation, executive director of the Security and Exchange Commission, and vice-president and general counsel for Middle South Utilities System. (In 1986 he was still a partner in the Hunton and Williams law firm in Washington, D.C.)

Richard E. Messick was with Kay, Scholer, Fierman, Hays and Handler, New York City law firm. He had held a variety of energy-related positions, including that of consultant to the International Energy Agency, and he had co-authored several publications on competition in the energy industry. (In 1986, he was chief counsel of the Senate Foreign Relations Committee.)

James L. Mitchell was a partner in Mayer, Brown, and Platt, a Washington, D.C. law firm. He had been associate director of OMB, general counsel and then under-secretary at HUD, and policy director for the secretary of commerce. (In 1986, he was with Citibank, N.A. in New York City.)

Diarmuid F. O'Scannlain was with the Portland, Oregon law firm of Ragen, Roberts, O'Scannlain, Robertson, and Neill. He had been a public utility commissioner of Oregon, director of the Oregon Department of Environmental Quality, and a member of the Oregon Nuclear and Thermal Energy Council. (In 1986, he was U.S. circuit judge for the Ninth Circuit Court of Appeals in San Francisco.)

Thomas A. Peacock was vice-president of government and public affairs for International Coal Refining Company. He had been a special assistant to the director of congressional affairs for the Department of Energy, director of Energy and Natural Resources for the National Association of Manufacturers, and served as director of House of Representatives Liaison in the Federal Energy Administration. (In 1986, he was director of market development for Signal Environmental Systems in Hampton, New Hampshire.)

Charles A. Trabandt was the minority staff counsel for Senator James McClure, Senate Committee on Energy and Natural Resources. He had been Republican counsel for the House Energy R&D Subcommittee, Republican counsel for the Senate Energy and Natural Resources Committee, program manager for an engineering consulting firm, a CIA Technical Operations Officer, and a Navy Officer. (In 1986, he was a commissioner on the Federal Energy Regulatory Commission.)

Jan B. Vlcek was a partner with Gardner, Carton, and Douglas of Washington, D.C. and Chicago, practicing energy and environmental law and representing both users and producers of energy. He had served as minority counsel to the House Commerce Committee with responsibility for energy legislation. (In 1986, he was with Sutherland, Asbill, and Brennan in Washington.)

C. M. (Mike) Butler III was administrative assistant to Senator John Tower. He had practiced law in the energy area in Houston and Washington for ten years before joining Tower. When Tower became chairman of the 1980 Republican Platform Committee,

Butler was called on to work on the energy plank, for which he wrote the first draft. (After the team's work was completed, he became administrative head of the Federal Energy Regulatory Commission. In 1986, he was manager of the Natural Gas Department for Kidder, Peabody, and Company in New York City.)

This was a powerhouse lineup and Halbouty had the good sense to appreciate it. He asked for advice, and he got it, but there was never any doubt as to who was in charge. These men, all top-notch in their own right, were amazed at Halbouty's boundless energy, his quick grasp of any given problem, his driving ambition "to get the job done right, and right now." Said one of the men, "He wanted us to shake things up until everything fell in the right place to provide a blueprint for action by the new administration. We shook, and they fell."

All of the loose ends, and some of the fast ones, were pulled together by two competent administrative assistants, Marsa Bintz and Anne Buchanan. Bintz, a paralegal, came to the team with Charles King Mallory from Hunton and Williams. "The team was just forming for the very first day and it was a madhouse—we had been given offices at DOE and phones, but not much else. Many cigar-smoke-filled meetings were going on, and here I was answering the phones by myself (which were constantly ringing off the hook), trying to remember everyone's name and wondering what in the hell I was doing there. However, I made it through the first day and, like manna from Heaven, the very next day in walked Anne Buchanan, and the rest, as they say, is history," said Bintz.

Buchanan's induction was even more precipitous. On her first day at work on a new job, working for James Atkin at Pillsbury, Madison, and Sutro in San Francisco, Atkin told her he was going to Washington to be Halbouty's deputy. Buchanan was startled, but not upset, even though she had just left a top position as executive secretary of the University of California Board of Regents to work for Atkin. She hesitated only slightly when he asked her if she wanted to go to Washington.

Atkin arrived on opening day, and Buchanan was there the next, just in time to preserve Marsa Bintz' sanity. They were joined later by Janet Onnie, and the trio—like the rest of the team—learned to live with Halbouty's stridency and profanity; they succumbed to his charm.

"We worked seven days a week until the inauguration and, I believe, it was the only team to become a family, not to mention produce a report that was read by the President," Bintz said. "Mr. H., being the whirlwind that he is, captivated our lives and our hearts, and I am sincerely proud to have been lucky enough to have spent that time with the team and especially Mr. H." (In 1986, Bintz was with David, Hagner, and Harvey in Washington, and Buchanan was administrative assistant to the DOE deputy secretary.)

Halbouty's task was made somewhat lighter by Carter's Secretary of Energy, Charles W. Duncan, who had moved to DOE from Defense where he had been deputy secretary. Duncan was a Houston businessman and a long-time Halbouty acquaintance. He was a gracious man, meeting with Halbouty at the oilman's request to answer questions and discuss ideas, and he instructed DOE employees to cooperate with the transition team. More often than not, they did.

As the weeks passed and the work progressed, two things became clear to Halbouty. One, he couldn't bear to be a part of a bureaucracy, even under the most favorable of circumstances. At one point he asked Duncan, "How many times in a year do you get called to the Hill?" Said Duncan, "Several hundred." Said Halbouty, "You don't have enough days to do that!" Duncan sighed. "Mike, I go when I can and send someone else occasionally. Just when I think I've got time to get something done, I get a call from the Hill."

Halbouty knew his impatience and short temper would not allow him to wrangle with Congressmen.

More importantly was his realization that he had been badly mistaken in his assessment of DOE—and so had misled Reagan. His judgment has been made solely on his personal experience with the department from an independent oilman's point of view. Now he knew that DOE was engaged in numerous energy areas, most of them essential. He determined that the transition team's efforts would streamline DOE operations without substantially altering the structure.

It was galling, but he knew he would have to report to Reagan just how wrong he had been over the years. He buckled up and went to see the President-elect. When he told Reagan of his conclusions, Reagan was incredulous. "But you've always insisted that we get rid of it, Mike!"

"I know that, but I was wrong. When you read our report you'll see why."

\*\*\*

Halbouty's marriage with Fay Renfro Kelly Halbouty had for many years been a distant one. The seven-day work-weeks his ambition demanded and his frequent travels left Halbouty little time to move in the social circles where Fay flourished. Neither, apparently, could understand the other's hopes and needs.

After the marriage had disintegrated, followed by years of separation, the Halboutys were divorced on November 21, 1980. During the separation, Halbouty met a sweet-faced blonde widow from Houston, Billye Stevens. She responded to his courtship, opening her heart to him. They became engaged before he went to Washington and she joined him there to lend him strength and share the plaudits his work was generating.

\*\*\*

Shortly after Halbouty had told Reagan that he no longer believed that DOE should be abolished, news stories quoting unidentified members of Reagan's "kitchen cabinet" reported that it appeared that Reagan had changed his mind about totally dismantling the department. Halbouty understood that because he knew Reagan had told some members of the "kitchen cabinet" of his report to Reagan. From other news reports, it also appeared that the inner circle was hedging on other promises Reagan had made on the campaign trail. Perhaps oil and gas should not be immediately decontrolled. Perhaps the "windfall profits tax" should not be repealed immediately; later, perhaps, the news reports indicated.

Halbouty bristled when he read and heard the news reports, but he kept his own counsel as he worked through the long days and nights with the transition team. It is likely that he held his tongue simply because he could not believe that Reagan would abandon the positions they both claimed to hold.

The "kitchen cabinet" also was at work selecting candidates for regular cabinet posts. The news media daily produced stories about various prospects for different administrative posts. Halbouty's name was mentioned early and often, and many in the media considered him the leading contender for the secretary of energy job.

Among others mentioned were John Sununu, a Tufts University professor and nuclear energy expert; Frank Zarb, Federal Energy Administration chief under Gerald Ford; Congressman Mickey Edwards of Oklahoma. Another name that surfaced as time went on was that of James B. Edwards, former governor of South Carolina who, as governor, had chaired the National Governors' Association's Subcommittee on Energy. Edwards had strong right-wing political support, particularly from South Carolina Senator Strom Thurmond, doyen of the super-conservatives.

In mid-December Halbouty was approached by Fred Fielding, attorney for Reagan's transition teams. "Mike," Fielding said, "the President is thinking about appointing you secretary of energy."

"Oh, no," Halbouty said. "I don't want it."

"Then you'd better let him know," Fielding said.

Halbouty did. "I think I can do more to help you on the outside than on the inside," he explained to Reagan. "And you know I'm a realist and a matter-of-fact person. If they called me to the Hill and some senator snapped at me, I'd tell him to go to hell. You'd have to ask me to resign, and I'm not going to let that happen. I don't want to embarrass you."

Fielding told Halbouty he had made a wise decision. Under "conflict of interest" laws, Halbouty would have been forced to place his business in a blind trust or get rid of it. Fielding told a press conference "it was just not possible" for Halbouty to undergo such a "massive" divestiture.

In a public statement, Halbouty listed only the "conflict of interest" as the reason for his request to be withdrawn from consideration for the post. Unspoken was his dislike for bureaucracy, his volatility that might make him a handicap to the administration.

Edwards was named secretary of energy. With his great political clout, he may have won the post regardless of what Halbouty did or didn't do. Only Reagan's inner circle knew.

Apparently no one in the inner circle had told Edwards that DOE was no longer expendable. He told reporters: "I'd like to go to Washington to close down the Energy Department and work myself out of a job. . . ."

\*\*\*

The rigorous work schedule began taking its toll on Halbouty. On December 21 he took leave and he and Billye flew in his plane to Las Hadas, Mexico. Their plan was to return to Washington on January 3. But on December 23, when they had hardly begun to relax, Halbouty received a phone call from his administrative assistant, Mary Stewart. Reagan had called the oilman's office and wanted Halbouty to call him on a private line. Reagan was in California.

Halbouty didn't propose to use his hotel telephone. Fortunately, he bumped into a Houston couple he knew, Sam and Betty Willson, in the hotel lobby. Willson was an executive with Coastal States, and he and Betty were staying in the vacation home of Dave Chalmers, president of Coral Petroleum, Inc. When Halbouty told the Willsons that he was looking for a private phone so he could call the President-elect, they gladly offered the use of one in Chalmers' house.

Reagan apologized for disturbing Halbouty. He wanted to know when the oilman was returning to Washington; he wanted an interim report on several DOE matters as soon as Halbouty could manage it. To Halbouty, that meant that he would return right away. "Thank you, Mike," Reagan said.

Halbouty had sent his plane back to Houston. Now he called Mary Stewart and told her he wanted the pilot to fly back to Mexico as soon as possible.

On Christmas Day the couple arrived in Washington and Halbouty went to work immediately on the mini-report. The report was completed on December 31, and that night found Billye and Halbouty in the 21 Club in New York City, prepared to welcome in the new year. They "closed up the club" at daybreak, and one of the club managers, Bruce Snyder, also leaving the club for his home, volunteered to drive them to their hotel.

\*\*\*

Edward Meese, the transition team's boss, had arranged for a videotaped history of the transition teams at work, with the finished product to be shown on the Public Broadcasting System. Reagan, meanwhile, was continuing to name people to hold cabinet posts. Reports flew that some of the new officials were anxious to get acquainted with their new surroundings and were ready to dismiss transition teams working in their departments. The tape showed Alexander Haig taking over his office at the State Department by shooing off the transition team like a farmer shooing off chickens.

Edwards was in Washington, and there were reports that he, too, was going to move right in at DOE. The transition videotape shows an angry Halbouty declaring that until one hour before the Reagan inauguration he would be in charge at DOE. "There's only going to be one boss here until then, and that's me!"

And that's the way it was.

(It was reported that Jimmy Carter, after viewing the transition videotape, remarked, "The only thing worthwhile in the entire tape is Mike Halbouty's statement. . . .''

\*\*\*

At one point before the inauguration, Halbouty went to Reagan to press once more that the recommendations of the Energy Policy Task Force advisory group be implemented. Particularly, Halbouty said, oil, gasoline, and propane should be decontrolled immediately after the inauguration.

Reagan wanted to know why the haste. "Oil control ends on September 30, Mike."

Said Halbouty, "All during the campaign you said you were going to deregulate this and deregulate that. Prove to the people you really *are* going to do it by taking some quick action."

Back at DOE, Halbouty and James Atkin sat down and wrote the executive order lifting controls on oil, gasoline, and propane. When Halbouty delivered it to Reagan, the President-elect asked, "When do you want me to sign this?"

"One hour after you're inaugurated," Halbouty said stoutly.

Reagan laughed.

Six days after the inauguration he signed the executive order.

But one hour after the inauguration, Halbouty celebrated. He and Billye hosted a party for the energy transition team in the Georgetown Club, a wonderful celebration for what the team considered a job well done. Every year afterward he and Billye hosted a party in Washington at the same time for a joyous reunion.

The gatherings were not to be missed. The team members had become so close to each other that each reunion was like an annual roundup of a large, loving family. Though they kept up with each other during the year, the January 20 meeting was a time for laughter and remembering, the recounting of old tales of tough jobs done and victories cherished. To Halbouty and his mates, it was the social high point of the year.

***

The great oil boom born in the Carter administration grew even wilder with oil decontrol. It was confined to the oil states, however, and thousands upon thousands of Americans rushed to them from other sections of the country where the economy was declining and unemployment growing. They found jobs in the oilfields and the plants and factories that were running around the clock to meet the demand for all kinds of oilfield equipment for current use and a boomier future.

Oilmen, bankers, and investment counselors predicted that oil would climb to $40 a barrel, $50 a barrel, $75 a barrel. The most optimistic saw $100 and $150 oil in their crystal balls.

The madness lasted for one year after oil decontrol. During the final week of December 1981, the rig count—land rigs in operation—stood at an unbelievable 4,530. The highest rig count before the boom had been back in the mid-1950s—2,620—when the Suez Crisis created a sudden demand for domestic production. But the rig count had declined after that, bottoming in 1971 with only 976 rigs in action.

In January 1982 the rig count dropped a trifle, then began a steady descent. Day by day it fell. By June it stood below 3,000, and still it dropped. Ten months later, in April 1982, it seemed to have reached its nadir when the count was 1,807.

Plants and factories closed. Banks folded. Oil companies disappeared. Bankruptcies were common. Those who had rushed to the oil states to escape the recession headed for home and uncertainty. Oil state citizens took their pink slips and tightened their belts.

Oil had dropped to $29 a barrel and the world was drowning in a glut that surpassed the glut of the 1930s. The price would have been even lower had not OPEC cut production and limited exports. Natural gas stayed in the ground; buyers who had contracted with producers to "take or pay" during the boom now could not do either because their markets had dwindled.

Why did the boom falter then die with a whimper? Everybody in the energy business and in government had a reason to present, it seemed, but one solid fact glared like a neon sign: the American people, faced with higher prices for gasoline and home heating oil, had heeded Jimmy Carter's plea to conserve.

Americans had consumed 18.8 million barrels of oil per day in 1978. In 1982 they consumed only 14.8 million barrels of oil per day.

The hikes in oil prices also brought some Third World countries to the brink of economic ruin. When they could no longer pay for the oil they needed, they paid for the oil they could barely get by on. And like America, other industrialized nations curbed their appetites for oil.

There was a gas glut, too, called a "gas bubble." When oil prices began falling, plants and factories switched from gas back to fuel oil.

And big investors with chunks of new money they had thrown into the oil patch in 1979, 1980, and 1981 reached back into the patch in 1982 and snatched out between $8 billion and $10 billion. They were tired of dry holes and "dog" wells that would never pay out.

In 1983 it appeared that the situation could not possibly worsen. But it could. It did.

***

The chief argument for decontrol of oil was that it would provide the money to explore for the new reserves the country desperately needed to lessen its dependence on foreign oil. But few oilmen sought the big fields that geologists for decades had averred were hidden in remote boondocks. Most of the wells were drilled in oil provinces where oil was most likely to be found. Thus, American reserve capacity was increased minimally if at all.

Meanwhile, it appeared that the Reagan administration had forgotten the industry and energy problems once the decontrol executive order was signed.

No solid, sensible energy program was promulgated.

Natural gas was not deregulated.

The "windfall profits tax" was not repealed.

Public lands remained untouched by the drill or coal shovel.

The Fuel Use Act was not repealed.

Offshore leasing practices were not substantially altered.

Congress received the brunt of the blame for the inaction, and certainly deserved some. But the Republicans had a Senate majority, and there were more than enough Republicans and conservative southern Democrats in the House for Reagan to have his will on almost every major issue, as was demonstrated time after time in other areas.

There was no doubt that Congress repulsed the administration's somewhat timid sallies on individual energy issues, but the simple fact was that Reagan, the most charismatic and powerful President in recent memory, failed to create and then push for an energy program as he had promised he would do. The "Great Communicator" never once stood before the American people and explained the country's energy plight and what, if anything, he proposed to do about it.

Nuclear energy languished. The great reserves of shale oil described in the Energy Advisory Group's report remained unmined.

And the country remained in thrall to OPEC.

It would not be until mid-September 1986—more than five years after his first inauguration—that Reagan would take a tentative step toward formulating an energy policy. He asked for a "study." By this time the oil industry was stumbling like a punch-drunk boxer, and oil was selling for $10 a barrel.

Cynics would point out that Reagan's move came just weeks before the November senatorial elections with the Republicans striving to retain control of that body. They were not amused when Reagan, campaigning in the southern states, took credit for lower gasoline prices then, in an unabashed volte-face, commiserated with the heartsick citizenry as he stumped the oil states. They saw it not as a clever political ploy but an exhibition of rank hypocrisy.

During all of these years—as we shall see—Halbouty continued to fight for the things in which he believed. He was in Washington often, sometimes at the invitation of Reagan or Vice-President George Bush, other times at his initiative to plead a cause. There were times when Reagan and Bush sought his advice. There were times when they got it unsolicited. And then there were times when the administration asked him to represent the country's interest at global energy sessions and at home.

Never once in those years did Halbouty publicly fault Reagan. He hid his keen disappointment and nourished a hope that the administration would, at long last, recognize its obligation to set a clear course toward a brighter energy future.

Privately, however, he occasionally allowed his feelings to surface. "If the administration had only followed the plan the advisory group set out, we'd be on our way to energy respectability," he grieved. "But nothing has been done. We never had a viable energy policy in the past, and we still don't."

Finally, however, his restraint broke. At the American Petroleum Institute's annual meeting in Houston on November 11, 1986, he went public. He told reporters, "What we (the industry) need is for President Reagan to get up and say this is what he wants. It's time for him to get up and be heard on the petroleum issue."

Once again he called for full restoration of the 27½% depletion allowance on new oil for both major and independent producers.

The depletion allowance, he said, would provide the tax incentive that would bring more cash into the industry without impacting oil prices. This argument had opened no ears in Washington in the past.

Halbouty spoke out even stronger a month later before an industry conference on imports in Washington sponsored by the Council on Alternate Energy and the *Oil Daily*. He was angered, along with other oilmen, because Energy Secretary John Herrington said he would advise President Reagan to leave out any reference to the state of the energy industry when he made his state-of-the-union speech in January. Herrington explained that Reagan's study group on energy matters—the study he had asked for in September—was behind schedule and would not report to the President for a couple of months or so.

Mention, or lack of mention, in the state-of-the-union address is often regarded as a barometer of White House concern on a given issue.

Halbouty declared that the administration should not wait any longer to take a stand on the industry's problems.

"We have seen the withering of the petroleum and its associated industries without a single positive firm action from the federal government to stop the continuous erosion," he said. "It is obvious that unless the United States government, specifically the legislative and executive branches, come up with a better brand of energy leadership than we have seen in the past, it could bring total disaster to us all. To continue these reversals is inviting and condoning the economic self-destruction of a nation. Yet, unfortunately, it is obvious the deterioration of the industry remains unabated. . . ."

People in the industry and the satellite businesses that serve it firmly believed that the Congress and the Reagan administration did not really realize the gravity of the situation, he declared.

Then he said, *"There have been yards and yards of rhetoric, but no solution. The industry and the millions who serve it and are a part of it feel that they have been let down, forgotten and ignored. . . ."*

He called on the President to state that he would use all of his influence to get Congress to repeal and correct inequities it previously had imposed on the industry.

But he added, "They also feel that the President should propose items which, if implemented, would be firm solutions toward a revitalization of the industry. . . ."

And, *"The President's declaration would give heart to those in the industry that he has not turned his back on them, and that he intends to keep his campaign promises to them. This declaration should be the first positive step toward formulating concrete and revitalizing solutions. . . ."*

It was a measure of his dismay and anger that he put them on public display within hollering distance of the White House.

He was speaking beyond his audience to the White House and the halls of Congress when he issued this warning: "One conclusion remains indisputable. Rising import levels combined with falling production produces a devastating equation, which is—

"Deterioration + Dependence = Disaster

"The bottom line result of this formula must be avoided at all costs!"

There was no response from President Reagan. By the time he made his state-of-the-union speech on January 27, 1987, the Democrats had won both houses of Congress and Reagan himself had lost the confidence of many Americans by his mishandling of foreign affairs.

He did not once mention energy in the speech.

\*\*\*

For Halbouty, the transition from the euphoria generated by the great Republican victory of 1980 and the early months of Reagan's tenure to the disillusionment that followed was made tolerable, for the most part, because Billye Stevens was by his side. For on December 27, 1981, they were married in Honolulu. Then, more than ever, she was able to strengthen him with her love and soothe the abrasions his combative nature engendered.

# CHAPTER SIX

Billye and Halbouty flew to Honolulu to get married without telling anyone of their intention to wed. Billye had two grown daughters, Shyrrel and Joy, and a grandson. Halbouty's only child, Linda Halbouty Hewitt, had a son and a daughter. They all learned of the marriage after the fact.

Halbouty had been baptized in a Greek Orthodox Church in Beaumont and had been reared in the faith. But there were no Greek Orthodox Churches in Houston when he established himself there, so he had become active in the Episcopal Church, eventually becoming a vestryman at St. John the Divine in River Oaks. Billye was a Baptist.

Before they left for Honolulu, Halbouty told Billye that his mother, long dead, had told him before she died to please marry in the faith of his infant baptism if he every married again. He said that is what he would like to do, but only with Billye's wholehearted approval and consent—which she readily gave.

In Honolulu Halbouty got in touch with Father Michael Rymer, priest at Saints Constantine and Helen Greek Orthodox Church. Father Rymer was happy to marry them in his tiny but beautiful church, the only Greek Orthodox Church on the island.

Halbouty called on a long-time friend, Robert Goodin, a San Francisco real estate investor-developer, to be his best man. Goodin's beautiful wife, Phyllis (called Fifi), was Billye's matron of honor. Father Rymer's mother, Marina, was her son's aide in the elaborate ritual of the marriage. No one else was present.

A Greek Orthodox wedding ceremony is a mixture of solemnity and joy, garnished with tears and flowers. Billye was radiant in an ankle-length old and new ecru lace dress with a high neck. Halbouty was as handsome as any prince or potentate.

The Halboutys and Goodins went to dinner, then Billye and Halbouty got on the phone and called the people they wanted to know about their marriage.

They welcomed the new year in Honolulu and following a brief honeymoon in the Islands they flew home.

The change in Halbouty after marriage was immediate and dramatic. There was no ripening process, no mellowing period.

Marriage blunted his irascibility, lowered his voice, softened his extreme attitudes. "I used to be afraid of Mike Halbouty," said a wife of a business associate. "I was scared to death when I was around him. Now," she said with a smile, "he's just a big teddy bear."

Marriage allowed his staff to see the man inside the boss. Not that he welcomed one and all into his office with cries of pleasure, but he could be approached without the trepidation that formerly marked their conduct. "He's still tough," said a ranking company officer, "but's he's not gruff about it anymore. There's a hell of a big difference."

Billye traveled with Halbouty wherever he went, and he was almost constantly in demand around the globe as a speaker, lecturer, or consultant. Their journeys took them to all the European capitols and most of those in the Orient. They were walkers. They walked the streets in foreign lands, avoiding the tourist traps when possible, savoring the sights and sounds with Halbouty as intent as a bird dog as they sought something that would remain vivid in their memories.

She liked Rome best. She told a friend, "We can walk down a street in Rome and meet Italians we know, people we met on other visits. We can go into a store or shop or restaurant and employees and owners will remember us by name. They never forget you. They don't move from job to job and location to location like people do in Houston. It's always nice to be remembered."

One incident in Rome seemed terribly serious when it occurred but was recalled with humor. They enjoyed climbing The Spanish Steps from the bottom at Piazza di Spagna to the Church of the Trinity at the top. The steps generally are crowded on sunny days with Romans taking their ease along with tourists. The steps on one side, however, are used less often and by fewer people. So on this particular bright day the Halboutys chose to mount the side stairway.

As they started up the stairs they saw that only four Gypsy children were sunning themselves. Billye guessed their ages as between 5 and 12. All were girls.

The Halboutys had been shopping, and the oilman had a shopping bag in each hand. The youngest girl held out her hand and spoke to Halbouty. Halbouty shook is head no; he had no wish to set down his bags.

"All of a sudden all four of them jumped all over Mike," Billye told her friends. "They were beating on him and trying to reach in his pockets and fists were flying everywhere. Mike was flinging his arms, trying to fend them off with the shopping bags. I was so amazed that I just stood there with my mouth open. Mike looked like a bear trying to fight off a pack of dogs."

The strange battle ended when a policeman at the top of the stairs started yelling at the Gypsies. They withdrew slowly, aware that the policeman was too far away to catch them.

"They just sauntered off," Billye said.

Halbouty was more flustered than he had ever been in an oilfield fist-fight or a honky-tonk brawl. After searching himself, he winked at Billye and said, "They didn't get a thing, honey."

They went to Moscow in August 1984 via Geneva and Helsinki. Halbouty was to deliver a paper before the 27th International Geological Congress; as it turned out, he was chosen to deliver the keynote address.

But first they had to stop over in Leningrad, one of the most beautiful cities on earth. They had heard and read too much about its cultural attractions to miss it. What they found was a city of stately architecture and, walkers as they were, they delighted in moving along the wide avenues and straight streets, stopping now and then at the splendid parks and gardens that seemed to spring up every few blocks.

There were more than a dozen theaters from which to choose, including the traditional home of the Russian Ballet.

And there were almost 50 museums. The two they would always remember were the Russian Museum, where only Russian art was displayed, and the Hermitage, considered to be one of the finest in the world with art from all countries and all periods ready for viewing.

"It was like being a guest at a great feast where every bite was a mouthful of glory and your hunger was never satisfied," Halbouty told friends later.

They left Leningrad reluctantly.

In Moscow they were given a special guide from the prestigious Society Academy of Science named Natasha, who taught English at the university. Her husband, an astrophysicist, had visited the United States to have a look at the American atomic facility at Los Alamos, New Mexico. One of their sons was a geophysicist, another a biophysicist. Her father had been a ranking general in the Red Army in World War II.

At Halbouty's request she took them to a Russian Orthodox Seminary complex about 45 miles out of Moscow. A bishop who had been a geologist for 17 years before taking up the cloth, went along with them. While he and Halbouty talked geology Billye went to a church where there were hundreds of silent worshipers.

Later Billye would tell friends, "It was a wonderful trip. Mike made a wonderful speech and was on Moscow television, and we saw people then that we knew from other such meetings—people from the States and other countries. I enjoyed Moscow very much."

\*\*\*

Halbouty was a seasoned China traveler. He went there first in 1980, returned in 1982 and 1984, and was back again two years later. Billye was with him for the last three trips.

Halbouty had dreamed of going to China since boyhood. Like many another youngster, he had thought of the vast area as a land of mystery and adventure. As a young geologist, he had read all that he could find of China's history and geology. He continued these studies as the years passed, and he became convinced that China was rich in petroleum and mineral resources.

When the Circum-Pacific Council for Energy and Mineral Resources was initiated in 1972, he worked doggedly to persuade the Chinese to become involved. A highly respected Chinese geoscientist, Zhai Guangming, became a council member. Halbouty beseeched the Chinese to find a way to bring a delegation of their scientists to the United States for an exchange of ideas and information.

In 1978, Halbouty had a special reason to push for a Chinese visit: the annual convention of the American Association of Petroleum Geologists (AAPG) and the Society of Economic Paleontologists and Mineralogists would be held in Houston April 1–4, 1979. The meeting would focus on "Giant Discoveries in the World of the Past Decade," and Halbouty had been selected to supervise and coordinate the session.

The People's Republic of China (still called Red China by most citizens of the western world) and the U.S. had been at swords' points from shortly after World War II when the Communists chased the national government off the mainland to Taiwan, through the bitter fighting in the Korean War, until 1972 when President Richard Nixon made his historic "Journey for Peace" to Peking. Nixon and the Chinese leader, Chou En-lai, had agreed to the lifting of trade embargoes and to cultural and educational exchanges. The People's Republic was admitted to the United Nations and the Nationalist Government on Taiwan was expelled.

Still, the U.S. continued to recognize the Nationalist Government on Taiwan and not the People's Republic on the mainland as the official Chinese government. This was anathema to the mainland Chinese. So, while the hostility between the U.S. and the People's Republic had diminished sharply, they still viewed each other with suspicion. And though trade and the cultural exchanges continued, the Chinese showed little concern for exchanges in scientific knowledge. Ping Pong teams and dancing troupes were not to be confused with groups of scientists discussing new discoveries and methodology.

Nevertheless, on October 3, 1978, Halbouty wrote a letter to Chang Wen-Ping, president of the China National Oil and Gas Exploration and Development Corporation. "In all probability," he wrote, "most of the proceedings of the session will be published in a special volume by AAPG which will be a sequel to Memoir 14, *Geology of Giant Petroleum Fields* which I was privileged to serve as special editor. . . .

"I would appreciate your advising me as soon as possible whether or not any geologist or geophysicist in your company will be permitted to present a paper at this session. . . ."

October passed. November came and went. Halbouty received no reply from Chang Wen-Ping. He continued planning for the convention. December was easing by.

Then, on the morning of December 15, Mary Stewart, Halbouty's administrative assistant, found among the letters in the early mail an envelope marked with stamps from the People's Republic. She opened it with nervous fingers. It was a message from Halbouty's Circum-Pacific Council colleague, Zhai Guangming, an officer of the Chinese entity. It said:

> Your letter dated Oct. 3 to Mr. Chang Wen-Ping, the president of China National Oil and Gas Exploration and Development Corp. has been received. Sincerely thank you for the invitation.
> 
> I would like to inform you that if no such complicated matters as "Two Chinas" or "one China one Taiwan" occur in the meeting, Taiwan attendants could write down only "China" in the nationality column of the meeting badges worn by them, and this is also the case with all the publications of this annual meeting, China Oil and Gas Exploration and Development Corporation will send a group of six petroleum geologists to attend the American Association of Petroleum Geologists annual meeting which will be held in April 1–4, 1979, on the basis of good wishes of seeking friendship and promoting exchanges, and shall present a paper. Kindly make due arrangements.

The letter had been written on December 5, but had not been mailed until December 12. Zhai Guangming apparently had intended for the letter to reach Halbouty on December 15, because shortly after Halbouty read the letter, President Jimmy Carter announced that the U.S. and the People's Republic of China had formally established full diplomatic relations, and the U.S. had severed all but unofficial relations with the Chinese Nationalist Government on Taiwan!

Elated, Halbouty conferred briefly with other AAPG leaders, and on the same day that he received the letter he sent a Telex message to Zhai Guangming. The key sentence was, "All terms mentioned in your letter will be complied with. . . ."

The Chinese came. They were led by Wang Tao, deputy chief geologist of the China National Oil and Gas Exploration and Development Corporation, later president of the China National Petroleum Corporation. His companions were Liang Shengzheng, CNOGEDC senior geologist; Hu Wenhai, a CNOGEDC geologist; Chen Sizhong, chief geologist of Shengli Oilfields; Wang Ping, senior geologist of Shengli Oilfields; and Miss Wang Jinxia, CNOGEDC interpreter.

Halbouty was in his element. He arranged for their living quarters and transportation. He took them to dinner. He saw to it that they arrived at the convention in proper style. And he arranged for a post-convention tour that took them to the Gulf Research and Development Corporation Laboratory; to a Houston Oil and Minerals offshore drilling rig in Matagorda Bay and to a production platform; to Shell Oil Company Research Center; and to Exxon Research Laboratory. Then he sent them on their way to California where he had arranged for tours of Chevron's La Habre Laboratory and the East Wilmington Oil Field, courtesy of Union Oil Company.

The delegation, as would be supposed, was the hit of the convention. Their paper, presented by Chen Sizhong and Wang Ping of Shengli Oilfields, was titled, "Geology of Gudao Oilfield and Surrounding Areas." They revealed that the field, in the coastal zone of the lower Yellow River Valley, held reserves of more than 700 million barrels of oil and had a daily production of more than 70,000 barrels. Though the Chinese were tight-lipped with reporters about petroleum matters other than Gudao Field, they did say there were several fields larger than Gudao, and that total Chinese production was estimated at 2.4 million barrels per day.

On the other hand, the delegation presented to AAPG a set of maps and books concerning the geology and paleontology of

China which was later displayed prominently in the AAPG library in Tulsa, Oklahoma.

Halbouty was highly pleased with the entire proceedings, and in his ebullient style told reporters, "Their visit was a success on both sides. It was simply wonderful! They were as eager as we were to exchange ideas and information, and they came offering friendship and a wish to continue our new relationship."

Then with a grin he added, "Maybe the State Department ought to turn over the handling of international relations to our earth scientists." As they left Houston, the Chinese told Halbouty that they hoped to see him soon in China as a lecturer.

\*\*\*

Near the end of 1979, Halbouty received a call from Martin F. Forrer, technical adviser for petroleum at the United Nations. Forrer, an old Texaco hand, had just returned from China. The UN and the Chinese were planning an international meeting on petroleum geology and the Chinese wanted Halbouty to participate as a principal lecturer, and so did the UN. Specifically, the meeting was a joint venture of China Oil and Gas Exploration and Development Corporation and the UN Department of Technical Cooperation for Development. Halbouty said he would participate if the timing was right.

After considerable correspondence, Halbouty received a formal invitation to the meeting on January 23, 1980. The meeting, he was informed, would be March 18–25, 1980. He wired his acceptance on February 13.

In Beijing (once Peking) he was joined by nine other principal lecturers—Professor Frederick M. Swain, University of Delaware; Dr. B. Tissot, Institut Français du Petrole, Paris; Dr. J. Connan, ELF-Acquitaine, Paris; Professor Robert L. Folk, University of Texas; Dr. H. Douglas Klemme, Weeks Petroleum Ltd.; Professor A. Hallam, University of Birmingham; Dr. Poh-Hsi Pan, Mobil Oil Corporation; Dr. Kenneth J. Bird, U.S. Geological Survey, and Dr. Hollis D. Hedberg, Professor Emeritus of Princeton University. (Hedberg later would serve with Halbouty on Ronald Reagan's Energy Advisory Policy Group). All of the men were geologists.

The meeting truly was international. In attendance were representatives from 21 developing countries and 9 from developed countries. The Chinese had brought in 20 scientists from various sections of the country.

Because of his association with the Chinese delegates at the AAPG convention in Houston—and because it was his nature—Halbouty acted as spokesman for his colleagues. (In a letter written to him more than a month after the meeting, Howard Brand, deputy director, Division of Natural Resources and Energy for the UN, said, "I want to express to you a special vote of thanks for the unique role you played during the proceedings in acting as spokesman for the participants—a role you performed with inimitable verve and good humor. . . .").

Evidence of Halbouty's good humor on the trip were the dozens of rolls of film he exposed and the great number of pictures he later sent to those he had photographed.

After the five days of lectures and discussions, the visitors were delivered to several oilfields and other installations. *The Wall Street Journal*, whose reporter had attended the sessions, wrote that the tour "was a demonstration of growing confidence in China's economic performance. . . ."

The reporter particularly noted that the Chinese proudly showed off their newest oilfield to foreigners for the first time, the Renqiu field in Hebei Province about 100 miles south of Beijing. The field was producing 20,000 barrels of oil per day.

The reporter interviewed Halbouty, who said, "I am very much impressed with the up-to-date equipment. The country has a great petroleum potential and much of it hasn't been explored."

The story also said, "Although visitors were allowed a close look, Chinese officials requested they not photograph maps or other sensitive objects, and some data were withheld from the foreigners. . . ."

Halbouty was pleased that the Chinese he had first met in Houston had welcomed him warmly, and had introduced him to their co-workers as a "friend, a good friend."

***

Halbouty returned to China in 1982—with Billye at his side—at the request of the China Oil and Gas Corporation. On the 1980 trip Chinese officials had asked him to return in 1981; they wanted to hear more from him, and they asked how much he would charge for lecturing their scientists on several topics.

"Nothing," Halbouty had said.

The Chinese had been startled. "Nothing?"

"Nothing," Halbouty had said firmly.

Business, however, delayed his return until 1982. Geologists from every oil-producing area in China were bussed in to Beijing to listen to Halbouty. He delivered three separate lectures, and gave unsparingly of his time in after-lecture talk sessions. The papers he presented were "Application of Remote Sensing to Petroleum Exploration;" "Exploration for the Subtle Trap—Stratigraphic, Paleogeomorphic, and Unconformity;" and "Basins and New Frontiers."

Chinese officials then asked Halbouty to speak to geology students at various schools in the general area. He did so, with his customary enthusiasm for such a task.

By now Halbouty was familiar with the established geological features of the country, and at this point he urged the Chinese—insisted is probably a better word—to drill to greater depths in the remote northwest provinces where only shallow production had been found. He continued to press his point during his stay, and returned to the subject many times in correspondence after his departure.

The Chinese learned that Halbouty was stubborn in other matters, as well. On their arrival, the Halboutys had been quartered in the State Guesthouse—a place of honor where President Nixon and Henry Kissinger had stayed. The Guesthouse is a collection of villas, some grander than others, that occupies what was once an imperial playground. It is surrounded by a wall and guarded day and night by soldiers or policemen.

The Halboutys' living quarters were satisfactory, but neither cared for the "compound" effect the wall and guards engendered. And when they wanted to walk outside the compound the gate guard suggested that for safety reasons they shouldn't do it. "It is better you stay inside," the guard said.

Halbouty got in touch with a Chinese official and announced that he wanted a suite in the old Beijing Hotel, the city's finest. He had stayed there in 1980 and like the location because of its nearness to the Forbidden City, giant Tiananmen Square, and the famous shopping street, Wangfujing. Halbouty reckoned Wangfujing Street to the most crowded avenue he had seen in all of his travels.

The official told Halbouty the Beijing Hotel was fully-occupied; perhaps another hotel would serve. No, said Halbouty firmly, only the Beijing Hotel would do. He refused to budge from his position during the discussions that followed, and won his point when he and Billye were moved into the old hotel's most luxurious accommodations.

He displayed his stubborn streak again when the Chinese said they wanted him to see a new oilfield. Halbouty was eager to see it. Fine, said the Chinese. You can be there in $19\frac{1}{2}$ hours by train.

Halbouty was aghast. Almost 20 hours by train! Not a chance, he said.

But there were no scheduled air flights to the oilfield vicinity, the Chinese said, and no other aircraft was available.

Halbouty shook his head. Not 20 hours on a train, he said again, and again he had his way. He was driven by auto far out into the boondocks from Beijing to a scraggly airfield where sat a military aircraft of dubious vintage. He was bowed courteously aboard, and was off to see the oilfield.

The Chinese were not affronted by his attitude. They apparently accepted his behavior as an amusing if bewildering eccentricity, and treated him with admiring deference at all times.

\*\*\*

The Circum-Pacific Energy and Mineral Resources Council staged its 1984 Symposium in Beijing in the autumn of that year with Halbouty as chairman. He had maintained a steady correspondence with Chinese energy officials in the intervening years, and had met with some of them at various times on their visits to the U.S. He had gained a special niche in their minds and hearts. It was not strange then that he was accorded the kind of treatment by the scientific community that Chinese political officials normally extended to visiting heads of state. Red carpets seemed to blossom in front of him at every meeting or banquet he attended. Billye shared in the warmth of his reception.

The symposium was declared a success. At its conclusion, the Halboutys were guests of honor at a banquet hosted by State Councillor Kang Shi'en. It was held in an old walled Guesthouse complete with guards to check one's credentials. The Chinese dignitaries were waiting in the foyer for the Halboutys to arrive. They were escorted to the head table and seated next to Kang Shi'en.

The Chinese drink toasts at banquets much like the Russians. The potable was Moutai, distilled from wheat and sorghum. A clear liquid like vodka, it weighs in at 106 proof—53% alcohol. It is served in a pony glass and the Chinese toss it off in one swallow.

There were a lot of toasts that evening. Halbouty's interpreter, Zhang Yancai, who also had served in that capacity in 1982, whispered to him, "Don't try to match them. They'll drink you under the table."

Halbouty was ready to believe him; his first swallow had left a fiery trail from his lips to his stomach. Thereafter he sipped his drink and kept his glass out of reach of attentive waiters. The toasts continued. A glass would be lifted. "Gan bai!" the toaster would exclaim, and down the Chinese throats the Moutai would flow. "Gan bai," Halbouty learned, meant "bottoms up."

Kang Shi'en, the state councillor, had a message for Halbouty. "He says he has good news and bad news," Zhang Yancai told Halbouty.

"What's the good news?" the ever-optimistic Halbouty asked.

"He says the experts drilled deeper in the northwest provinces as you told them to do, and they found an excellent producing zone."

Halbouty was delighted, but he asked, "What's the bad news then?"

"He says the well has blown out."

There was hearty laughter the length of the table when everyone understood the exchange.

(Shortly thereafter the wild well was brought under control and sites for other deep wells were planned.)

Halbouty had other lecture commitments in China, but first the Halboutys paid a memorable three-day visit to Guilin, a magic city on the Lijang River. Peng Zuoming of the Foreign Affairs Office was their interpreter and guide as they made their way about the charming city. The deputy mayor of Guilin, Li Jian He, was their official host, and he honored them with an eleven-course banquet.

The Halboutys also made a boat trip on the Lijang River from Guilin to Yangshuo. The Guilin area is regarded by Chinese and visitors alike as the most beautiful section of the country. It is a land of green hills, clear rivers and lakes, intriguing caverns, and spectacular rocks. For Halbouty it was like a giant classroom, for the region is a marvelous example of Karst topography, topography that is formed over limestone, dolomite or gypsum by dissolving or solution, and it is characterized by pinnacles, closed depressions, caves, and underground drainage.

Halbouty deduced that the region was once on the ocean floor, that about 200 million years ago limestone deposits at the bottom of the sea rose to form the present-day land, and then erosion commenced, leaving thousands of caves of thousands of shapes, and towering limestone stalagmites, tubular stalactites, stone flowers and curtains, sandy rocks, timber fossils and eroded rocks alive with color—red, green, yellow, white.

He could see all of this from the boat deck, an unraveling of the past, page after fascinating page. Halbouty, who loved music and poetry, recalled the lines from Samuel Taylor Coleridge. He tilted back his head and recited:

In Xanadu did Kubla Khan a stately pleasure dome decree

Where Alph, the sacred river, ran

Through caverns measureless to man

Down to a sunless sea. . . .

Billye later told a friend, "We so enjoyed the river trip. Mike was lost in the wonder of it in his geologist's mind. He said it was a geologist's paradise, and I'm sure it was. Every curve of the river brought different scenes, and to him different ages in the earth's history.''

From Guilin they flew to Gangzhou (formerly Canton), an industrial city of three million on the Southeast China coast. Petroleum scientists from that area were brought in to Gangzhou for Halbouty's lecture.

The Gangzhou visit was a happy one for Halbouty because two of the geologists who had attended the 1979 AAPG convention in Houston had been promoted and held key positions in the area. They were headquartered in Gangzhou. One was Wang Tao, who had headed the 1979 delegation; now he was general manager of Nanhai East Oil Corporation of China National Oil and Gas Corporation. The other was Chen Sizhong, who had delivered the paper on the "Geology of Gudao Oilfield" in 1979; now he was manager of the Exploration Department of Nanhai East Oil Corporation. (In 1985 Wang Tao would be named China's Minister of Petroleum.)

Wang Tao was host at a banquet for the Halbouty's in the White Swan Hotel on the Pearl River, but it is likely that the meal the Halboutys savored the most on their entire China stay was one they had at the New China Hotel in Gangzhou. It was a western-style hotel, and they passed up more exotic fare to dine on king-size hamburgers and french fries, the first non-Chinese food they had eaten since their arrival on the mainland.

From Gangzhou they flew to Hong Kong, where they stayed several days, then flew back to Houston.

***

In following years Halbouty was in almost constant contact with Chinese energy officials. He was their mentor in the United States. Groups came to his office for advice, and he would make arrangements for them to visit various petroleum-related installations around the country. By mail and Telex messages he answered the questions that came from scientists and students in China. Chinese delegations who visited with major oil companies in the U.S. oftimes would ask their hosts to invite Halbouty to the sessions so they could question him.

One such session created a proud moment for Halbouty. He had received a phone call from Esso Exploration saying that State Councillor Kang Shi'en was leading a delegation to New York for meetings with Esso executives. Esso had received two Telex messages from Kang Shi'en. One said, "I would like to meet with Michel Halbouty in New York, a famous geologist in Houston, for ½-day session on the latest developments on petroleum geology today."

The second message said, "Meeting to discuss with Michel Halbouty the recent new theories of petroleum exploration and petroleum geology in the USA, *and to present a certificate to Mr. Halbouty for being the Honorary Advisor of the Scientific Research Institute of Petroleum Exploration and Development.*"

Halbouty went to New York. He discussed what the Chinese wanted to discuss. And he accepted with pleasure the honorary advisor certificate.

The Chinese characters attesting to Halbouty's distinction are in blackest ink on a beige parchment. It is in the form of a book whose cover of lambent beige silk bears curious Chinese figures of subdued blue.

It has its place, near photographs of President Reagan, in Halbouty's outer office.

# CHAPTER SEVEN

In the summer of 1981, between the inauguration of President Reagan and his marriage, Halbouty became involved in a problem that would affect him profoundly. It had its beginning in late November of 1980 while he was busy running the transition team. Several Indians representing the Council of Energy Resource Tribes (CERT) called on him unannounced. It was at the time when the media was reporting that Halbouty was the leading candidate for the secretary of energy job.

Indian affairs are regulated by the Department of the Interior, but the Indians apparently believed that Halbouty, if he became head of DOE, could be of assistance to them. Halbouty was aware that several months earlier, in June, the media had reported that an inspector for the United States Geological Survey had caught a thief stealing oil from the Wind River Reservation in Wyoming.

Now the Indians told Halbouty that their lands had been systematically plundered for 20 years or more. Oil thievery was widespread, they said, and cheating on oil royalty payments cost the tribes hundreds of millions of dollars a year. Royalty income, they said, played a critical role in enabling the tribal governments to function efficiently and in the best interests of their people.

They wanted the thievery stopped and a fair shake on royalty payments. Could Halbouty use his considerable influence to help them?

Halbouty said he would do his best.

There was more, the Indians said. Thievery and inadequate royalty payments were common on federal lands leased for oil exploration. The federal government and the states where the lands were leased were the losers in these instances for they shared the royalty payments.

Halbouty thanked them for coming to see him.

He had been outwardly calm, but inside he was seething. He had never drilled on Indian lands, but his firm belief in self-determination and a free market told him that the Indians should be handling their affairs without having to obtain permission from several layers of government. He found that condition offensive. That condition was worsened, he thought, when the government failed to act responsibly.

He was wrapped up in transition team labors, and it was not until six months later in June 1981 that he had an opportunity to live up to his promise to the Indians. James G. Watt had been appointed secretary of the interior and he asked Halbouty to have breakfast with him and the undersecretary, Donald Hodel. Halbouty had met Watt only once before; Watt had taken him to lunch to pick his brain about energy resources.

At the breakfast meeting, Halbouty told Watt and Hodel about his Indian callers. He was outraged, it was obvious, and Watt asked him what he would do about the problem. Halbouty told him, and Watt asked him to put it in writing. Halbouty said he would.

He put his thoughts in a 7-point memorandum. In an accompanying letter he encouraged Watt to deal directly with the oil companies involved, as he had done at the breakfast meeting. "The thrust," he wrote, "is to lay it hard on the companies that it is their responsibility to prevent the thefts. After all, there are 37,000 wells on federal and Indian lands nation-wide, and the USGS has only 45 inspectors to check those wells, which you and I know is impossible. It would cost the federal government literally millions of dollars to hire competent reservoir engineers to monitor such a vast number of wells. Therefore, I strongly feel it is appropriate to place full responsibility on the companies to prevent the thefts. . . ."

The memorandum showed that he had done his homework. It said:

> I recommend the following be discussed at the meeting with operators concerning oil theft:

1. The outright theft of crude oil and unauthorized transfer of crude oil from the point of production to another point for the purpose of circumventing control of oil *must be stopped.*

    Theft of crude oil from federal and Indian leases is estimated to be as high as $400 million per year. Of the 10,000 federal oil leases inspected by the USGS since September 1980, technical violations were reported on more than 3,500 leases. The problem is compounded by the fact that the USGS has only 45 inspectors to check on more than 37,000 producing wells on federal and Indian land nationwide.

    To add additional inspectors would cost the federal government literally hundreds of thousand of dollars, as the most competent investigators for this area would be reservoir engineers who are familiar with federal properties as well as the production characteristics of all outside operated leases in the same field.

2. Oil theft has been generally appraised to be the result of combinations of unapproved oil storage facilities; unapproved metering systems; fraudulent run tickets or no run tickets at all; fraudulent reporting of wells that are not producing; misrepresentations by oil reclaimers; improper drainage or storage tanks by by-pass meters; and lack of locks or seals on oil storage tanks, or the misplacement of these locks or seals on tanks.

3. Cite that the Department of Interior has appropriate legislative authority to fully investigate all irregularities and prosecute violators.

    Further, the Department of Interior intends to utilize that power to see to it that good oil field surveillance practices are adhered to.

4. The Department of Interior feels the companies should have the first opportunity to straighten out and prevent further theft on their leases.

5. The Department of Interior recommends:

    (a) The companies police their own leases with their own people;

    (b) The companies must send their own employees and/or engineers to the field to monitor the entire production operation and to determine where the weaknesses exist;

    (c) The companies report to the Department of Interior within 45 days that they have done everything possible to stop these thefts and also report to the Department of Interior any offenses incurred by other parties;

(d) The companies are liable for these thefts and if the Department of Interior is forced to make its own investigations and prove the alleged offenses, then the Department of Interior could hold the companies liable for all thefts and would expect payment to be made by the companies for all past losses as well as all future thefts that might occur.

6. The Department of Interior would be glad to assist the companies in their policing efforts; however, the burden of policing leases rests entirely with the companies.

7. If the companies cannot stop the thefts, then the Department of Interior will take over full investigation and all alleged violators will be prosecuted to the fullest extent and all losses incurred will be the responsibility of the companies to repay to the U.S. government.

Halbouty heard from Watt within the week. Watt had decided not to confront the companies. Instead, he was going to appoint a commission to investigate the complaints. He wanted Halbouty to serve as a member. Halbouty said he would.

The Commission on Fiscal Accountability of the Nation's Energy Resources was chartered on July 8, 1981, or about a month after Halbouty's breakfast meeting with Watt and Hodel. The Commission's tasks were to "examine the allegations of massive irregularities in royalties on the nation's energy resources which are owed to the federal government, Indian tribes, and states; to investigate the allegations of theft of oil from federal and Indian lands; to make recommendations for improving the fiscal accountability of the nation's energy resources."

Watt wanted a final report from the Commission in six months, January 1982.

Chairman of the Commission was David F. Linowes, professor of political economy and public policy at the University of Illinois. Linowes had served as chairman of the U.S. Privacy Protection Study Commission, chairman of the Trial Board of American Institute of Certified Public Accountants, and on behalf of the U.S.

and the United Nations had headed economic development missions to Turkey, India, Greece, Pakistan, and Iran.

Others on the Commission with Halbouty were Mary Gardiner Jones, president of the Consumer Interest Research Institute, vice-president for Consumer Affairs for Western Union Telegraph Company, a former Federal Trade Commissioner and an attorney with the Department of Justice; Charles J. Mankin, director of the Oklahoma Geological Survey, executive director of the Energy Resources Center, professor of geology at the University of Oklahoma, past-president of the American Geological Institute and past-chairman of the Board of Mineral and Energy Resources of the National Academy of Sciences; Elmer B. Staats, former comptroller general of the U.S., former deputy director of the Bureau of the Budget and former executive director of the Operations Coordinating Board of the National Security Council.

One of the Indians who had made the surprise visit to Halbouty was Peter MacDonald, chairman of the Navajo Nation and of the Council of Energy Resource Tribes. In a letter to Watt, he applauded Watt's decision to create a high-level commission, but added, "At the same time, however, I must be candid in expressing to you my surprise and disappointment that not a single American Indian was appointed to this five-member body, especially in light of the fact that the problem—to the extent it is understood today—is first and foremost a problem of grave concern to the American Indian people."

He also wrote, "I am confident that you have chosen individuals of high caliber and extensive experience to serve on this Commission. One of them, Mr. Michel Halbouty, has already demonstrated a keen sensitivity to the tribal perspective on energy-related issues."

Like MacDonald, Halbouty was disappointed that no Indian had been appointed to the Commission.

Three months later, in October, when the Commission was deep in hearing testimony from scores of witnesses at various locations, MacDonald invited Halbouty to speak at the annual CERT meeting in Denver where representatives from 26 tribes had gathered.

Halbouty got right to the heart of the matter as he saw it. "The ultimate responsibility for dealing with your resources should lie with tribal leaders. The status of the Indian tribes will always remain grim as long as they depend on the government."

Government controls were necessary to protect Indians from being exploited in the early days, Halbouty said, "but those controls have served their purpose." The federal government must live up to its full obligation under the tribal-federal trust relationship, he said, "but that doesn't mean perpetuating tribal dependence forever on direct federal handouts for subsistence and survival."

Where the tribes have the capacity to run their affairs themselves, he said, "they should do everything possible to free themselves from government shackles.

"The tribes must be independent to conduct their own affairs, especially in leasing the rights of their lands. Your lands are your lands, and you should have as much right to govern and use those lands as I have to govern and use the land I own."

The Indians liked what they heard because they already had started a movement aimed at obtaining increased energy resource development on terms more favorable to the tribes.

Halbouty went back to work. What the Commission uncovered was gross mismanagement and worse. Its report, delivered to Watt on January 21, 1982, began with this summary:

> Management of royalties for the nation's energy resources has been a failure for more than 20 years. Because the federal government has not adequately managed this multibillion-dollar enterprise, the oil and gas industry is not paying all the royalties it rightly owes.
>
> The government's royalty record keeping for federal and Indian oil and gas leases is in disarray. For this reason, the exact amount of underpayment is unknown. The results of individual audits, which have often uncovered large underpayments, suggest that hundreds of millions of dollars due the U.S. Treasury, the states, and Indian tribes are going uncollected every year.
>
> In addition, oil thefts are occurring on federal and Indian leases. The extent of theft and the amount of royalty losses from theft are unknown, but it is well-documented that security at many federal and Indian lease sites is lax and is an open invitation to theft.
>
> The nation can no longer afford mismanagement of royalties for its energy resources. The stakes are too high. With the rapid

escalation of energy prices, oil and gas royalties have risen from less than $500 million in 1971 to more than $4 billion in 1981.

The government's royalty management system needs a thorough overhaul. This report details 60 specific recommendations for revising and rebuilding the system. Underlying these recommendations are some fundamental conclusions the Commission reached in the course of its intensive inquiry:

1. *The government's royalty management system must have qualified managers.* The scientifically oriented Geological Survey, which now manages royalties, has never been able to supply the active, sophisticated management that is needed. It is largely for this reason that the commission recommends removing the royalty management function from the Geological Survey. In a separate office with a clearly defined mission, royalty management could attract managers with the training and experience required.

2. *The federal government should work more closely with states and Indian tribes.* In fulfilling its royalty management responsibilities, it should cooperate much more than it has in the past with states and Indian tribes, sharing both information and specific tasks, such as auditing and site inspection.

3. *The federal government should perform an oversight role.* It must not waste its limited resources on tasks that are industry's responsibility. In managing royalty collection, it should not remain mired in bookkeeping details that rightly belong to the lessee. Instead, it should develop systematic, independent cross checks of royalties paid and reports submitted by companies, and it should impose meaningful penalties for false statements or gross errors. In helping to prevent theft, the government should not issue detailed, rigid regulations for security of lease sites. Rather, it should monitor the companies' performances in carrying out their own site security plans and should penalize violations.

4. *The oil and gas industry should carry out its obligation, as lessee, to pay royalties in full and on time.* The industry, not the government, has primary responsibility for the detailed record-keeping needed to assure that all royalties are paid. The industry also has the obligation to assure the security of lease sites. The industry, not the government, is best suited to develop

effective site security plans, subject to the government's minimum standards.

If there is one concept that sums up the Commission's overall approach, it is accountability. Oil and gas companies must be held accountable for the obligations they undertake when they lease federal and Indian lands for minerals production. The federal government must be held accountable for fulfilling a public trust, that is, assuring that royalties for the nation's energy resources are fully and fairly collected on behalf of the people of the United States.

The federal government has not fulfilled this trust in the past 20 years. It is now taking steps to better its performance. Complex and demanding as the task may be, it is achievable if the internal controls, site security standards, and sanctions recommended here are made part of an improved royalty management system.

Halbouty was elated, the Indians joyous, when Congress took action as a result of the hearings. In December 1982 the Federal Oil and Gas Management Act, encompassing more than 80% of the Commission's recommendations, was passed into law. Still in the reform spirit, the Congress also passed the Indian Mineral Development Act which permitted Indians to lease their own lands and conduct their own energy affairs subject to Department of Interior approval. This freedom, however, applied only to new leasing; those lands already leased remained under strict governmental control, and those lands constituted the bulk of Indian holdings.

So what happened?

Not much, if anything, according to A. David Lester, executive director of CERT. Month after month went by and became years, and Watts and his successors did not promulgate the regulations to implement the Federal Oil and Gas Management Act, Lester said, and the monumental foulups so decried by the Commission remained virtually unchanged.

In 1986 the Navajos and Indians of Western Oklahoma were suing the Department of the Interior, asking that the Department be forced to comply with the provisions of the Act, according to Lester.

The tribes were still not receiving timely payment of royalties, Lester said. When they received checks there was no explanation of the payment. There was a constantly growing backlog of payments and, without explanations, the Indians had no way of knowing how much interest they should be receiving on late royalty payments, Lester said.

There had been no improvement in security, Lester said. The Bureau of Land Management's inspection corp was still understaffed. The inspectors' goal was to try to visit each lease once a year!

Halbouty had not kept in touch with Indian affairs chiefly because Peter MacDonald had been defeated in the November 1982 election and CERT had a new chairman. It was not until mid-1986 that Halbouty learned of Interior's dereliction. He was saddened, and he reproached himself for his neglect.

On July 4, Halbouty was watching on television the giant celebration at the Statue of Liberty. The son of Lebanese immigrants, he was reveling in the sights and sounds when he suddenly thought of the Indians with whom he felt such empathy.

He went to his typewriter and wrote a letter to the *Houston Chronicle*. The letter was published and picked up by other newspapers across the country. The letter said:

> It is indeed gratifying to be an American and share in the freedoms America affords. This last fourth of July which marked 210 years of independence for America and 100 years of the Statue of Liberty was celebrated by millions of immigrants and their descendants who were given their freedoms and their choice of a life to make for themselves.
>
> On that day of celebration and patriotic rhetoric, I solemnly reflected upon the category in which we placed the only real native Americans—the Indians—who did not have to see the Statue of Liberty to enter a land of freedom. They had known freedom long before the first ship landed at Plymouth Rock.
>
> Yet the arrival of that first immigrant who came to our shores seeking freedom began the deprivation and disintegration of freedom for the native American.
>
> Our Indians are really not free. They have been abused for over 200 years by an intolerant government—deprived of those very freedoms which our founding fathers proclaimed—and are still looked upon as wards of the nation.
>
> During that Fourth of July celebration, I reflected upon the hardships and oppression to which native Americans were subjected

for over two centuries and I thought that it is appropriate for *all* of us to stop a moment and pay a silent tribute to those Indians who still do not share in the total freedoms of the immigrants who came from across the seas and adopted this land as their own.

"For a time after he wrote the letter he brooded," Mary Stewart said. "I knew he was trying to figure out what he could do, if anything, to goad the Interior Department into action. But he was still in the thick of the fight for an intelligent energy policy—and he was still in the oil business, with lots of responsibilities. He never told me so, but I think he finally decided, that for the time being, he couldn't afford to spread himself too thin. So he reluctantly put the Indian's oil problems on a back burner with the idea of tackling them later." She smiled. "And of course, you can bet he will."

# CHAPTER EIGHT

Michel T. Halbouty the wildcatter became Michel T. Halbouty Energy Company on February 23, 1981 at the height of the great boom. He was drilling more wells and hunting new fields, and he needed more people in his employ. The increase in staff prompted him to incorporate. All of his key people were given stock interest in the corporation.

Before the change there were 20 employees. With incorporation the staff rapidly expanded to 51.

*As 1986 drew to a close, there were still 51 members on the Halbouty corporate team.* That number is significant because by 1986 the oil industry had suffered—and was suffering—from not one but two economic broadsides.

The collapse of the boom in 1982 had brought on company closings, bankruptcies, and unemployment of hundreds of thousands in the oil states. The strongest and most astute, and the luckiest, rode out that storm, wounded though they were. OPEC curtailed production to maintain prices, and oil settled down at $28 a barrel.

Then so-called "corporate raiders," attempting "hostile takeovers" of long-established oil companies, forced new rounds of layoffs and reductions of exploratory funds.

Meanwhile, OPEC would not maintain curtailment because Great Britain and Norway, with their North Sea fields producing without restraint, began gaining larger and larger shares of the global oil market.

Oil was still selling for $28 a barrel when OPEC opened its valves in December 1985 to regain its market share. By July 1986 oil prices had plummeted to less than $10 a barrel!

Great Britain and Norway continued to ignore OPEC entreaties to cut production, and American independents and smaller oil companies were driven to their knees. The majors also were bloodied.

The layoffs this time cut deeply into the ranks of long-time employees in all segments of the industry. Funds allocated for exploratory drilling again were drastically reduced.

Halbouty deplored the layoffs—"retrenchment" it was called—and he abhorred the corporate raiders. He publicly chastised the oil companies for retrenchment, and he blasted the raiders wherever he could find a forum. He was the first to denounce the raiders, and for many bitter months he stood alone. His harsh criticisms were published in newspapers and magazines and were seen and heard on television and radio.

His thoughts on retrenchment were fully expressed in a speech made at the AAPG Annual Meeting in Atlanta on July 16, 1986. Some of his remarks were stinging rebukes. Portions of the speech follow:

> Many of us in this room have been around long enough to have witnessed first-hand the cycles of the petroleum industry. We have become knowledgeable enough to know that any successful turnaround for the industry will require that it be adequately prepared to mount aggressive exploration programs. But with the unusual and devastating retrenchment that is going on today, there is no way to mount any kind of an exploration program, much less an aggressive one.
>
> Today, domestic oil production is falling.
>
> Drilling is down to a dramatic low equal only to that of the levels experienced after World War II.
>
> Our oil imports are gradually increasing.
>
> Independents are going under.
>
> Massive layoffs are regular occurrences.
>
> Budget cutbacks in exploration and production, as well as in research and development, are almost daily reported.
>
> Today's dangerous retrenchment trend was precipitated by the hostile raids on the industry, raids which saddled companies with huge debts, triggering cutbacks and personnel layoffs.

The recent oil price slide has only accentuated the problem and accelerated the attrition.

The gross retrenchment by the large integrated companies is appalling and increases our dependency on factors beyond our control. In all of this maneuvering, what disturbs me most is the complete disregard for the human element. It is a sad commentary of our morality in doing business that the welfare of those who sustain the growth of business is being neglected at best and ignored at worst.

There appears to be total disregard for the employees, the only real asset of any company. Companies condemn themselves to lesser success and lower achievement with each round of terminations. The time will come when those companies that are bleeding themselves of their lifeblood will desperately need those employees. But these dedicated, experienced professionals will not be around when they are needed. Instead the companies will have to rely on newly-hired, inexperienced, and untrained personnel.

In the final analysis, greater sums will be spent trying to catch up than were saved by cutting back.

This country was built on long-term planning, and those same companies also were built on long-term planning. The short-term policy currently adopted by most of the majors is associated with a pessimistic doom and gloom attitude. The pessimism that now prevails is so thick it can be cut with a 6-inch board; you don't need a knife. This is *not* the kind of thinking that forged this industry into a worldwide giant. It is tragic that the companies have embraced such a negative philosophy and have discarded the two basic doctrines that made our industry the greatest of them all, long-term planning and optimism.

The impact of exploration cuts and employee layoffs is felt in all sectors of the oil and oil-related industries. The multiplier effect of these cuts is heavily felt in the communities where those cuts were and are being made. Eventually the nation as a whole will again experience another but greater shock caused by the retrenchment policies now being adopted. It seems that the mistakes of the early sixties and seventies are being repeated again, this time with unrelenting fervor and fury!

The job loss toll is in the hundreds of thousands, and for those who are still on the payrolls, the doubt, apprehension, and worry are causing heartaches and grief. They are asking, Who will be let go, retired early, or transferred? Am I one of those who'll be laid off? What about my family, my children in school, my children away at college? Where can I get another job? Or even worse, Are there *any* industry jobs out there for me to get at all?

And the most devastating mental anguish is the anxiety associated with waiting for the answers. There are many who are totally devastated by losing their jobs, and, in turn, are finding that there is little hope of obtaining work in their chosen professions.

I can understand companies that were hostile-takeover targets and saddled with tremendous debts, such as Unocal and Phillips, cutting back somewhat. But it is difficult for me to understand other major companies, ones that were not exposed to raids, takeover attempts or threats, retrenching as much as they are.

For example, Exxon's profit last quarter was one of the highest in the corporation's history, yet a few days after releasing information on this profit it announced that thousands of employees were being terminated and billions of dollars cut from exploration programs. It seems that the human element is being disregarded by many companies, and I decry the immorality of shattering the lives of loyal employees and their families for the sake of quarterly earnings and fixed dividends.

With the round of reductions in exploration that has taken place and will take place, be assured that soon there will come a day of reckoning when our dependence on foreign imports increases beyond acceptable economic limits and adversely affects our national security interests.

There's *more* at stake than whether a company continues a maximum dividend policy!

There's *more* at stake than loss of jobs and relocation of families!

What *is* at stake is our accepted future methodology of doing business in America. The raiders believe the *one and only* duty of management is to the shareholders, meaning that the highest dividend be paid and the price of the stock kept as high as possible. They ignore other, more important responsibilities.

The foremost responsibility of the company is to the nation; second to the communities in which the company operates; third to the employees and their welfare. Then, fourth and last, the company should attempt to provide for a reasonable profit and growth for the shareholders.

Currently, the first three are being ignored, and the ravaging of the most successful industry in America's history appears to be well underway.

But it doesn't have to be that way. Instead of terminating thousands of employees and drastically cutting back on exploration, production and R&D, companies could reduce dividends and thereby maintain employees and sustain reasonable and effective exploration activities.

Or they could cut back on the salaries of everybody in the company, regardless of position. Salaries could be reduced by 5, 6, or 7%, or whatever, across the board from top to bottom! No one to be exempt. At the same time it should be announced that there will be no layoffs. Thus, the reduction enables the company to maintain a reasonable exploration program and keep its staff intact.

A company could reduce both dividends and salaries, but not as much as if they had been acted upon separately. This would keep the employees working and also maintain a reasonable, effective exploration program.

Either one of these proposals, or a combination thereof, would permit the companies to continue to contribute to the welfare of their employees and the nation.

What is now going on is harmful to both the employees and the nation and, in my opinion, to the companies as well. If any of these methods were implemented, instead of massive retrenchment, we would be planning for the upturn; instead of sacrificing our most creative and innovative manpower, we would be fostering greater creativity and innovation. *This* is indeed long-term planning as it should be.

Instead of liquidating companies, we would be strengthening them. Instead of waiting for the ax to fall, we would be taking action to see that our industry will be ready when the cycle changes. Instead of shutting down hundreds of rigs, we would be exploring for new petroleum supplies.

Again I repeat, without qualification, that the current retrenchment in the petroleum industry is another step leading this nation into excessive dependence like we experienced in the 1970s. Yet with exploration programs at home and abroad practically at a standstill, and a dramatically reduced work force, the U.S. petroleum industry cannot possibly forestall the inevitable decline in domestic oil production.

With this decline, the rise of imports of crude oil and products is inevitable. These events following one another will create a price shock that will make the oil-price increases of the 1970s pale in comparison.

So I say to all Americans, BEWARE that we do not follow the same course of the past and find ourselves creating an over-dependence of our petroleum supplies from those upon whom we cannot permanently depend. In this regard, there is no doubt that this over-dependence has commenced and is increased by the current retrenchment process.

Have the majors reached the point where they have become callous to their moral and ethical responsibilities? Have they ignored the far-reaching effects their retrenchment is having on individuals, their families, the industry, and the nation?

The saddest of answers is the only logical one that comes to mind. Evidently, knowingly and irrespective of the consequences, long-range planning has been cast aside together with the very element without which they cannot possibly hope to survive—the human element.

So we geologists can ask ourselves, where do we go from here? Do we put out tails between our legs and run? Or do we stand tall and show our stout-hearted spirit?

Through this ill-created mess in which the industry finds itself, I trust that all of us will attempt to stand tall because this profession of ours is absolutely indispensable to any success the industry will enjoy in the future.

Those of us who are accustomed to looking to the long-term know that probably the only good aspect of the current dilemma is that when sanity once again prevails in world markets and industry strength is restored, the oil and gas prospects that are not searched for, or found, in this retrenchment era, will still be there waiting for us to discover.

*** 

After such a speech, or after newspaper and television interviews, Halbouty's office would be swamped with mail. The bulk of it was laudatory, and one suspects that many of the writers had themselves been caught up in retrenchment. But some argued that oil industry employee ranks had long been over-populated. Retrenchment, they said, should have been practiced years back.

A few writers chided him for what they considered his innocence. An Oklahoma oilman wrote, "I read with great interest your article in the June/July issue of *Shale Shaker*. I certainly agree with your assessment that the cutbacks we are currently experiencing in our industry are tragic. The ultimate results will include a long-term loss of expertise and a further reduction of this nation's energy independence.

"However, your comments concerning the duty and responsibility of American companies bordered on the incredible. Your statement that a company owes primary responsibility to the nation and the community is in absolute contradiction to the reason companies are formed. It is elementary that corporations are begun to further the financial interests of their stockholders. They prosper and provide employment to growing numbers of people because they return a profit or promise of profit to their owners. I seriously doubt you follow the criteria stated in your article when you make your personal stock investments. . . ."

A touching letter was written by an elderly woman in California. "I fear," she wrote, "that your big heart has placed you in danger. We live in perilous times, and criticism of powerful people and institutions is not appreciated by the targets. So, be careful, dear sir, because the country needs persons such as yourself. . . ."

Halbouty wrote back, "I am not accustomed to having people worrying over me, so I'll cherish your letter—and I'll be careful. . . ."

One writer was blunt. "I'm a damned good oilman sitting out here on my ass and losing confidence in my ability with every passing day. So give me a job or help me find one. . . ." He enclosed an impressive résumé, but when Halbouty got in touch with him he already had found a job in the electronics field. He thanked Halbouty for calling him, but said, "I've said goodbye to the oil patch for good."

"There are far too many who feel like he does," Halbouty told a friend.

\*\*\*

When Halbouty spoke of corporate raiders—there were several operating in the mid-1980s—there was no doubt that he was thinking of one in particular, T. Boone Pickens, chairman of Mesa Petroleum Company. In a series of hostile takeover stabs, Pickens and his partners raked in $750 million for an after-tax profit of $435 million. Among the targets were Cities Service, Unocal, Gulf, and Phillips Petroleum Company.

Halbouty could not fault the legality of Pickens' moves, but he questioned their morality. He was incensed by the resulting unemployment and the routing of money earmarked for exploration and research and development into shareholders' pockets and Pickens' money bag. He considered the moves detrimental to national security.

Pickens, like Halbouty, began his career as a geologist. He formed Mesa Petroleum in 1964 and built it into a powerful independent company engaged in exploration, drilling, and production. He came to national attention with his takeover attempts on major companies.

His ploy was to acquire stock in a major company such as Gulf and demand that management create a "royalty trust," a move that permits companies to transfer a portion of its cash flow directly to shareholders with the limited residue going into the normal operating channels. Gulf did not succumb to Pickens' blandishments. Instead, the management sold the company to Chevron. Gulf headquarters was closed, divisions were sold, and large numbers of employees were stricken from the payrolls.

Mesa made an after-tax profit of $214 million from the merger.

Halbouty inferred from public statements made by Pickens that the raider believed there was little oil and gas left to be found in the country and no need to waste money searching for it. Halbouty could not accept that he belonged to a "dying industry."

Though his criticism of the raiders appeared in dozens of magazines and newspapers across the land, his most powerful denunciation of Pickens and his ilk—although Pickens was not mentioned by name—was in a speech before the Houston Geological Society on June 10, 1985 where he had been a member for 54 years. It went, in part, like this:

> During the more than 50 years I have spent in the petroleum industry I have spoken out whenever I felt injustices were being committed against any aspect of our rights, freedoms, the petroleum industry or my profession.
>
> I come from a generation of Americans who believe in integrity in business, of professional pride in a job well done, of willingness to work for family, community and nation and, above all, never to profit or gain by intentionally injuring or depriving others.
>
> I have seen cycles of boom and bust—depressions, wars, recessions, recoveries. As a nation we have prospered through the workings of the free enterprise system, a system based on the principle of free choice, of mutual and voluntary arrangements.
>
> I have always been and still am a staunch advocate of the right to trade, the right to build, the right to expand. I also have been and still am a strong advocate of the least government control of business and least regulation of our industries.
>
> Today I am compelled to pause and reflect on what is happening in the market place, as it is obvious that the manner of doing business is in total disregard of those inherent principles that are the heart and soul of the American free enterprise system.
>
> It seems there is no sense of conscience in those who want to gain an immediate profit regardless of the adverse outcome to others or the nation. The manner in which such a profit is gained can well be referred to as seeking "instant gratification" regardless of the consequences.
>
> From the vantage point of many years of experience, I can say with certainty I have never seen such avarice and greed as I now see in the current hostile raiding attacks on business.
>
> The fair treatment of all participants in all negotiations is today in jeopardy and, if permitted to continue, those tactics will destroy the will of people to invest, to trade, and to negotiate without fear. We are witnessing a blight on our national economy and our national security.

And that blight is caused by raiders, arbitragers, sharks—cold, calculating profiteers who are weakening us all in the name of "shareholders rights." Morality is being totally ignored.

Free enterprise is being misinterpreted by the raiders as meaning free in the sense of license to act and do as one pleases.

But free enterprise means, instead, the freedom for individuals to operate in an ethical environment with due respect for the equal rights of others. This system is both the instrument and result of our individual liberty.

The basic and undisputed reason for American's growth is that we have continually built up its economic structure. Companies built their assets by investing their profits in their businesses.

Shareholders shared in the profits and in the growth of those businesses. As the industrial complex grew, employment increased and the nation became economically and strategically stronger.

*Now we see companies that took decades to build, companies that enhanced the welfare of communities, states, and the nation, raided and dismembered for the instant benefit of a select few.*

It is obvious that the raiders care less about what happens to employees or customers of the company—or to the company itself or the community it serves.

*And I don't believe they give a continental damn about the shareholders, either. They use the shareholders as pawns. Ironically, the shareholders' quick profits serve to weaken a viable company from which they would have been able to gain much more in the long run. The raiders have perceived that it is easier to buy assets than to work for and build them, and equally easy to abandon or liquidate companies than to stay and labor for long-term gains and growth.*

Each time a hostile or self-inflicted takeover occurs, the welfare of the nation is damaged because of the retrenchment that occurs in the infrastructure of the company.

I was shocked by ARCO's statement last month that it intended to reduce, among other things, its exploration and development budget by as much as 35 to 40%—an estimated $800 million in just one year!

As a geoscientist and explorationist, I can only gasp in horror at the significant oil and gas reserves that will not be found as a result.

It appears that ARCO's management has created its own takeover out of fear of a hostile move and is restructuring the company under the same or more restrictive conditions—and with the same results—that would have occurred under a hostile takeover. The company may increase its debt to total more than twice its net worth—and rob itself of its future.

The greatest absurdity of it all is that the raiders claim they are restructuring the industry. Well, the petroleum industry has been restructuring itself since its inception and will continue to do so as the need requires. It needs no assistance from takeover artists, raiders, opportunists, or arbitragers posing as oilmen, and certainly not from oilmen turned into the pawns of Wall Street!

A company can restructure up, or as ARCO did, restructure down. In the raiders' methods, the restructuring is always down!

What I object to most in this type of short-term planning is the substantial reduction of exploration which, by the way, has been the policy of every company involved in a hostile takeover.

*With the round of reductions in exploration that is taking place, let me assure you that there will come a day of reckoning. Petroleum imports will steadily rise beyond expectations and will drastically increase the nation's foreign deficit payments and consequently the inflation rate.*

Meanwhile, let's not forget that the hostile raiders have an ally. I'm talking about banks in particular. When a local bank supports a hostile takeover it becomes a partner of the raiders, and therefore is equally responsible for the suffering and damage that result. It is almost inconceivable to me that any local banking institution would participate in supporting a raider when it is obvious that the after-effects will injure the local economy.

Bank customers and depositors should not permit use of their money to foster elements against them. They can respond by informing the bank of their displeasure and withdrawing their deposits and business and going to other local banks that have refused to work with the raiders.

Lately, I have wondered just how much pure, cold greed enters into a decision to cause financial institutions to ignore the very principles that founded them, inasmuch that their charters were granted on the premise that they serve, enhance and build the communities in which they are located.

Another legacy of the raiders is the heavy cut-back in research and development. A tragic case in point is what is happening at Phillips Petroleum Company.

Two months ago, Charles Kittrel, executive vice-president and a director of the company, publicly stated that two Phillips projects to benefit humanity are among projects affected by the excessive debt incurred in thwarting two hostile takeover attempts.

The company has scrubbed construction of a plant for producing a single-cell protein that was hailed as a possible solution to world hunger. More than 25 years of work has been halted. A second project—a joint research venture in nuclear fission—is endangered by lack of funds and may be abandoned.

*Therefore, the raid on Phillips halted a safe energy resource for the future and a way to feed the world's hungry, two projects that were so close to commercial reality. These tragic losses to society are also a part of the raider legacy.*

I also have been informed that in Houston certain research and development projects also will come to a halt. As a result of the acquisition of Gulf by Chevron, the Gulf Research Center in southwest Houston will be transferred to La Habre, California. Who can say whether the innovative concepts that might have been forthcoming in the Houston lab will now ever be realized?

Of the 5,000 Gulf employees once working in our community it is estimated that at least one-third or more will be terminated, one-half will be transferred to other locations, leaving only a small number in Houston.

Houston was base headquarters for Gulf's world-wide exploration effort. Now it will be just one of Chevron's four divisions, with a substantial loss in personnel.

And in Pittsburgh, Gulf's venerable home base building is empty save for a few caretakers.

Those who raid have poked fun at those of us who still believe there is a substantial amount of oil and gas yet to be found in this country. Indeed, their disbelief is the reason given for their raiding tactics, or so they say.

But new oil and gas fields are being discovered almost daily all over the world, onshore and offshore in both producing areas and in the frontier regions. As one familiar with the world's geologic potential, I firmly believe we will find domestically, as well as world-wide, at least as much oil and substantially more gas than we have produced to date.

*You in this room and I have shared a common sense of conviction to search for and discover the oil and gas this nation has needed to sustain its growth and strategic leadership. That is what separates us from those who produce on Wall Street. We discover and produce—they buy and liquidate. Drilling for oil on Wall Street does not add one drop of new oil to our reserve base, nor is one dollar added to the national wealth.*

A raider has said that companies are throwing away huge cash flows in exploring for new reserves in high-risk areas, that the price of oil today does not warrant exploring and drilling in frontier areas. I say that frontier areas in the past were successfully drilled when oil was selling below $3 a barrel, and under worse economic conditions than now exist.

We've been told by this same raider that there are no more prospects to be drilled in this country. You and I know that there are thousands of prospects yet to be drilled in the United States.

This same raider has called our industry a "sunset industry," that replacing reserves is all but impossible, that we have no hope of survival.

We should not accept the glib mouthings of the raiders that no favorable prospects remain.

We should not accept the babbling of the raiders that we are in a state of self-liquidation as an industry.

We should not accept the ridiculous drivel of the raiders that replacing reserves is all but impossible.

We should not accept the poppycock of the raiders that in essence we should stop exploring the frontiers.

We should not accept the twaddle of the raiders that our industry is all but gone, that our professions are becoming extinct like the dodo bird.

I have spoken out as a citizen, as a representative of our professions, and as a member of the petroleum industry.

I've been told that my voice is one and alone in the wilderness. I've been told that no one gives a damn what goes on.

Well, I don't believe that!

I believe the millions who work in our industrial complex care. Employees who have lost their jobs care. Families that have been disrupted care. The cities of Pittsburgh and Houston and Tulsa and Bartlesville and Los Angeles care, as well as other communities hurt by the raiders.

And I fully believe that the majority of Americans would care if they were fully aware of the adverse impact the hostile raids will have on their future.

Can the raiders be stopped?

Yes, emphatically yes. And very easily, by the people, all of us, sending out a message to the media that the raiders, in flouting the inherent principles of moral, social, and ethical standards of conducting business, are not protecting the investors or the workers. If that message was forcibly expressed, the raiders would be held up to public scorn and, like robber barons of the 19th century, would be remembered only for the chaos they created in their greedy quest for the fast buck.

When men assume special privileges, without regard for the welfare of others, they usually harm themselves in the end.

Lust for riches is its own nemesis. It may fatten temporarily on an apathetic public conscience, but it commits hari-kari because it doesn't know when to stop.

There are other things besides money, even in this dollar-chasing age. A clear conscience and the respect of one's fellow citizens are still worth striving for.

He who raises the black flag in any avenue of life is riding hard for a fall because retribution—though not the highest of laws, human or divine—is as inevitable as fate itself!

\*\*\*

Though Halbouty did not name a banking institution in his speech, he had, six months earlier, been quoted in the *Houston Post* as slamming Texas Commerce Bancshares "for its participation in a banking group helping to finance (T. Boone) Pickens' latest move against Phillips Petroleum Co."

The story also said that Pickens held a seat on the board of directors at the bank holding company.

The story said, "With this city suffering a recession caused by the slowdown in that industry, Halbouty said, 'it is unfortunate that Texas Commerce would aid one of its board members to further undermine the one industry which is so vital to the welfare of Houston. I believe it is time for those who depend on the petroleum industry for their livelihood to stand up and let those who are assisting Pickens know exactly how they feel about the erosion of their industry.'"

Ben F. Love, chairman of Texas Bancshares defended the bank's actions: "If our customers are abiding by the law of the land and are creditworthy, then we have an obligation to those customers to supply funds without in an arbitrary way attempting to play God. We have had as much as $3 1/2 billion in energy loans to every sector of the energy industry. Very few of those dollars were in the acquisition sector. Those facts clearly demonstrate Texas Commerce's support and commitment to the industry."

A few weeks later Pickens was not on the Texas Commerce Bancshares' board.

Halbouty and many others hoped that the furor over Pickens' activities would prompt the Congress to pass legislation that would check the takeover process. The House Subcommittee on Telecommunications, Consumer Protection, and Finance, held a series of hearings on the subject in 1985, but nothing came of them.

It seemed that time, perhaps, would slow down Pickens. In the September 1986 issue of *Petroleum Management* he was quoted as saying there probably wouldn't be any more hostile takeovers, at least in the near future. He was busy in promoting the T. Boone Pickens, Jr. United Shareholders Association, which he had formed a month earlier. He was quoted as saying, "I'm tired of them (hostile takeovers). It's not an easy game. It's like Super Bowl Sunday every day of the week; 24 hours a day. The pressure is on all the time. You can't relax a second. It is a very physically and mentally demanding operation. And the way Mesa is structured now (it's a master limited partnership) would indicate that we probably wouldn't take the MLP into a hostile attempt."

Three months later he launched a hostile takeover attempt on Diamond Shamrock Corporation, a small major oil company based in Dallas, with the usual fanfare.

He failed in that attempt. He made two more sallies, but in both cases was thwarted by Diamond Shamrock directors. He quietly retreated.

# CHAPTER NINE

The fog of gloom that settled on the oil states when OPEC kicked open its valves and drove the price of oil down to $9 a barrel found oilmen stumbling around in search of a ray of salvation. Since the industry's infancy, oilmen had absorbed with their mothers' milk the conviction that the government had no place in their business. They had fought against every regulation, every restraint, and oil-state legislators had fought at their sides.

But only a month after the precipitous price decline began, many of them were rallying around Texas Senator Lloyd Bentsen, a conservative Democrat and industry supporter, who announced his advocacy of a price floor and an import tax on foreign oil. Speaking at the 22nd annual Houston Chamber of Commerce Outlook Conference, Bentsen said, "Set a price for oil, then add the tax. If oil were $22 a barrel, and it went down to $16, the import tax would be $6, which would make up for the decline. When it got back up to $22 a barrel, then you would take off the import tax."

His arguments in favor of his proposal were persuasive. The tax, he said, could help trim the federal deficit while stabilizing the economies of the oil states and banks in the Northeast and on the West Coast that also were hurt by the price decline.

The deficit, which had soared under the Reagan administration, certainly needed trimming, and independent oilmen certainly needed help from somewhere. And with the thought of rising prices there was the vision of bits drilling, factories humming, and the unemployed settling back to their old jobs.

Domestic oil groups began marching in the parade, some quickly, some reluctantly and with misgivings. High-octane independent oilmen like George Mitchell of Mitchell Energy and Oscar Wyatt of Coastal States heartily endorsed the proposed tax and urged its quick adoption. Some petroleum-oriented publications threw their support behind it. Oil-state legislators spoke favorably of it. Columnist William F. Buckley, to whom tax was normally a dirty word, demanded it, and the *New York Times*, as liberal as Buckley was conservative, seemed to call for it in an editorial titled, "Tax Oil to Save Oil."

George Mitchell, a long-time friend of Halbouty's and also a Texas A&M alumnus, sent Halbouty a copy of a telegram he had sent to President Reagan on July 21, 1986. It succinctly stated the pro-tax case. It said:

> As head of one of the nation's largest petroleum independents and a member of your National Petroleum Council, I urge you to take immediate action to counter the one-two punches of rising oil imports and the decline in domestic exploration. Imports of crude oil to the United States jumped in June almost 50% over those in June 1985. Total imports including products were 6.5 million barrels daily, up more than one-third. Domestic production declined.
>
> Meanwhile, the search for future supplies goes on at barely more than 15% of the industry's capacity. The modest increase in the drilling rig count last week is hardly cause for optimism—it only underscores the fact that exploration and development continue to scrape along at near record lows.
>
> By 1990, only 3½ years from now, the United States will be dependent on imports for more than 50% or more of its petroleum needs. By that time the domestic industry's hardware will have rusted away, sources of capital will have dried up, and its human resources—the men and women who know how to find and produce oil—will be working elsewhere.
>
> The threat to our economic and military security is intolerable. We are gambling away our future for the sake of a cheap gallon of gas. An import fee now is the only practical means available to assure our nation some degree of energy independence.

From the beginning of the push for the tax, Halbouty had been petitioned by Mitchell, Oscar Wyatt, and scores of other oilmen to lend his considerable weight to their position.

And from the beginning, Halbouty had refused. He spoke against the tax privately and he spoke against it publicly in forums from Los Angeles to Tulsa to New Orleans. He spoke in places where, but for the audiences' regard for him, he likely would have been ill-received.

He spoke against the tax knowing that its imposition would put money in his company's till and in his personal pocket. He telephoned, wrote letters, and made personal visits to senators and congressmen and to President Reagan, advising against support of such a measure. His arguments were published in newspapers and magazines and voiced on radio and television.

Mexico and Canada, both exporters to the U.S., came out against the tax. Mexico's oil chief, Mario Ramon Beteta, said in Houston, "A tariff could adversely affect Mexico and Canada. Speaking for my own country, I can tell you a tariff on oil imports would reduce our capacity to buy goods and equipment abroad, a majority of which comes from the United States. It would also weaken our capacity to fully service our debt obligations. . . ."

Most major oil companies opposed the tax, not with Halbouty's passion nor the drumbeat of his rhetoric, but for some of the same reasons.

And in late July 1986, President Reagan said he had decided to oppose it. However, when he asked for his energy "study" in September, the tax was thrown into the grab bag for discussion.

Meanwhile, Norway told OPEC that it would cut production by 10%. Britain stood fast for full production, but observers felt sure that Britain would do privately what it would not admit to doing publicly.

And in early August OPEC announced its decision to cut production by 4 million barrels a day in September and October, and in October announced it would extend the cutback until the end of the year.

Oil prices rebounded by about $5 a barrel. OPEC let it be known that it was aiming at an $18-a-barrel price level. Independents let it be known that they were thinking in terms of $22-a-barrel oil and would much prefer to return to the $28 a barrel they were getting before OPEC lowered the boom in December 1985.

So the call for the import tax continued.

No one was more aware than Halbouty the dangers to the country's economic and military security the drilling slowdown presented. No one felt more strongly than he that exploratory drilling must be greatly increased—and rapidly—for those dangers to be lessened. But the import tax, he argued, would cause the country more harm than good.

In lieu of the tax he offered his own program, one that would stimulate drilling and production without upsetting other segments of the country's economy, he said.

The import tax would bring hardships to home-owners in the Northeast and Midwest who use more heating oil than the national average, and to motorists of the Southwest who consume more gasoline, he said.

Farmers would have to pay more for fertilizers, operating machinery, irrigation equipment, and crop-drying. The competitiveness of U.S. agricultural exports would suffer from an increase in both production and inland transportation costs.

The price of coal and other energy sources would rise, and eventually the price level for all goods and services would be pushed upward, and economic growth could falter. "Don't forget," he warned, "that the higher oil price is passed on to the final prices of other goods, leading to a general increase in prices. That means the raising of nominal interest rates, the driving down of investments, and the reduction of the real worth of consumers."

He was particularly concerned about the petrochemical industry. Petrochemical producers would have to raise their output price and would be at a competitive disadvantage with foreign competitors who would have access to raw materials at below-market prices. "So imports of petrochemicals would increase since foreign producers would be able to supply products cheaper than U.S. manufacturers," he said. "Finally, the manufacturers of everything made from petrochemicals, from plastics to pharmaceuticals, would raise their prices, and that would ripple through the economy."

With the tax, then, exports would suffer, imports other than oil would surge, jobs would be lost, and living costs would rise and rise, he said.

He made other points—he once compiled a list of 42 reasons why the tax should not be imposed—and from time to time he touched on his alternative plan.

But at a gathering of the Rotary Club of Houston, the largest Rotary Club in the world, he delivered an address that was a full disclosure of what he thought the American energy policy should and should not be. The meeting was in the Astro Village Hotel.

The well-reasoned speech was calmly made in contrast to his usual fiery addresses. He spoke without anger or rancor, and there was a hint of sadness in his words. The only enemy he denounced was a numbing apathy that had seeped into the public will.

It was apparent that he felt his more than five decades in the oil business qualified him to voice his views with some authority.

This is what he said:

> The title of this presentation is "The Petroleum Industry at Its Crossroads." There is no question in my mind that under current conditions of the petroleum industry the title is most appropriate. Over the past few months I have been asked many times about the outlook for the domestic petroleum industry and the impact that a weakened industry will have on the nation. Reporters, colleagues, businessmen, senators, congressmen, and members of the Administration have asked me questions such as, Is there any real threat to our national security from rising imports of crude oil and products from the Middle East? Aren't we being somewhat over-emotional about the decline of the petroleum industry? Aren't we being hasty in talking about a looming energy crisis when the world is flooded with oil?
>
> In each instance I've answered by explicitly pointing out the serious condition of the petroleum industry. So let's examine the problems, understand what caused them, and see what must be done to solve them. Let's look back to the beginning of the beginning of the oil industry's slide, back a few years ago to the initial breakdown of the industry where the groundwork for our present problems was laid.
>
> The dangerous retrenchment trend that has become prevalent throughout the entire industry was precipitated by a surge of hostile takeover raids and threats against companies. These raids and threats undermined productivity, created depressions in communities and

states, and burdened the victim companies with billions of dollars of excess, and unnecessary, debt.

These raids crippled every segment of the industry and in turn affected every service company and satellite entity associated with it. The harm will be felt for years to come. Thousands upon thousands of workers were laid off or dismissed completely. Exploration budgets were cut to skeleton levels. The impact of these cuts was indeed demoralizing.

Those who perpetuated the raids sowed the seeds of discord, fear, anxiety, and pessimism and also fostered our great petroleum industry's downward slide. *That* was the commencement of the industry's current problems.

Then OPEC flooded the world oil markets, causing a severe drop in oil prices. This "double whammy" by the raiders and OPEC badly damaged the economies of our major oil producing states, especially Oklahoma, Louisiana, and Texas, and in addition literally brought the petroleum industry to its knees. Independents and service companies went out of business at an alarming rate. State and local government are suffering from fallen revenues and job losses have produced record unemployment and intense negativism throughout the entire industry.

Financial support for the industry has practically evaporated. Banks, insurance companies and other funding entities have no desire to invest in an ailing industry. Sooner or later, what has happened in this one industry will affect every person, home, and entity in the country. Still, the apathy in some quarters is disturbing and unrealistic.

This was illustrated by the *Washington Post* when, the day after the recent congressional election, it published a long list of important issues to be addressed by this Administration and energy was not even mentioned. When one of this nation's most powerful and influential newspapers, located in the national capital, fails to recognize that energy is a vital issue to be reckoned with, it clearly illustrates how little the problem is understood.

The newspaper should have researched and informed the public that domestic exploration for oil and gas is at a standstill and that the nation's oil import dependence is steadily increasing, and if continued, will generate an unacceptable risk for the country. It also should have stressed that without secure petroleum supplies to fuel our military complex, our national strategic security is jeopardized and that in the event of hostilities or outright war, we would stand little chance of sustaining, much less winning, any confrontation.

Although I have singled out the *Washington Post* for its sin of omission, I also blame the entire media for treating this issue too lightly. I would think that the media in Houston and Texas and elsewhere would highlight the seriousness of the matter daily so as to inform the public that a crisis is upon us. This should be done on the front pages of the papers where it will receive the best overall coverage instead of in the business section which is read selectively by people who already understand the problems.

I should also point out that the President of the United States did not make a single mention of energy in his state-of-the-union speech despite urging from leaders from all sectors of the industry. He never even uttered the word. I was so disappointed, it made me want to cry.

It is sad but true, that in the years since the 1973 oil embargo, we failed as a nation to develop and implement a coherent energy policy. It seems that everybody and every entity in Washington is either unaware that a policy does not exist or just doesn't care to establish one. If we had had a strong workable and effective energy policy, the President, the Congress, and more particularly the public, would have recognized that we are experiencing a negative turnaround in our entire energy arena.

They would also have known that as a result of lower oil prices, most of our alternate-energy research and development projects have been curtailed or cancelled. They would have definitely known that of all activities engaged in by the petroleum industry, the exploration for new reserves of oil and gas is the most essential to the nation's welfare. Furthermore, they would surely have known that each day we are not extensively exploring for petroleum is another setback to the nation's energy strength.

They would without a doubt have known that as our production continues to decline, our import level increases and our foreign trade deficit rises. Also, they would have known that imports of crude oil and products rose substantially all last year, reaching 7.9 million barrels a day in September, a record high of 49.8% of our daily requirement, and they would have done something to slow down the climb. And, they would have been shocked to know that in one year domestic production has declined 817,000 barrels a day and our demand has increased from 15.6 million barrels a day to approximately 16.3 million barrels a day. Also, in that same period, our imports have increased 1.1 million barrels a day, and when these figures are added together, they total a negative turnaround of 2.6 million barrels a day. This is *indeed* alarming!

And most of all they would have known and concluded that to continue along this path is inviting and condoning the lessening of our national security and inviting the economic upheaval of this nation. National security and economic concerns are not the only issues. Ahead of us is a slow-down in our overall industry growth and a gigantic responsibility to cut back our overwhelming trade deficit which now approximates $175 billion. Furthermore, our oil reserves are being depleted without any exploration to add to them. Consequently, the nation is placing itself in an uncompromising and untenable position of great risk. But most of all, what concerns me is that with all of what is happening the public apparently does not know what is going on or if it does know, it doesn't give a damn!

I have criss-crossed the country over the past year speaking to industry and professional groups of all kinds about the plight of the domestic oil industry. And everywhere I have spoken I have proposed what I consider to be reasonable solutions for our dilemma. While others have called for quotas and import fees, I have called instead for increased incentives to help the industry without the government being involved with the price structure. We have learned from past experience that when the government controls or manipulates the prices of oil and gas, the results have not been beneficial.

I am a staunch believer in the free enterprise system, but I must say most emphatically that there is a great different between the free enterprise system and the world oil market. The fact is that there *is* no free market in oil. There has never been a free market in oil as long as I can remember. The free market in oil passed into oblivion when the Texas Railroad Commission issued its first statewide proration order in April of 1928.

When OPEC exercised its strength during the 1973 embargo, the disruption in the market forces was accentuated. Today, non-OPEC countries are competing against tremendous OPEC reserves and as long as that market is controlled by OPEC, there is no free market. Maybe sometime in the future when world oil reserves have declined to the point where demand for oil cannot be met, then the free market on oil will return.

Until that time, stopgap measures and quick-fix approaches will not help the U.S. oil industry. For example, there is a clamor for an import fee. Strong support has come from petroleum independents, a few majors, politicians and state governors, including our own. Although I personally might be helped by an increase in oil prices brought about by an import fee, it will do far more harm than good to the industry as well as to the country. Congress will *never* pass an oil import fee without placing another kind of tax on domestic oil producers. The exemptions to the import fee could include large numbers of charitable institutions, churches, schools, farmers, to say nothing of friendly-nation exemptions. The bureaucracy to handle the bookkeeping could be as large as the Pentagon. An oil import fee would add one more regulation, one more control, and one more tax to this industry, and there is no assurance that the funds derived from the fee would be plowed back into exploration.

What I want is for the government to come up with a better brand of energy leadership than we have seen in the past. Now, this is what I think the Congress and the President should join hands to do:

1. Repeal the Windfall Profits Tax and the Fuel Use Act. The first is simply an excise tax and the second is a major detriment to the proper use of oil and gas.
2. Deregulate all remaining natural gas and let it seek and find its natural price level.
3. Help us to work in harmony with enlightened environmentalists so we can prove that public lands can be drilled without damage to seas and fish life, without damage to forests and foliage and scenic delights, and without damage to all creatures great and small. It can be done. It *has* been done!
4. But the most important action they should take, the greatest incentive they could provide us to find the oil and gas we so desperately need to develop and produce, would be the restoration of the full 27½% statutory depletion allowance to all producers!

For those of you who are not producers of oil and gas or familiar with the meaning of the statutory percentage depletion, I will take a moment to enlighten you as to what it means and accomplishes. From 1926 until 1969, percentage depletion allowable for oil and gas was set at 27½% of income from production. The Tax Reform

Act of 1969 reduced it to a 22% rate. Then, in 1975, it eliminated all integrated oil companies (in essence, the majors) and reduced the percentage to 15% to apply only to independent producers. The elimination of depletion percentage from the integrated oil companies in 1975 was a knee-jerk political reaction by the Congress to the dramatic increases in world oil prices that occurred during and after the 1973–74 Arab oil embargo.

The percentage depletion recognizes the depleting nature of oil and gas and allows for the partial return of the producer's capital investment and provides an incentive to invest capital in high risk business. The depletion allows a taxpayer-producer a deduction equal to a specific percentage of the gross income from the production of oil and gas. While there are many limitations and complications, in general, an independent, for example, is allowed a deduction equal to 15% of the gross income from the production attributable to a maximum of 1,000 barrels of production a day. The percentage depletion deduction is treated as any other business deduction in computing a taxpayer's taxable income. For example, for each $100 of gross oil or gas income a deduction of $27.50 would be allowed for a full 27½% depletion deduction.

Thus, in the past, producers were provided with a source of funds free of tax which were generally used for additional exploration and drilling. This was the very reason it was enacted by the Congress in 1926 and it served the nation well while it was in effect. It was responsible for new exploration and the discovery of significant new reserves which otherwise would not have been timely discovered. The statutory depletion percentage was one of the most effective incentives responsible for exploring in frontier and offshore areas. Also it was the catalyst that strengthened independents and kept them drilling 80% of all the wells drilled in the country.

Therefore, I felt that what was needed to encourage more exploration, more reserves, and more production was the restoration of the tax deductible percentage depletion provision. I also felt certain that an import fee would never be passed by the Congress or approved by the Administration, so more than a year ago, I began advocating the restoration of the depletion percentage to all producers. I was the first in the industry to publicly call for such action. I concluded that the depletion percentage would not manipulate or interfere with the price structure of oil and gas, nor would it provide government control on prices. I knew that it would stimulate industry activity without making gasoline and home heating oil prices shoot through the roof, as an import tax most likely would.

The import fee would be a temporary fix. It would cause prices to rise and fall like a monkey on a string. On the other hand, the statutory depletion percentage will bring stability and continuity back to the industry.

When I first proposed the restoration I was told by friends and foes alike that I had lost my mind, that it would never be restored. Well, I've kept right on advocating it, and it's surprising how many now think that maybe, just maybe, it could be possible.

Now there are many who are pushing and supporting its passage. It's the most positive incentive the Congress and the Administration can give to a vital industry. I must remind you that geologically from a single drop of water the Grand Canyon was initiated and eventually formed. So I hope that with a single push an avalanche will form to support the restoration of the statutory depletion percentage. And I would also hope it wouldn't take as long as the creation of the Grand Canyon.

My studies indicate that the restoration of the depletion percentage would create investment confidence among the financial community and new money for exploration would flow into the industry. As more money was made from production, more taxes would be paid, thus there would be no reduction to the Treasury. To the contrary, the overall swing would mean more income to the government. Although it would stimulate more activity to have the depletion percentage to apply to all wells now producing, I am calling for the percentage to be *applied only* to wells which produce *after* the date of the restoration of the depletion percentage.

The independent producing up to 1,000 bbl/day would keep his 15% depletion rights on his old wells after the passage and would gain the full 27½% on new producers. Therefore, with new producers, independents and majors alike would have the full 27½% benefit. The passage of the depletion percentage would create an immediate positive design for financiers to come back into exploration. Also it would stimulate the entire industry. The economic stability of this city, this state and the nation would be enhanced.

We cannot afford to lose more production and become more dependent on imports from sources beyond our control. That is tantamount to ransoming our energy security. It places our nation at risk. I think that all of us here agree that the depressed conditions that exist in the petroleum industry will affect the long-term welfare of the nation. We already know how this city and the state have been adversely affected. Without the incentives I have mentioned, and particularly the restoration of the depletion allowance, U.S. exploration will remain stagnant, our dependence on imports will continue to increase, and our vulnerability to oil price shocks and possible oil shortages or stoppages will rise to an excessively dangerous level.

There may be time to avoid a national crisis, but what little time there is must be used prudently. Positive action must be taken *now*.

I want to emphasize that those in the industry, including those in the thousands of satellite businesses which serve it, firmly believe that the Congress and the Administration do not realize the gravity of the depressed condition of the industry and the long-term negative effect it will have on the nation.

They also feel that the President should state that he will ask the Congress to help him in this mission. God knows it's not a partisan matter. The people of this nation do not want outside forces to control their future. I am sure of that. If they knew the facts they would not sit idly by and watch the continuing deterioration of the U.S. petroleum industry and with it the strategic welfare of the nation!

So it is time for the President and the Congress to assist the industry in solving its problems and, without further delay, to tell the 240 million people in this country what is happening, how it is affecting their security, and how it will affect their future.

I am convinced that the steps I have outlined would provide the starting point for the revitalization of the domestic petroleum industry. If we do not take positive action *soon*, we will lose the most precious legacy of all—freedom and independence.

We, as a nation, are 210 years old, and history had shown that at the average life of 200 years, each of the world's great civilizations either faltered or began to falter. I hope and trust that it does not occur to us, and that we will last forever. However, when a nation's most vital industry falters, that nation begins to falter.

In this regard, we had a viable, highly productive petroleum industry. It helped to sustain our freedoms, but the government and the people lost the desire and the passion to preserve it. So, as it dies, many of our freedoms die with it.

The petroleum industry is at its cross-roads. Which way it goes, nobody knows, but I do believe that if it continues on the road it is now traveling, it will end in disaster. It will be the beginning of the end of the United States as a world super-power. We will then become a second-rate country by our own hands.

He had spoken to a packed house, and at the conclusion of his speech the audience rose as one and gave him a ringing ovation. Those in the audience who knew him best were surprised—and apparently pleased—by his restraint. He had not castigated environmentalists as he had in the past; he had asked them to meet with oilmen to pursue a course that would permit industry access to government lands without damage to nature. He had asked the Administration to join hands with the Congress to make the people aware of the coming energy crisis, and to work together to forestall it.

Noticeably, he had ended his speech without the optimistic flourish that normally marked the conclusion of his addresses. Even in the darkest hours of the past he had whipped out his rose-colored glasses as he neared the end. This time he had ended on a warning note; if the government and the people did not take immediate action, we were risking becoming a second-rate country by our own hands.

He had reserved his sternest censure for President Reagan, noting that when Reagan failed to even mention the word "energy" in his state-of-the-union address, "I was so disappointed, it made me want to cry."

\*\*\*

He was cheered up after the speech to learn that Interior Secretary Donald Hodel had told the *Houston Post* that he favored "a look at potential tax incentives for exploratory activity, including an improved depletion allowance with a plowback clause." The "plowback clause" would be legislative insurance that oilmen would spend the depletion allowance money on exploration rather than yachts, horses, women, and castles in Spain as some had spent it before the allowance had been disapproved.

Halbouty had discussed the "plowback clause" with Hodel and others in the Administration all through 1986. He had strongly supported it. Hodel was a strong voice in President Reagan's energy "study group." Now his public statement produced new hope for Halbouty that at long last an intelligent energy policy might be around the corner.

"It's a beginning," he told Mary Stewart.

Now he teamed up with Phil Gramm, the junior senator from Texas, to add more pressure on the Administration. Lloyd Bentsen, the senior Texas senator, was the initial advocate of the import tax, as we have seen. Gramm had opposed the import tax but had never made it clear what he considered a benign alternative. In late February, Gramm, with Halbouty's strong support, publicly advocated the restoration of the depletion allowance, and said he had other measures to include in bills he was preparing. Halbouty, meanwhile, continued his argument for restoration in interviews and speeches.

Then, on March 17, 1987, Energy Secretary John Herrington released a 300-page report, the product of the administration's "study." It virtually turned thumbs down on an import tax, but looked favorably on restoration of the depletion allowance and other tax advantages, as well as other measures Halbouty had long called for.

Supporters of the import tax had little but scorn for the report. Halbouty, understandably, was jubilant, but his joy was tempered by his experience with six years of administration neglect and knowledge that a very low row remained to be hoed. For one thing, the report would have to undergo further study and debate by the full Cabinet, and that meant weeks, perhaps months, of waiting. Formidable opposition could be expected from the Treasury Department; the potential revenue loss from the depletion allowance was estimated from $3½ billion to $7 billion. (Halbouty believed this loss would be made up by taxes paid by rehired workers and rejuvenated segments of the industry.)

And, of course, there was President Reagan's obvious reluctance to open up the 1986 tax overhaul for amendments of any kind.

Shortly after the report was made public, Senator Bentsen announced that he was through fighting for the import tax because he saw no chance of its passage. He was pessimistic, too, about chances for restoration of the depletion allowance, but he had hopes that other tax credits to boost exploration and drilling would win administration approval.

That same day, Herrington acknowledged to reporters that he was facing a skeptical audience in trying to sell others in the administration on a program of tax breaks for the oil industry. "You're talking about going back into a tax code and you're talking about increased government spending. If I were the White House, I'd be cool, too." But he added that he thought the facts contained in the report, plus his salesmanship, would win the day.

And on March 24, before a sullen audience in Houston, Herrington made a strong pitch for the depletion allowance while putting the sword to the import tax. About 500 representatives of the Houston chapters of the American Petroleum Institute and the International Association of Drilling Contractors were his listeners, and after his speech a majority of them evinced their displeasure with his stand by endorsing a resolution calling on President Reagan to impose an oil import tax.

None of these things, however, could dampen Halbouty's natural optimism. He had always been able to shake off hard blows himself, and he believed sincerely that the industry that was his life was capable of the same. His rosy attitude was much in evidence in an article he wrote for the Opposite Editorial Page of the *Houston Post* in the March 29, 1987 edition:

> In recent years the U.S. oil industry has been in an extremely depressed state. Hostile raids and threats of hostile takeovers spawned massive retrenchment throughout the industry. Many major oil companies restructured and took on huge debt burdens in order to be as unattractive as possible to the raiders. Massive personnel layoffs and budget cutbacks became commonplace.
>
> Then OPEC flooded the world with crude oil and the price of a barrel of oil plummeted. Business and banking failures escalated. Hundreds of independents were forced to close their doors. Domestic exploration all but stopped. Nationwide petroleum pro-

duction declined more than 700,000 barrels per day last year and imports of crude oil and refined products rose dramatically. The Texas economy has been stifled, and Houston in particular has taken a severe beating. Pessimists abound saying "give up"—there isn't a chance that oil prices will rise fast enough to preserve the U.S. petroleum industry, drilling will go down instead of up, and the industry can't be revived.

In contrast to these doomsayers, there are many others who *don't* believe the industry is dead. Those who did *not* succumb to the liquidation fever engendered by the corporate raiders still believe in the viability of the industry that made this country second to none.

Today, amid the reports of devastation there is a ray of hope. The slump in the oil industry and its related service sectors appears to have bottomed out, and for Houston that's cause for relief. We're overdue for a turnaround.

Evidence that the downhill slide has stopped has come from many areas. The Texas Railroad Commission's "State of the Industry" meeting held recently in Dallas produced a consensus that the Texas oil industry is in better health than it was a year ago.

Numerous petroleum industry analysts have revised their predictions of doom and gloom, so prevalent just weeks ago. New forecasts indicate that the rig count will start to rise soon—going as high as 2,000 by the early '90s—as a response to the disappearing natural gas "bubble" in this country. Others are projecting an oil price rise in response to the decline in drilling worldwide, which is prompting increased import dependence in many areas of the world, thus inevitably the shifting of oil pricing power once again to the Middle East.

But before the U.S. petroleum industry can rebound, strong measures must be taken. Recommendations have come from all sectors of the industry and most recently from the federal government.

Two back-to-back reports—the National Petroleum Council's report to Secretary John Herrington of the Department of Energy in mid-February and the DOE's own task force report on energy-related national security concerns, released March 17—indicate that steps must be taken immediately not only to help preserve the domestic oil industry, but by doing so to also safeguard and enhance our national security and our national economy. The impact of these reports, combined with OPEC's sustained efforts to stabilize oil production and oil prices, has inspired new confidence throughout the petroleum industry.

Bringing the situation closer to home, I want to state that there is no question in my mind that what is good for the oil industry is good for Houston. Although we have a multitude of other assets—the Port of Houston, our world-renowned medical center, our magnificent museums and cultural centers, our convention and sports facilities—the highest percentage of Houston's economic base is oil-related. Put another way, whatever affects the local oil industry—for the good or bad—affects every other segment of the city's economy.

The turnaround is about to begin, but the recovery will be a slow one. Just as the recession did not happen overnight, neither will our economy blossom instantly. We've learned difficult lessons and we know what we have to do. Houston is no stranger to hard work and dedicated effort. The city will come through the ordeal stronger for having been so severely tested. The bottom has been reached. From this day forward there will be a gradual and steady economic climb for Houston and Texas.

\*\*\*

At the time of the article, it appeared that only OPEC could turn Halbouty's professed optimism into reality. Only OPEC had the ready ability to hike the price of oil and thus increase domestic exploration and production. OPEC obviously was trying to keep the price in the $18 range, not a price that would send domestic explorationists out in droves to find new oil even if the administration and the Congress granted tax advantages to the industry.

So Halbouty was basing his hopes on a stabilized OPEC continuing to lower production to facilitate price increases, and the administration and the Congress doing their duty as he saw it.

# CHAPTER TEN

It was a character oddity that Halbouty, who loved to see his name in print because he thought it belonged there, shied away from publicity about his public generosities. Yet, he regularly donated six-figure amounts to the public welfare. Even less known were the many gifts to down-on-their-luck associates and loans that he never expected to be repaid.

He made his first contribution to the public good in 1949 when his income was smaller than his public image and, like most wildcatters, was living just one step ahead of his creditors. Indeed, there were those who said he borrowed the money, something he never confirmed nor denied. The contribution was to St. Luke's Episcopal Hospital.

His daughter, Linda Fay, was born in St. Joseph's Hospital, prematurely and weighing in at less than four pounds. The obstetrician, Dr. Herman Gardner, called on Halbouty shortly after the child was safely at home. Dr. Gardner assumed that Halbouty was wealthy because he was an oilman and lived at a fine address. He explained that he had been named chief of obstetrics and gynecology at St. Luke's Hospital, which was in its formative stage. He wanted to have an outstanding premature nursery at St. Luke's, and he wanted Halbouty to finance its beginning.

Halbouty didn't hesitate. He contributed enough money to get the project underway, and continued to contribute as the years passed and his fortune grew. The Linda Fay Halbouty Premature Nursery at St. Luke's became the finest in the Southwest.

Over the years he received letters from grateful parents, such as this one from a young couple in El Campo, Texas: "Dear Mr. Halbouty, the people at St. Luke's said you were responsible for getting the premature nursery started. We were told that your premature daughter is growing up to be a lovely youngster. Because of you and the nursery, our son Charles survived, and we are sure he will be a fine boy and a fine man. We are taking this way to say thank you, thank you, thank you."

Halbouty was appreciative of such mail, but he was unaware that his capable administrative assistant, Mary Stewart, retained the letters and kept them in a separate file. "I'm keeping them for his grandchildren," she said. "I think it'll be nice for them to have them when they're old enough to understand their significance."

\*\*\*

It will be recalled that back in the 1940s, when he was scraping to make a living and to pay a secretary—his only employee—that Halbouty established a postgraduate fellowship in geology at Texas A&M for students who had worked while in school obtaining their bachelor degrees. And the school, in later years, named its geological science building the Michel T. Halbouty Geoscience Building. Some time later Halbouty provided funds for interior construction and furnishing of an addition to the building, a restful lounge-library of subdued opulence. It was a haven for teachers and students. Teachers retreated there to grade papers, to discuss issues; for small talk and private thinking. The library was a bonanza for students. It was stocked with hundreds of books and papers on every aspect of the earth sciences, and it also held the innumerable papers Halbouty had written over the years. Further, there were stacks of scrapbooks featuring Halbouty but also constituting a clear, concise history of the domestic and foreign oil industry. The lounge-library, then, was an educational oasis.

On October 28, 1984, versions of this story appeared in newspapers around Texas and elsewhere. It was datelined College Station, Texas, home of Texas A&M University, and said:

> Michel T. Halbouty is now the donor of the largest individually endowed academic chair at Texas A&M with the announcement that he has increased his endowment in geology to $1.1 million.

The Michel T. Halbouty Chair, originally endowed in 1981 with $500,000 from the internationally prominent Houston earth scientist and engineer, is held by Dr. Robert R. Berg, widely acclaimed geologist and former president of the American Institute of Professional Geologists. The announcement of Halbouty's new gift came during the dedication of a $7.1 million expansion of the Michel T. Halbouty Geosciences Building.

The increase in the chair to $1.1 million identifies it as one of the most outstanding chairs in geology in the United States, and will afford Texas A&M the opportunity for expanded geological research. It will also assist the College of Geosciences to maintain its standard of excellence.

Halbouty is a 1930 graduate of A&M and has been designated one of the University's distinguished alumni.

At the beginning of the ceremony, telegrams of congratulations were read from President Ronald Reagan, Vice-President George Bush, and the Secretary of Energy.

Speaking to more than 100 persons gathered inside the Halbouty complex, Jack M. Rains, president of 3/D International and a 1960 A&M graduate, said he first heard of Halbouty in the 1950s when he arrived at A&M. "He was a legend then, and he has always been one of my heroes," Rains said.

Rains told a story of Halbouty's first days at A&M as a freshman when he was $50 short of funds to register.

"He kept hearing everybody say Prexy Walton did this and Prexy Walton did that, so Halbouty decided to find this person to see if he could help. Not knowing that Prexy was a nickname for president, he went to Prexy Walton's secretary and told her his story.

"President Walton heard Halbouty outside his door and came out to meet the young man, and ended up lending Halbouty $50 out of his pocket. I submit that was the best investment Texas A&M ever made."

Halbouty earned his bachelor's and master's degrees at A&M before earning a doctorate of engineering at Montana College of Mineral Science and Technology.

A staunch supporter of his alma mater since graduation, Halbouty's generosity includes the giving of two scholarships in geology and petroleum engineering each year for more than 35 years and funding of a President's Endowed Scholarship.

Halbouty has received numerous honors including the Hoover Medal for engineering excellence and public service from the American Association of Engineering Societies, the Geosciences and Earth Resources Medal for Distinguished Achievement, and the American Association of Petroleum Geologists' President's Award for his special publication, "Giant Oil and Gas Fields of the Decade 1968–1978."

He has presented his personal papers, reflecting his illustrious career and involvement in worldwide energy matters, to A&M's Sterling C. Evans Library.

"Mike's love for Texas A&M began as a student on campus and has grown every year since," said Dr. Robert Walker, vice-president for development. "He is very generous with his time and his resources and his interest in everything for the good of Texas A&M."

Dean Mel Friedman said with the new 40,000-square-foot Halbouty addition and the renovation of the older wing, the College of Geosciences at A&M will have facilities for teaching and research that are second to none in the nation.

\*\*\*

Halbouty had loved to write since his high school days, and his ability to put his thoughts and ideas on paper oftimes provided him with an income during his lean periods. His first venture was prompted by a desperate need for $500. His reputation as a geologist was spreading, so he was not turned away when he went to the office of Warren Baker, editor of *The Oil Weekly* (now *World Oil*), with a proposal that he write a series of articles for the magazine that would then be published as a book. He asked for a $500 advance on book royalties, and got it.

The book was brought out with a formidable title, *Petrographic and Physical Characteristics of Sands from Seven Gulf Coast Producing Horizons.* Sales were surprisingly brisk, and the book was still in print in the 1980s.

During another tough period, shortly before World War II, Halbouty had to turn to his typewriter. He was in debt and his secretary had taken a pay cut from $125 a month to $85. He began writing articles for trade magazines. Most of them he wrote alone, others he wrote in collaboration with recognized older scientists who welcomed his help.

With his background, the writing of pure scientific papers for scholarly perusal was done with ease.

He moved into the popular field of writing in 1952 when he and James A. Clark, a friend and a noted oil historian, wrote the best-seller *Spindletop*, published by Random House. The book, a history of the field, was still selling in the 1980s.

The pair collaborated again in 1972. Once again Random House was the publisher. The book was *The Last Boom*, a rich and fascinating history of the great East Texas oilfield. It became a collector's item until it was reprinted in 1984.

Halbouty moved from fact to fiction in 1981 when he co-authored a novel with an international oil background. The book was *Grady Barr*, published by Arbor House. He gave to fiction the color and excitement that he saw in reality.

His most important work, however, was published in 1967 to worldwide industry acclaim. It was *Salt Domes (Gulf Region, United States, and Mexico)*, published by Gulf Publishing Company. It was the culmination of years of study of the geological phenomenon and it was a complete and ready reference in one volume.

Said the *Oil Daily*, "Halbouty has 'programmed' his book deliberately and carefully to appeal to a wide audience, one which includes not only the Gulf Coast geologist and geophysicist, but also earth scientists working in any diapiric province in the world. It is clear that he has familiarized himself with every aspect of his subject. . . ."

And Dr. A. A. Meyerhoff, editor of the AAPG *Bulletin*, wrote: "This exceptional, compact, and tasteful book is a well of information that will never run dry. To the writer's knowledge, this is the first book of this scope every published on the description of salt domes. The person who purchases it will not regret his decision. . . ."

This accolade came from Dr. Carey Croneis, Chancellor and Weiss Professor of Geology at Rice University: "*Salt Domes* is a big book about a big subject by a leading student of the structures involved. Moreover, the author's encyclopedic knowledge of their notable intricacies has been responsible for significant financial rewards as well as important scientific concepts. In the present volume Halbouty generously shares the latter with a predictably large audience. Careful readers are also likely to share the former because, as the author makes clear, there is much more black gold to be found associated with the grey salt. If the reader cannot find what he is looking for regarding salt domes in this new volume, it is certainly not the fault of the author. . . .''

The book, with revisions and appendages, was reprinted in 1979, and once again was well received.

Halbouty was a voracious reader, his taste catholic. He had never taken "speed reading" courses, but in friendly competition with associates who had, he invariably was the victor. His power of retention was amazing. He went through several newspapers daily; he read industry and scientific publications; histories, fiction, and non-fiction. He loved poetry, and was able to recall long passages from works as diverse as Homer's *Iliad* and T. S. Eliot's *The Waste Land*. He was particularly fond of Shakespeares' *Sonnets*, and often quoted from Robert W. Service's *Spell of the Yukon* and *Rhymes of a Remittance Man*.

For a college newspaper reporter Halbouty once listed his best remembered books as Dostoevski's *The Brothers Karamazov, The Song of Roland* by Turold, Dickens' *A Tale of Two Cities*, Machiavelli's *The Prince* (though he detested the author's reasoning and conclusions, he was vastly impressed by his style and talent), *All The King's Men* by Robert Penn Warren, "and anything by Winston Churchill." As for latter-day works, he said that *Lonesome Dove* by Larry McMurtry not only was "the finest novel of the West" he ever had read but was, he believed, "destined to be enjoyed for decades by intelligent, imaginative readers. . . ."

***

A visitor to Michel T. Halbouty Energy Company would find the walk from the foyer to the head man's office pleasant and surprising. The right wall was dotted with Maurice Utrillo prints of the artist's beloved Montmartre. In contrast, the left wall was alive with the works of Bob Wygant—vivid, realistic depictions of the Venezuelan oil scene and the savage beauty of the land.

But the sight that greeted the visitor as he entered the corridor was a colorful mosaic of the North East-South West cross section of the great Spindletop Salt Dome and the formations it penetrated and shattered as it made its way toward the earth's surface over the eons. People not in the oil industry were apt to pause and study its singularity. For oilmen the thrusting white stalk of salt and the shaded fractured strata told the story of the country's first great field.

Halbouty was partial to mosaics. On his private office walls hung the provocative mosaic works of Cassio and Luziano. Oils by Cassio and Carbellini hushed and softened the stark modernity of the conference room. A wintry scene by Luziano in the outer office, or waiting room, countered the rows of photographs of the Halboutys with the Reagans and Bushes and others that almost dominated one wall.

But the pride of Halbouty's private office was a panorama of the old Forum, a magnificent work of art and craftsmanship fashioned from rocks from the earth in the old Roman School manner. It strains the imagination to conceive the years of painstaking, loving labor behind this masterpiece. Each minute piece of rock was selected for the proper coloration that makes the micromosaic almost as realistic as a superior oil painting or photograph.

Halbouty found his prize in a Roman jewelry store. While the shop owner was showing his wares to Billye, the oilman, wandering idly about the shop, almost stepped on the micromosaic. It was on the floor, almost obscured by dust blown in from the windy street.

He thought at first it was a painting. He bent down and brushed aside some dust with his handkerchief. "When I saw what it was, I had to have it," he told a friend. "It obviously was a masterpiece." Without dickering with the shop owner, he made the purchase for a fraction of the micromosaic's worth.

At the Vatican School of Mosaic, Halbouty learned that his find's last owner of record was the Austro-Hungarian Ambassador to the Vatican who obtained it in 1824. He was told that there were 138,000 pieces of rock in the micromosaic, some containing minerals such as azurite, cinnabar, and fluorite. The rocks were embedded in a basalt base.

Halbouty placed no dollar value on the micromosaic, but Mary Stewart said it had been appraised at a very high figure.

Before and after his location of the prize, Halbouty obtained other micromosaics for his home from the Vatican School of Mosaics on his countless trips to Rome. He made so very many visits, in fact, that he was well remembered by the museum staff, and particularly by a veteran guide.

In 1954, on his first trip, Halbouty was in a group of tourists being shepherded around the Vatican museum. The guide stopped the group before an imposing piece of solid stone, green in color and shaped somewhat like an urn. He explained that the group was looking at a piece of fine green marble.

Halbouty politely edged through the group to have a closer look. As the other tourists began shuffling away behind the guide, Halbouty called out to him. "This isn't green marble," the oilman said. "This is malachite." The other tourists stared at him, shocked by such effrontery. And the guide, made lofty by such cheek, declared, "It has been here for more than a hundred years, and for more than a hundred years it has been green marble. It is green marble today."

Halbouty loved to argue, but he knew he could gain nothing by arguing with the guide. He handed him his card. "I'm a geologist," he said. "Give that card to the curator, and ask him to call be at the Excelsior Hotel when he gets time."

The tour went on. That evening the curator phoned Halbouty. They agreed on lunch the next day and an examination of the lustrous stone. It was clear that the curator believed he was placating a hard-headed tourist of some reputation.

It also was clear the next day that the curator had interviewed some experts during the intervening hours. No examination was necessary, the curator said. "We have been wrong for one hundred and ten years." And he added with a smile, "Please don't look so sharply on your next tour."

About 25 years later a group of geologists from the Houston Geological Society were touring the museum. The same guide showed off the green museum piece. "Every day for many years I have been telling my groups that once we thought this piece was of green marble," he said, "but a smart man from Texas convinced us that it is malachite."

The men in the group looked at each other. One said, "From Texas—whereabouts in Texas?"

"A geologist from Houston," said the guide.

"What geologist? Did he have a name? Do you remember it?"

"Of course," the guide said smugly. "Mister Halbouty of Houston, Texas. A friend of the curator."

"By God," said the questioner, "if that isn't Mike all over." And his companions chuckled.

It was such a good story, one so typical of the Mike Halbouty they had known so long and so well, that one of them wrote an article about the incident which was published in *Geotimes* Magazine.

# CHAPTER ELEVEN

If his belligerency faded somewhat with the years, his irascibility was not diminished by any measure until his marriage. One person whose irascibility matched his was undoubtedly his most intimate friend, James A. Clark. They had been boyhood friends in Beaumont. Later, Clark chose to write about oil instead of hunting it. He became a newspaper oil editor and for the *Houston Post* wrote a column, *Tales of the Oil Country*. He and Halbouty teamed up to write *Spindletop* and *The Last Boom*.

They saw each other several times a week when Halbouty was in town, if a quarrel hadn't made them stiff-necked. The quiet times when they relaxed together in the warmth of their friendship oftimes were shattered by furious disputes. They ranted and called each other names that would have caused them to raise their fists had someone else uttered them. No one had any reason to question the identity of Halbouty's visitor if Clark were on the premises. Not that their cuss fights were all in private; they stormed at each other in public places to the astonishment—and sometimes amusement—of onlisteners.

When Clark died in 1978, Halbouty cloaked his grief in the language of their quarrels: "He was the only son of a bitch who was more irascible than I am, and I'll tell you one thing—he never kissed *anybody's* ass. That's why we got along so well. Whatever happened, we always loved and respected each other."

Halbouty would often say that one woman and six men helped shape his life. The woman was "Miss Emma," his science teacher when he was a junior in high school. "She prompted me to learn things for myself," he said. He was speaking specifically of an incident that occurred while the class was studying the rudiments of astronomy. He understood the lesson, perhaps too well for his tender years, and he was upset by the implications in her lecture that the Earth was much older than he had been taught in Sunday school Bible class. After class he had a question: "Miss Emma, how old is the Earth?"

In her wisdom, "Miss Emma" sent the troubled youngster to the public library where he discovered geology and fell in love with the grandeur of the discipline and, presumably, found the answer to his question.

The six men were:

T. O. Walton, president of Texas A&M University, who loaned Halbouty $50 to add to his $75 to pay his entrance fee to the school. Halbouty remained convinced thereafter that if Walton had not loaned him the money—which he repaid before the first term was over—he would have been forced to return home to the life of a grocer's helper.

Dr. John L. Lonsdale, head of A&M's geological department, who arranged for a fellowship so that Halbouty could work and obtain his Master of Science degree. He gave Halbouty the job of mapping the geology of Atascosa County for the U.S. Geological Survey and the state of Texas as his thesis. Halbouty made the first base map of what would be called the Charlotte-Jourdanton-Leming fault system. Some years later, a geologist with Humble Oil and Refining Company found a copy of the thesis in the university library, and the company used it to find the first of many oilfields in the county.

Miles Frank Yount, kingpin of the successful Yount-Lee Oil Company of Beaumont, who promoted Halbouty to chief geologist after Halbouty, a mere chain-puller on a surveying crew, "discovered" the High Island field. Yount had little formal education, but he was a self-educated geologist, a "creekologist," whose ability to find oil made some think he used a "wiggle stick" or "doodle bug." He taught Halbouty the mysteries of salt domes and nurtured his career in other ways. Yount also was a collector of fine art and a lover of music and literature, and he exposed Halbouty to these mysteries as well. When Yount died in November 1933 in his 53rd year, Halbouty shed his first adult tears.

Dad Kellam, Yount-Lee's field supervisor of Texas exploration and production, who almost thwarted Halbouty's discovery of the High Island field by ignoring Halbouty's geological deductions until Yount intervened in Halbouty's favor. "He was the most fair-minded man I ever knew," Halbouty would say of Kellam. "It didn't rankle him for a smart-ass kid to win a round. He taught me everything he could, and always saw to it that I was put in positions where I had to learn."

Max Schliecher, Kellam's counterpart in Yount-Lee's Louisiana operations, an aging veteran with no formal education who had taught himself to read and write as an adult. He was proud of Halbouty's scholastic accomplishments, not envious, and he spent hours day and night on the drilling rigs teaching the young man hands-on field petroleum engineering. Once at a small gathering he commented disparagingly that he considered himself an uneducated man. Halbouty got indignant. "Don't ever say that again, Mr. Schliecher! Here I am with two degrees and I'm having hell's own time of learning just a little bit of what you know! You're better than any engineer coming out of school. You know *exactly* what to do all the time about everything about a well. Nobody knows what to do better than you do. In your field you're an educated man. I'll never be as educated as you."

Max Schliecher smiled. "Let's wait and see, Mike."

Marrs McLean, like Miles Frank Yount an untrained "creekologist" who built a fortune on his uncanny ability to find oil. It was on his leases at Spindletop that Yount brought in the wells in 1925 that created the second great boom in that field, and it was on leases McLean dealt to Yount at High Island that Halbouty discovered the field by solving the riddle of the complex structure. Many years later McLean would deal a lease on Spindletop to Halbouty, and the younger man would revive the oil field by sinking his bit into 210 feet of oil-saturated virgin sand. McLean had been a hero to Halbouty from the day they first met in 1931. Late in life, Halbouty told a reporter, "I never got over my amazement that Marrs McLean, with no formal education in geology, was able to fathom the intricacies of salt domes. . . ."

\*\*\*

Many of his peers in the earth sciences with whom he sat in worldwide energy conferences won his respect and admiration, but there was little doubt that he considered himself first among equals. It was his nature to take charge of the work at hand.

Some of the directors of the Circum-Pacific Council, for example, were well known to fame in their respective regions—people like Nikita A. Bogdanov of the U.S.S.R.; Rafael S. Bueno of Colombia; Maria Teresa Canas of Chile; William W. Hutchinson of Canada; David Kear of New Zealand; Harold M. Lian, president of Unocal's company in Thailand; Tamotsu Nozawa of Japan; Roye W. R. Rutland of Australia; Guillermo P. Salas of Mexico; Arthur Saldivar-Sali of the Philippines; V. G. Swindon of Australia; Zhai Guangming of China, and George Gryc, John Reinemund, John H. Silcox and Carlos del Solar, all of the U.S.

There were two other men with whom Halbouty had lasting relationships. The friendships were not as intense at the one with Clark, but he valued them highly. Both men were geologists. One was Merrill Haas of Exxon; he and Halbouty worked together on many AAPG projects, and Haas accompanied him on what were considered delicate missions when Halbouty was the AAPG president. The other was Dr. William Brown, a European geologist associated with Robertson Research, Ltd. of Wales. The two men visited each other often, spoke on the phone often, and Brown was in his corner when Halbouty addressed the OPEC conference in Vienna in 1977.

Politics or strong differences of opinion was never a barrier between Halbouty and other acquaintances. Two men he admired and counted as friends, for example, were staunch proponents of the oil import tax. Feelings sometimes ran high over the issue. But George Mitchell of Mitchell Energy Corporation and Fred Hartley, chief executive of Unocal, remained high in his esteem, as he did in theirs.

During the late 1970s and through the 1980s Halbouty was on television so often, and his photograph so often appeared in newspapers and magazines, that he was recognized by someone wherever he went. In restaurants, for example, strangers would approach his table and introduce themselves. It would not be fair to say he accepted such attention as his due, but he obviously didn't feel that it was inappropriate.

***

In his journeys around the globe where he met so many people, Halbouty found only one country that he absolutely detested—Czechoslovakia. He had liked Russia and loved China. He had heard poetry in the austere Russian landscape, and the Chinese people, he often said, were the most courteous on earth.

Czechoslovakia was another matter. His experience there was limited to a shortened stay in Bratislava, capital of what is called the West Slovak Region. It is a border city, and the Halboutys had been chauffeured there from Austria, a country he always had found delightful. It was a spur-of-the-moment excursion.

The city was a dismal gray. The people wore black, "because they felt that way," he said. Women stood in line for hours in front of shops to buy food. "No one ever smiled," he said. And everywhere they went two men—always the same men—appeared to be following them.

They had intended to stay two days but decided to leave immediately. They couldn't leave immediately because they couldn't regain their passports, which they had surrendered on entry. Hours passed as they were shuttled from one office to another, and their apprehension mounted with every passing minute.

"We walked all over the entry area trying to get those damned passports," he said, "and everybody sent us to someone else. We felt like we'd never get them. I really became concerned because I had committed a stupid blunder. I hadn't told anyone—not a soul—where we were going, and if we disappeared, no one could trace us."

At one stop, however, as they were being instructed to go somewhere else, Billye saw an official put two U.S. passports in a wire cage. He was the official who had taken their passports on entry.

"Those are our passports," Billye said indignantly. "You give me those passports right now!"

Halbouty stood dumbfounded as the official took the passports from the cage and handed them to Billye without a word. "Let's go, sweetheart," Billye said.

The Austrian chauffeur had been terrified all during the brief stay. He was soon to be married, he had told the Halboutys on first meeting them, and planned to honeymoon in Czechoslovakia. Now he was as happy to leave as they were. He swore he would never return.

There were three barriers to pass through before they could safely say they were back in Austria. "Even after we got through the first one, I still felt trapped," Halbouty said. "I felt only a little relief when we got through the second. But when we got through that third one, we were full of joy. We knew what freedom means. By God, we felt like birds out of a cage!"

"I wouldn't go back to that country if they'd pay me ten thousand dollars a second as a consultant!" he told Mary Stewart.

\*\*\*

No classroom could have contained him, nor could he have abided routine, but Halbouty was an excellent teacher in his fashion. He loved to lecture, but he wanted to see new faces in his audiences, seek new approaches to making his points.

Some of his happiest days were spent traveling around the country and to distant parts as "Distinguished Lecturer" for the Society of Petroleum Engineers and "Distinguished Lecturer" for the American Association of Petroleum Geologists in 1965 and 1966. It was an honored role, and he played it to the hilt. In 1982, SPE named him its first "Distinguished Lecturer Emeritus."

His classmates at Texas A&M University recall that Halbouty was a sophomore when courses in petroleum engineering were introduced in the school. The teachers were well grounded in theory, but had no practical experience to speak of. So they called on Halbouty to lecture on the basics of oilwell drilling because he had learned them while working as a roustabout at Spindletop to help pay his way through school. That was his first teaching experience.

He would lecture at the school many times after he had gained prominence as an earth scientist, and on two occasions appeared on programs sponsored by the Student Conference on National Affairs

(SCONA). SCONA's goals are to "create intelligent interest in the complexities of problems and policies, national and international, rather than offer solutions or accept ready-made answers; and to develop enlightened, responsible leaders by free expression and a meaningful exchange of ideas among students of different backgrounds. . . ." Halbouty contributed annually to the support of the programs.

To ensure that Halbouty's influence on his alma mater would continue, the internationally renowned painter/sculptor David Adickes was commissioned to create a three-quarter size figure of the earth scientist to be unveiled in the Grand Foyer of the Michel T. Halbouty Geoscience Building with appropriate ceremony.

In this bronze likeness, Halbouty is standing at a lectern as if he were teaching class. In his hands is the lecture material—the bronzed electric log of this third productive well in the South Boling field, a huge salt dome in Wharton County, Texas. The well, completed in late November 1951, was a geological phenomenon. The first two wells had produced from a rich Frio sand that lay above a much older formation of Jackson Shale. The drill bit on the third well, however, reached the Jackson Shale without finding any indication of the Frio sand. Oilmen generally quit drilling under these conditions, assuming no Frio existed in the area.

Halbouty's bit pierced the Jackson Shale and below it found the rich Frio sand which would produce more than 4 million barrels of oil.

As reported in the AAPG Bulletin: "Never before had such a phenomenon been reported in the Texas and Louisiana Gulf Coast province. The presence of multiple, thick, highly permeable and porous oil sands under an older overthrust formation revealed a heretofore unrecognized Gulf Coast geologic condition. . . ."

Halbouty concluded that a thrust fault of more than 1,000 feet had occurred and had moved the older Jackson Shales over the younger Frio beds.

It seemed that every geologist, paleontologist, and wildcatter wanted to hear about the strange well. So did oil writers for newspapers and magazines. Halbouty discussed it before a score of scientific societies.

To him, teaching about the geology of the field was almost as much fun as finding it!

\*\*\*

Perhaps the best indication of Halbouty's desire to teach occurred during a period when he spoke to thousands of youngsters in dozens of high schools and junior high schools in Texas and neighboring oil states. A more sophisticated version of his speech was delivered in several colleges and universities.

His theme was one dear to his heart—"They said it Couldn't Be Done!" Whereupon he would prove that "they" were wrong, and that "it" could be done. After he had delivered the speech, he would hold a question and answer session and, as he told Mary Stewart, he was always amazed at the sharpness of the youngsters' minds.

In language much more colorful than that in their school texts, Halbouty spoke of Columbus, who was jeered for his theories concerning the shape of the earth and plans for a voyage to the New World; Robert Fulton and his plans for a steamboat; Thomas A. Edison for his plan for electric light; Alexander Graham Bell for his plan for the telephone; Samuel Morse and his plan for a telegraph; Guglielmo Marconi for his plan for the radio; the Wright Brothers for their dreams of an airplane; Charles Lindberg for his plan for a trans-Atlantic flight; Jules Verne for his predictions of interplanetary flights and underwater vessels.

And he did not neglect oil industry heroes, all of whom had been vilified by some for their beliefs. He told the students about Colonel Edwin L. Drake and his well near Titusville, Pennsylvania, the first well ever drilled for the express purpose of finding oil; Pattillo Higgins and Captain Anthony Lucas at Spindletop; Columbus M. (Dad) Joiner at Rusk County, Texas and the great East Texas oilfield.

Some of the students had heard of these oil heroes, of course, but Halbouty told them of others who were not in any of their school books. One was William Knox D'Arcy. Of him, Halbouty said:

> In the 1890s D'Arcy's spirit of adventure led him to Australia where he made a remarkable fortune in gold. And that was probably under some circumstance which was considered impossible, too.

With that fortune in his possession, D'Arcy, an adventurous Englishman, returned to his native country to retire. But before he could get settled comfortably he became obsessed with the idea that oil could be found in Persia. A French archaeologist told him of oil seeps there similar to those he had read about in Pennsylvania and elsewhere where oil had been discovered.

So D'Arcy set forth for Persia and finally got a concession from the Shah on May 28, 1901 at a time when the reports of incredible fortunes being made at Spindletop were circling the globe. His 'little lease' covered a half million square miles.

While his friends were urging him not to waste his fortune in the search for oil in a terrain so forbidding that no other civilized man would even go there if the oil were waiting for him in million barrel tanks, D'Arcy spudded his first wildcat late in November of 1902, some 18 months after getting the concession.

The climate was horrible, the terrain terrible, and natives composed of tribes so fierce that a man would have felt far safer in a pool of man-eating sharks. That first well, as all first wells always seem to be, was a failure. Again his friends started urging him to get out. They said it couldn't be done. There were more dry holes, but D'Arcy wouldn't give up.

D'Arcy finally got some help from his government, which prevailed upon the Burmah Oil Company, Ltd. to finance him.

After more dry holes, early in 1908, Burmah Oil could no longer stand the burden of the terrific expense. It dispatched a messenger to D'Arcy telling him to give up the project. But that very day his drill hit the famous Asmari lime. It happened in a remote area near an old fire temple in the Bakhtiari hills near Maidan-i-Naftun. It was May 26, 1908, two days short of seven years from the very day he had started. The oil gushed forth like the torrent at Spindletop.

The great Persian Gulf area had been tapped. No man ever found a greater treasure on this earth.

Halbouty moved to another part of the world and another hero:

Let's take a look at Lake Maracaibo in western Venezuela. It was back in the 1920s after Shell Oil Company's subsidiaries had first found commercial oil in Venezuela in 1914 and then electrified the world with another Lucas gusher type of discovery on the edge of the lake in 1922.

In the meantime everyone was finding oil in western Venezuela except Standard Oil of New Jersey, now Exxon. Back home at the office the managers were worried. Company after company in Venezuela, most of them solid competitors, were cleaning up. One day it occurred to the heads of an Exxon subsidiary, after $40,000,000 had been spent on dry holes in a country where everyone else was finding oil, that maybe it would be a good idea to try to purchase production. But no one wanted to sell anything.

There was one man, a pioneer geologist by the name of Charles Eckes, who had traveled the world looking for oil for other companies but decided to settle the remaining years of his life in Venezuela. He studied the Maracaibo Basin and came to a startling conclusion. He was sure there was oil beneath the bottom of Lake Maracaibo, and he spent eleven years attempting to sell every oil company in Venezuela on this idea.

All the companies laughed at him and in despair he formed a small oil company and called it British Equatorial. The first thing he did was to get a concession for most of the lake's submerged lands. He then put enough equipment together to start drilling out in the water. The critics hooted and hollered at the idea of virtually drilling in the open lake. His first test was a tremendous discovery. It came in on April 22, 1924, and it made 2,400 barrels of oil a day and the hecklers and disbelievers were again stopped in their tracks.

Eventually British Equatorial sold this concession to the Pan American Oil Company for millions. Later Pan American sold all the wells and the concession to Exxon for $43,000,000. It was only then that Exxon was able to obtain production in the Maracaibo district. And as luck would have it, the purchase was a great bargain. The reserves are in billions of barrels. The faith of one man had paid off again. Today there are wells being drilled in deep waters in many parts of the world because of this faith.

Let us go on to another story. And another hero. Maybe it has no great significance at this moment, but I believe the story of oil's beginning in Colombia proves again that you cannot listen to those who said it couldn't be done.

It is a fascinating story of a Frenchman named Roberto DeMares who found oil seeps so big that they gurgled constantly or spouted oil into the high branches of trees deep in the Colombian jungle in the Las Infantas area. DeMares paid his last dollar for a concession covering 2,061 square miles and then started trying to raise the money to explore for oil.

Wherever he went they laughed at him. It was impossible, they said, to even get a rig to the concession, much less drilling or getting oil out if it were found.

DeMares got his concession in 1905. Then he started looking for financial help but everyone turned him down, including Exxon. One day on a boat trip he met a geologist with Benedum and Trees, two great wildcatters, and mentioned, casually, his story of the oil seeps in the jungles of Colombia. The geologist was fascinated. He asked for a look at the area. After DeMares showed it to him, he went home and told his bosses, Mike Benedum and Joe Trees. In 1916 they made a deal with DeMares. In 1918, after an almost impossible experience in jungle warfare, tugging at equipment piece by piece to get it to location, and ignoring how they were going to get the oil out, Tropical Oil Company, a subsidiary of Benedum and Trees, hit a 5,000-barrel well.

Within a few months the concession had been sold to Exxon for $33 million and the pessimists were again put to rout.

He cited story after story, all with the same theme—"stick by your convictions." The faculty members often were as engrossed as the students.

Pressed for an explanation why a busy man would undertake such a speaking program that consumed so much of his time, Halbouty said, "I believe the students needed it, and I wanted to do it. Maybe all of us need to be reminded now and then that the best of us and the worst of us require a booster shot occasionally. I know damned well I do."

\*\*\*

Recognizing the scholar/teacher in Halbouty, President Reagan in 1981 selected him to serve on the President's Commission on White House Fellowships. Each year a group of outstanding young leaders in their separate communities are winnowed from a much larger group to work at the highest levels of the federal government for a 12-month period. In theory—and in fact—they return home to enrich their communities and society as a whole.

The program was established by President Lyndon B. Johnson in 1964 "to draw individuals of exceptionally high promise to Washington for one year of personal involvement in the process of government." Succeeding Presidents enthusiastically supported the program. Partisan politics play no part in the selection process.

Halbouty enjoyed the screening process. "There's no other way I could have met so many fine young people," he told Mary Stewart. "It's a shame we couldn't pick them all."

\*\*\*

Halbouty through the years was presented with so many awards that it is amazing that he found the time to accept them all. Some shone more brightly than others. One of the brightest was the coveted Hoover Medal, presented by the American Association of Engineering Societies. Named for the late President Herbert Hoover, it is one of the highest honors an engineer can receive. Hoover, before his entry into public service in the 1920s, was considered the engineer *nonpareil*. He had worked on major projects in the U.S., Australia, China, Russia, India, New Zealand, South Africa, Canada, Great Britain, Belgium, and Mexico. The great dam on the Colorado River at the Nevada-Arizona border was named in his honor. Like Halbouty, Hoover was a born teacher, and he lectured frequently at various universities.

The awards appeared to come in clusters. Soon after receiving the Hoover Medal in 1982, he was awarded Honorary Membership in the Gulf Coast Association of Geological Societies, and in the following year the Paul Carrington Chapter of the Sons of the American Revolution presented him with its Distinguished Service Award; he received the Texas Heritage Award from the Angleton Chamber of Commerce; was selected as Distinguished Texas Scientist of the Year by the Texas Academy of Sciences; was awarded Honorary Membership by the Society of Exploration Geophysicists. (See Appendix at end of book for complete listing of honors and awards.)

***

In early 1987, as Halbouty approached his 78th year, a young woman reporter asked him, "How do you want to be remembered, Mr. Halbouty?"

Halbouty grew thoughtful. "To tell you the truth, it hasn't crossed my mind that often. I suspect that all people who have tried to do their best in life want to be remembered for more than one thing. But what I hope for most is to be remembered as an earth scientist whose contributions added to the heritage of the science of geology and to the profession he loved." He nodded his head. "That about sums it up."

# CHAPTER TWELVE

At 78, in 1987, Michel T. Halbouty was still hunting oil and gas. His love of the search had not diminished. He could look back on almost six decades of thrilling successes and heart-numbing failures, but he seldom did so. His eye was on the future, and he continued to imbue his associates with his boundless hope and enthusiasm.

On the other hand, he could not accept with good grace the rejection of his major proposals by the Administration and the Congress. For six and half years he had had access to President Reagan, Vice-President Bush, and all the members of the Cabinet, especially Interior's Hodel and Energy's Herrington. He was on a first-name basis with scores of senators and congressmen, particularly those from the oil states. All of these at times had asked him for his advice and counsel, and he had not been reluctant at other times to volunteer them.

When his advice had been acted on, which was often, the Administration had proceeded timidly, and congressmen who had no direct links with the oil industry had little trouble blocking the path.

One of the sharpest rebuffs was Reagan's out-of-hand dismissal of restoration of the depletion allowance as a means to stimulate domestic exploratory drilling and thus infuse fresh blood into the ailing industry. This came in early May 1987 after Halbouty had lobbied valiantly for more than a year for the measure. He had been the first to propose restoration. He had gained adherents in the industry and the media and, he thought, at the White House. Both Hodel and Herrington had spoken out publicly for the allowance on various occasions.

But it was reported in the *New York Times*, and not denied, that Herrington did not make restoration of the allowance a part of his package of energy proposals at a Cabinet-level White House meeting because Reagan had dismissed the idea in advance.

"I can't believe they haven't come up with some positive initiatives," Halbouty told reporters. "All the things the President did accept in Herrington's package simply give us back just a little of what they took from us. They won't increase exploration by any means."

His anger and disappointment was shared by spokesmen for virtually every segment of the industry. His staunch friend, George Mitchell, told reporters the measures the President supported were "very pitiful." Mitchell, it will be remembered, had lobbied strongly for the import tax while Halbouty had opposed it from the moment it was first proposed. Now both the import tax and restoration of the depletion allowance appeared to be dead issues.

It was a gauge of Halbouty's disappointment when he told reporters, "This will severely affect industry support for Republicans, especially in Oklahoma, Louisiana, and Texas, the states that are hardest hit by the oilfield depression. The party must remind itself that in the past no Republican candidate for President has been elected without Texas." This was a harsh warning from a man who was Republican to the core.

The *Houston Post*, normally a Reagan supporter, summed up much of the outrage expressed throughout the industry in a brief editorial:

> President Reagan's "compromise" package to provide relief for the distressed energy industry is fine as far as it goes. The trouble is, that isn't very far at all—not nearly enough for a country becoming increasingly dependent on foreign energy.
>
> The measures are relatively painless. They won't hurt anything and they might do some good. They are, however, a little like giving a patient an aspirin when in fact he needs a heart transplant.
>
> The President repeated his call for repeal of the windfall profits tax, which makes sense; the tax hadn't been collected lately, but it required extensive and complex record-keeping. And he called again for deregulation of natural gas, which is long overdue.
>
> Increasing strategic petroleum purchases, which he conditionally recommended, makes sense, as does reducing the minimum bid in

offshore lease sales. But taken together, these and other measures are a pathetic response to a problem of great magnitude.

What is needed? Major tax breaks would be a start. Restoration of the percentage depletion allowance is an obvious candidate, as is a tax credit on new energy production. Such measures might help start an upturn in efforts to find and produce domestic energy.

The modest proposals of the President, even if they are all enacted by a hostile Congress, certainly won't.

\*\*\*

Halbouty did not allow his bitterness to deter him. He swallowed his disappointment; he had another string on his bow.

It will be recalled that he had teamed with Phil Gramm, the junior senator from Texas, in preparing a package of energy measures that Gramm was to introduce in the Senate. The package was to contain a provision for restoration of the depletion allowance. Halbouty had hopes that Gramm could generate enough support and enthusiasm to send the bill through the Congress with enough votes to discourage a presidential veto.

One day after what he considered "a presidential debacle," Halbouty sent Gramm a telegram urging him to meet quickly with Senator Bentsen and the senators from Oklahoma and Louisiana to "agree on positive initiatives to submit to the Senate and the Administration." And he wired Gramm, "Your leading role is imperative to obtain action for the benefit of the entire nation."

Gramm called Halbouty and told him he was trying to get positive action to assist the petroleum industry. He didn't get it.

\*\*\*

On another front, Halbouty was gladdened by a bill presented to the Congress that would sharply curtail corporate raiders and inside dealers. The bill was introduced by Representatives John Dingell of Michigan and Representative Edward J. Markey of Massachusetts, both Democrats.

Under current law, a corporate raider such as Boone Pickens had 10 days in which to make a public disclosure of his intentions after buying a 5% stake in the target company. Within those 10 days a raider could acquire huge blocks of stock relatively cheaply because shareholders were unaware that a takeover, which would send stock prices soaring, was underway.

The Dingell-Markey bill would require the disclosure within 24 hours after a raider hits the 5% mark, and forbids him from acquiring additional stock for two days after filing.

The bill also forbids "greenmail," the practice of a company repurchasing its stock from a raider at a premium price to avoid a takeover, and prohibits "golden parachutes," lavish severance benefits for managers who could lose their jobs in the event of a successful takeover.

The bill gained major editorial support quickly. The *Houston Post* said, "Representatives John Dingell and Edward Markey deserve praise for fielding this measure, which in no way impedes legitimate, above-board acquisitions of one company by another. . . ." Others in the media offered similar plaudits.

For Halbouty, who detested corporate raiders and had spoken out against them at every opportunity, the Dingell-Markey bill was a "milestone."

\*\*\*

Dr. William Brown, the geologist associated with Robertson Research, Ltd. of Wales and a long-time Halbouty friend, was speaking:

> Wherever I go around the world, I am continually asked questions about Mike Halbouty. Those who have met him want to know more about him; some who haven't are desirous of meeting him. Women, particularly, want to know if he looks like his photographs. It seems as if everywhere his name is mentioned in a gathering that almost everyone has a story to tell about him.
>
> What can I say about the man? The most remarkable thing about him is that he is as active and enthusiastic in his 70s as he was in his 30s. There's no denying his brilliance, of course, because it has been demonstrated time and time again. There is no denying his humanity; those who know him best are deeply aware of his generosity of spirit, his willingness to help in any worthwhile

project, his ability to take the lead and push something through to fruition, his strong love of country that has kept him working in its best interests all of his adult life.

I know young earth scientists who idolize him just as his peers respect and admire him. Both know that few men have made as great contributions to their disciplines as Halbouty. Most men who become legends early in their careers cannot maintain the mystique. Halbouty has. His reputation has grown more formidable with every passing year because his actions in behalf of his profession, his country, and I might say the world at large, have never slackened.

Were I asked, I might say that I think of him as a global treasure.

\*\*\*

Almost 27 years after he delivered his prophetic address before the American Association of Petroleum Geologists in Los Angeles, Michel Halbouty returned to that city to speak once again to his fellow geoscientists. The date was June 9, 1987. The audience this time was much larger, swelled as it was by newcomers to the profession, but there were many in attendance who had been present when Halbouty delivered his memorable speech back on November 3, 1960.

If any of the old-timers had written him off as an alarmist in 1960, they were prepared now to accept his judgment and heed his warnings. He had been right too often to be labeled a doomsayer. And he had given too much of himself to the profession and to the petroleum industry as a whole, and yes, to the country, to be deemed a self-server. It had been said of him more than once that no single man had done more than he for the betterment of every segment of the petroleum industry.

This time, as always, he tried to speak beyond his audience, hoping, perhaps forlornly, that his words might stir the greater public to actions he considered vital to the country's welfare.

He was at his oratorical best, and when he had spoken his final word his audience gave him a thunderous ovation. This is what he said:

> Ladies and Gentlemen, fellow geoscientists, I am entering my 58th year as a member of our profession and as an explorer for

petroleum. During this more than half a century, I have also devoted much of my time and resources in activities, both civil and political, in the attempt to enhance the industry which many of us in this room claim as our own. As I venture forth in the golden years of my life, I unfortunately find that our profession and our industry have undergone and still are subjected to the most depressive conditions in the history of both entities.

My most profound concern is *not* for our profession nor for the industry, but for our nation's security which is now at risk. Its vulnerability increases as our dependence on imports increases. The welfare of the nation is paramount because you and I know that whatever affects the nation affects our industry and our professional disciplines—and the entire world. So I speak to you today of the significance of that concern.

In the late '50s exploration was down and imports were rising steadily and the slow deterioration of the petroleum industry was beginning to take its toll. The Congress and the Eisenhower Administration did not care to recognize the conditions that prevailed and, as it is today, the people could have cared less.

During this perilous and unstable time in our industry, when thousands of geologists were laid off and dismay and despair permeated the profession, I was asked to make the keynote address to the 37th annual meeting of the AAPG Pacific Section, in conjunction with the local sections of the Society of Economic Paleontologists and Mineralogists and the Society of Exploration Geophysicists. The date was November 3, 1960, here in Los Angeles. After detailing the ominous conditions which prevailed, I predicted what the nation would face by concluding my remarks with the following:

"I want to end this presentation by making it perfectly clear that, in my opinion, this country is reaching toward a severe economic crisis, as well as an imposition of our national security by our not doing everything possible to increase our domestic production now. To continue along the downward exploratory curve which we are now experiencing will surely result in economic chaos in the years ahead. The impact of an energy shortage in this country would be absolutely disastrous.

"Unless there is an appreciable and sustained turnaround in our exploratory activities, I can safely predict that between now and 1975, we will have an energy crisis in this country which will cause repercussions throughout the width and breadth of this great nation of ours like a devastating earthquake.

"I have stated this before and I will say it again, it is appalling to me that the American people can be so apathetic to what is so obvious to some of us in industry. The people of this country just do not care. They are not experiencing shortages now and evidently they care less what will happen in the future. Some of these days the shortages will catch up with us and then the people will say, 'The industry is to blame! Why weren't we told?'

"Well, I am telling them now."

The energy crisis of 1973–74 will be written in all our history books and will record the long gas lines which were paramount news for the media. The hue and cry of the public was "Why? How could this happen to us?" And as I predicted, the petroleum industry *was* blamed! We could not say the industry was entirely blameless. The international oil companies had flooded this country with foreign oil, prompting the decline in domestic exploration and the layoffs in our profession. But no segment of the industry was spared the public censure. All of us were branded as conniving manipulators who cared only for ourselves. But the worst culprit, the United States government, covered itself as an innocent babe and punished the industry by imposing laws, regulations, and controls that are now fueling the impending new crisis.

I am compelled to pause at this point and refer to a remark made by that great philosopher Yogi Berra who, after being told that the Yankees lost a crucial game to the Red Sox by the same score as the year before, replied, "Yeah, it's deja vu all over again." Believe me when I tell you that what our nation, our industry, and our profession are now experiencing is deja vu all over again, but much more deja vu than before.

Today, 27 years later, after that speech, we are in the midst of the making of another, more severe crisis. This one will make the 70s debacle seem like a Sunday picnic in the park. Its beginning was spawned in 1983 by the raiders who caused massive personnel layoffs and budget cutbacks which reduced exploration to skeleton levels. This was accentuated by OPEC reductions in prices, which further reduced exploration and production. In the months and years which followed, the only increase was in imports. The decline in exploration has brought that segment of the industry to a virtual standstill.

We have seen the petroleum industry slowly sink to its knees, carrying its satellite industries along with it. The impact has been devastating, and the lethargy of Washington and the people is hard to accept. The hardest pill to swallow is the rebuke from politicians the oil patch materially assisted in electing to their high offices in Washington. New and incumbent candidates visited our petroleum regions with their hats in hand, asking for our help. They made all kinds of promises and some were even bold enough to make those same promises nationally to all of the people. But when they were elected, those promises were put on the shelf and forgotten. Our industry became an item for derisive and revengeful jokes. Over the country they laughed at us—that we were at last getting our comeuppance. Our elected officials who promised so much turned their backs to us without regard to the effect our industry's continued deterioration will have on the strategic and economic welfare of the nation.

In the meantime, industry impairment has accelerated, unemployment still looms high in our oil producing states, yet it looks as if neither the Congress nor the Administration is willing to do anything to change the direction. Also they evidently do not realize the gravity of the industry's condition and from all outward appearances do not care to strengthen it. And even more astonishing is that Americans are unaware of the industry's continued deterioration and the negative impact it will have on themselves and the nation.

As this deterioration continues unabated, there is no assistance from any source. Congress and the Administration are willing to sit idly by, hands in their pockets, looking the other way, while the very life-blood industry of this nation is being drained. The petroleum industry is the only source to provide this nation the bulk of its oil supplies, and every effort should be made by the government to encourage and assist it in that vital effort, but instead the industry is discouraged, penalized, taxed, and pummeled with excessive restrictions and regulations at every turn.

The Administration's response to two significant and most revealing energy security studies was weak and certainly must have been influenced by not wanting to affect the budget and the new tax code. The release from the White House, outlining possible changes, was disheartening and meaningless. It gave the industry little, if any, encouragement. The response caused the rig count to fall and further spread despondency throughout the oil patch. Petroleum people in the 33 oil and gas producing states felt that at long last the Administration let them down.

We do not need Middle East oil if efforts are made to sustain our own domestic production at 9 million barrels a day or better. We can do this if we maintain a vigorous domestic exploration program. The industry cannot survive without viable and sustained exploration activities. Otherwise, we will be forced to increase our imports and depend upon them, thus letting domestic production fade away. If this occurs, we will have an industry that only refines imported crudes from foreign countries. It will be an industry without exploration. Geologists, geophysicists, petroleum engineers, landmen, drilling contractors, and many other petro-professionals will cease to be part of an industry that had made this nation second to none in industrial and overall power. At a time when national attention should be focused on the future viability of our most essential industry, we who are part of it find ourselves drifting without a wind to reach port.

Many, including some congressmen and senators, unbelievably contend Middle East oil is cheaper to import than to produce our own. This is an illusion, as it does not include the costs of our fleets in the Mediterranean to protect the flow of these imports into our country. The cost of imported oil does not include the tremendous damage to our domestic industry which has seen exploration virtually eliminated, the disappearance of thousands of independent domestic operators, and the exodus of experienced and needed drilling contractors from the energy picture. It does not include the thousand other untold costs to our economy and, above all, our security. It does not include the precipitous increase in our foreign balance of payments, which places the economic stability of the nation at great risk.

Former Navy Secretary John Lehman recently stated that the cost of U.S. military presence to enforce the Persian Gulf oil supply lines is $40 billion a year. I want to repeat that figure, $40 billion a year! That $40 billion only brings us 800,000 barrels of oil per day from the Persian Gulf because this country gets less than 6% of its imported oil from that region! The bulk of our imports come from Mexico, Canada, and Venezuela. On the other hand, Japan imports more than half of its oil requirement through the Persian Gulf, and Western Europe more than 30%. Simple mathematics shows that the oil imported from the Persian Gulf by the U.S. costs Americans $137 a barrel, plus another $18, making the total cost $155 per barrel! I contend, therefore, that oil from the Middle East is the most costly imported commodity Americans have in the world today!

So the questions arise: What are the nation's priorities? Is the vulnerability of an all-out war more effective to the nation's security than to instigate positive initiatives to revitalize exploration? Are the billions of dollars that it is costing the American taxpayer to move Middle East oil cheaper than extending a meaningful and workable petroleum policy in our country? Such a policy could include a positive tax preferential initiative which would cause an immediate surge in exploration. Even if the initiative took a few hundred million dollars a year out of the treasury, it would be much better and far cheaper than the billions it is now taking to protect the movement of oil from the Persian Gulf area.

Are we to assume that the Congress and the Administration do not know what is going on? If they do, how can they ignore the tremendous costs imposed upon the people of this nation without correcting it? If they do not know what is taking place, are we to believe that they are not informed? If they are informed, are we to believe that they ignore the conditions that exist and that they just don't give a damn?

I asked myself these questions repeatedly and I got no answers. What scares me more than anything else is the fact that the people of this country do not realize the enormity of it all, and how this continuous drop in domestic production and continued increase in imports will affect their lives and the nation's welfare. Really, I am confused and bewildered! As a citizen who has spent most of his career in fostering the industry and the two disciplines he represents, and devoting his resources and time to government and political issues for the benefit of the entire nation, I am literally disgusted with all the rhetoric and lack of positive initiatives from Washington.

Americans must beware! The apathy which now prevails will lead to hardships and heartaches. An industry is dying and the nation will surely start dying with it. One of our industry problems is that evidently we are not getting the message over to the public. As long as the public is apathetic about what the industry is going through, and as long as they can fill their automobiles at a service station without waiting in a line, they are not going to listen to what we are saying.

E. W. Scripps, who founded one of the most aggressive and influential chains of newspapers in this country, is best remembered for his strict adherence to the basic journalistic principle—total objectivity in reporting the news. He incorporated this ideas into a slogan of his newspapers: "Give the people light, and they will find their own way." He did not believe anyone had the privilege to tell other people right from wrong, or how to vote, or where to spend their money, or with whom to associate or even what to drink. He believed that if the press gave the people the facts without fear or favor, the people were capable of finding their own way to whatever conclusion these facts dictated. Today the petroleum industry has reached the point where it must give the people light so they can find their way.

To those of you in the media who may be in this room today, I implore you to inform the people of this country that a severe energy and security crisis is evident and the outcome to the nation could be a disaster. You should tell the people to arise and make their voices heard by their representatives in Washington to do whatever is necessary to avert this impending doom.

We geoscientists are indispensable to the future energy stability of this nation. We are needed to find the oil and gas that remains to be found, both onshore and offshore. Without us no oil and gas would be discovered and produced. In this regard, our profession cannot survive without exploration and neither can the energy security of this nation. We are tied together; if one falters, so does the other.

When our imports control the country's industrial might, we will find ourselves in the hands of those who control those imports. Then it will be too late for exploration to remedy the disaster.

I hope that Americans will recognize the severity of the import increases as well as the deterioration of the petroleum industry and, thus, also realize that deterioration plus dependence equal disaster. Consequently, I trust that if and when that realization becomes evident, the people will force the government to prevent this disaster from occurring.

This is the year we celebrate the 200th anniversary of the signing of the Constitution of this great land. This historic document starts off with these inspiring words—"We the people." As long as we the people have the right to elect our representatives and officials in Washington, we the people can control the destiny of this nation, our industry and our profession. I hope and pray that the will of the people will be felt and that this country's energy security will be restored through a once-again healthy and viable petroleum industry which, in time past, materially assisted in making this great nation of ours the world's most dominant power.

And to my fellow geoscientists, I say to you: Take heart. Our time will come. The nation needs us more *now* than ever before. Our challenge becomes larger and more formidable. We have always overcome the challenges thrust upon us in the past and given the opportunity, can overcome the one before us now.

\*\*\*

Some time later, while delegates were still talking about his speech, one of Halbouty's peers asked him, "Mike, what can we *really* do to bring people to their senses?"

"We've got to keep on fighting in every way we can," Halbouty said grimly.

"It seems like we've been fighting forever, Mike."

Halbouty nodded. "It's like a war without end."

# EPILOGUE

On June 21, 1989, Halbouty passed his 80th birthday. He was still active as an explorer for and producer of petroleum. He was still pressing with undiminished zeal to establish America's energy security. His own amazing energy belied his years.

During the Presidential campaign of 1988 he strove mightily for the election of George Bush, a Republican, though Republican presidents in the past had sorely disappointed him with their almost total disregard for the country's energy welfare. But Bush was a long-time friend, once an oilman himself, and Halbouty appeared convinced that Bush would act to alleviate what Halbouty perceived as a graver peril than budget deficits and trade imbalances.

Meanwhile, he had committed himself to a schedule of activities that extended well into 1994!

There was a symposium to chair in 1989 in San Jose, Costa Rica on "Energy and Mineral Resources Potential of the Central American-Caribbean Region," and yet another in 1990 on "Giant Oil and Gas Fields of the Decade: 1978-1988," in Stavenger, Norway.

He was to organize and co-chair another in the Soviet Union dealing with "Tectonics, Energy and Mineral Resources of the Northwest Pacific." While there he was to visit various petroleum provinces at the invitation of the Minister of Geology and others. And his beloved Circum-Pacific Council for Energy and Mineral Resources, which he founded in 1972, was to convene abroad in 1991 in Thailand and in China in 1992 and in Australia in 1994. As always, Billye would accompany him on his journeys.

They made a trip of significance to Moscow in the spring of 1990. There, with unanimous approval, the Presidium of the U.S.S.R. Academy of Science bestowed on Halbouty the honorary degree of Doctor of Geosciences "for his many contributions to and achievements in the science of geology." It was the first honor of its kind awarded to a foreigner by the Academy.

He remained in demand as a speaker in the United States and elsewhere. He had limited his appearances, however, to forums he believed would "spread the word" about his ideas to revive the American petroleum industry and create a comprehensive national energy policy. And, as always, he favored speaking to students and other young people, hoping they would embrace his stout belief in the free enterprise system and be receptive to his arguments against a frightening dependence on unreliable foreign petroleum sources.

And, as he had for decades past, he continued to journey to Washington to plead his case. He went there on August 1, 1989 at the invitation of President Bush's Secretary of Energy, James Watkins, to testify at the National Energy Strategy Public Hearing.

It appeared that events and moods would militate against immediate, positive results from the hearing. Oil spills in Alaska and elsewhere had upset not only environmentalists but ordinary citizens from coast to coast. Support for opening up wildlife preserves and other federal lands, never strong, dwindled as public outrage swelled.

Tax breaks for the petroleum industry to encourage drilling were not a priority for a Congress operating in a tight budget climate, and prospects for increased production of nuclear energy were still tarnished by memories of Three-Mile-Island and Chernobyl.

And public indifference remained a stumbling block in Halbouty's crusade. With tanks full of gasoline, motorists apparently didn't care if the crude oil from which it was derived came from the Middle East or East Texas.

Still undaunted, Halbouty fought on like the warrior he was.

After some introductory remarks, this is what he told those assembled for the public hearing:

> All of our vast domestic energy resources—petroleum, coal, nuclear, solar, hydropower, wind, and biomass, to name only a few—should be continuously researched for improved usage. However, our key resources—petroleum, coal, and nuclear energy—are not being produced in quantities or in manners adequate to meet

our energy demands. I want to speak briefly on the importance of each of these resources.

Our petroleum resource base has a special place in the hierarchy of domestic energy sources. Crude oil and natural gas today supply about 66% of our entire fuel mix. Yet, unfortunately, our domestic crude oil production is declining at a precipitous rate, and our supplies of natural gas in most cases cannot immediately be substituted for oil usage. As a result, our crude oil and product imports are dramatically rising almost daily.

The impact of increased imports is demonstrated by the fact that our domestic production has dropped from 8.9 million barrels a day in 1985 to our current production of 7.5 million barrels a day, a drop of 1.4 million barrels a day. Of our production, some 1.9 million barrels a day comes from Alaska. Therefore, we are producing less than 6 million barrels a day in the conterminous U.S. and the drop is accelerating. We are now producing 500,000 barrels a day less than we did in 1988. Our imports have risen from an average of 5.1 million barrels a day in 1985 to today's average of 7.9 million barrels a day. This is a negative turnaround of an astounding 4.2 million barrels a day in just 4 years! It is incongruous that this situation can be further tolerated!

Currently, our demand is 17.2 million barrels per day. We are producing 7.5 million barrels per day and we are now importing 7.9 million barrels per day—a combined total of 15.4 million barrels a day. Our imports represent 46% of our demand. We now have a 1.8 million barrel per day deficit which must be made up from our existing crude oil stocks and our natural gas liquids production. In addition, it is possible that we could be importing close to 9 million barrels per day before the end of this year! Furthermore, it is estimated that in the lower 48 states, production has been dropping at the rate of 40,000 barrels per day *each* month. In a year or so, a decline will finally set in on the North Slope, which will further accentuate the import dependence. And it is estimated that by the end of 1990 the United States will be importing from 9 million to 10 million barrels per day. This is indeed frightening! This could approximate 60% of our total daily consumption.

We cannot continue to just produce our remaining reserves without trying to replace them through more exploration. It is most evident that when imports increase, exploration decreases, which in turn reduces the strength of our petroleum industry and thus jeopardizes our economic and national security.

Let me cite a few more statistics: In 1981 we drilled 91,600 wells. Last year we drilled 25,186. For the first quarter of 1989, the total was 5,529, and there are estimates of only about 20,000 wells drilled for the year. Today there are fewer than 900 rigs running. Because of this very low rate of exploration, the independent segment of the industry has not only been decimated but virtually wiped out.

I should here remind you that the independents throughout the history of the petroleum industry have drilled 80% of the wells and discovered 75% of all the oil and gas in this country. Where there were once 60,000 independents actively drilling for oil and gas, there are now less than 1,000. Where there were once more than 40 major companies, there are now less than a dozen.

For more than 30 years, from one administration to another, the government has thrust one disincentive after another at the industry. These disincentives did not appear suddenly. Rather, it was a gradual process which caused a deterioration, particularly in the exploration and production segments. It is really baffling that a nation that is considered to have the most intelligent people on earth can permit this deterioration of the industry when they—the people—realize that in the long-run that whatever hurts the petroleum industry will eventually hurt them. Such thinking is irrational.

Yet there are those, many even in high places, who say ''don't drill,'' ''don't explore anymore,'' meaning let the U.S. petroleum exploration and production segments of the industry die. They say just keep on increasing imports—the oil is cheaper. This concept is most dangerous in that it does not take into account where our dependency lies, and how it could affect our economic and strategic securities. Those who favor greater imports do not realize that we just cannot ever place this nation's destiny in the hands of others who have their own interests above ours. But, unfortunately, this is exactly what is happening. We are gradually ceding some of our liberties to those who control and own the supplies of oil that are shipped to this country.

It is evident that the appropriate and obligatory role of the federal government in our quest for energy supplies is to create an atmosphere and an energy policy which will encourage the private sector to seek, produce and develop all of our energy sources without undue interference. The policy must provide core pieces of legislation through which was can rationally evaluate our energy-resource options. Such a policy should be truly bipartisan, formulated solely for the protection and best interests of the national welfare. It must be viewed as a means of survival for this country.

From geoscientific studies of our land and water areas, it is evident that there is the potential to find as much oil and gas as we have produced to date. Much of our petroleum potential lies in our federal lands and waters. Yet we have been prevented from exploring for energy and minerals on some of these lands because of federal restraints. For example, geoscientists from industry, academia and government are in common agreement that the Coastal Plain of the Arctic National Wildlife Refuge (ANWR) is the most promising onshore petroleum frontier in the United States. Yet federal restraints prevent drilling in this region.

Our growing energy needs indicate that nuclear energy and coal will progressively have to be substituted for petroleum in the post-petroleum era. The proper long-range development of these sources has been sorely neglected.

Nuclear-generated electricity has already saved America over three billion barrels of oil, with billions more to be saved before the turn of the century. Our existing nuclear plants are preventing more than 2 million barrels of oil per day from being imported into the country.

Public fear has prevented the construction of additional plants. I firmly believe reform of nuclear permitting regulations and standardization of design could revive the industry. If we were to establish *one*, and only *one*, design, we could rapidly build the 100 new plants we now need, which could save us another 3 million barrels per day and thus solidify our domestic energy base.

Now let's talk about coal. Coal is the most abundant yet least utilized of our domestic energy resources. We should be using more coal than we are today, and, therefore, should be planning to use more in the future. In terms of proven reserves, we have 60 times more coal than oil on an energy equivalent basis and more than 40 times more coal than natural gas on an energy equivalent basis. Considerable research is necessary to determine the most efficient use of coal and its compliance with approved environmental standards. Coal also can make a positive contribution by becoming a major export which would be a boon to reducing our foreign deficits.

In addition to what nuclear energy and coal can provide, if we could increase our energy supply from other sources equivalent to another 2 to 3 million barrels of oil per day, we would be energy secure, and that security would increase year by year.

The invitation to participate here today stated we should give our opinion on "what should the priorities be for National Energy Strategies."

Therefore, my recommendations for priorities for the creation of an Integrated National Energy Strategy which would also serve as guidelines to form a most constructive national energy policy are as follows:

1. Enhancement of federal leasing policies to provide for more energy and minerals exploration.
2. Completion of the filling of the Strategic Petroleum Reserve.
3. Environmental controls and regulatory policies based on a scientific cost-benefit basis. Government should encourage and strongly recommend that environmentalists and industry leaders get together and both parties use every possible means to arrive at a compatible understanding and solution to a dispute or a problem or a situation instead of one or the other adopting a "go to hell" attitude or a standoffish impasse attitude.
4. Increased efforts to provide safe and economic nuclear power and encourage industry to build 100 new, standard-design plants.
5. Development of clean coal technology, greater utilization of our coal resources, and promotion of U.S. coal exports.
6. More research and development programs to fully exploit our energy alternatives, energy conservation, and enhanced oil recovery technology.
7. And, most importantly, reasonable tax measures such as:
   (a) Removing oil and gas preference items from Alternative Minimum Tax computations.
   (b) Providing investment tax credits for research and development activity, especially in the area of enhanced oil recovery.
   (c) Allowing immediate expensing of 100% of Intangible Drilling Costs in tax calculations, and expanding the definition to include geological and geophysical costs and unrecovered surface casing.
   (d) For increasing the depletion percentage for oil and gas to $22\frac{1}{2}\%$.

(e) Returning temporarily abandoned stripper wells to production under a 22½% preferential tax credit on all production and equipment costs.

(f) Providing a 20% exploration incentive credit on all drilling and equipment costs expended for a discovery well and for subsequent development of the new field.

If the above mentioned tax incentives are granted, it is my opinion that within 18 months of enactment there will be 2,500 rigs operating in this country, searching for, discovering and producing oil and gas from new fields and, thereby, reducing our import levels and our foreign deficit with each new discovery.

Furthermore, if all of the above mentioned recommendations are adopted, they will materially restore and sustain the nation's energy strength and security as well as set the permanent foundation for a viable, effective national energy plan for now and in the future.

I appreciate the invitation from Secretary Watkins to participate in this hearing.

\*\*\*

He had fired his best weapons. Now it was time to re-load for battles he was yet to fight in the War Without End.

# Awards, Honors, Activities

1930 Texas A&M University, Bachelor of Science Degree (Geology and Petroleum Engineering)

1931 Texas A&M University, Master of Science Degree (Geology and Petroleum Engineering)

1956 Texas A&M University, Professional Degree in Geological Engineering

1966 Montana College of Mineral Science and Technology, Doctor of Engineering, Honoris Causa

1965 Texas Mid-Continent Oil and Gas Association's Distinguished Service Award for 1965, presented to an independent for outstanding services and contributions to his industry and profession

1968 Engineer of the Year, Texas Society of Professional Engineers and the Engineer's Council of Houston

1968 Texas A&M University's Distinguished Alumni Award

1969 Honorary Membership in The American Association of Petroleum Geologists

1970 Honorary Life Membership in the Houston Geological Society

1971 DeGolyer Distinguished Service Medal of the Society of Petroleum Engineers of AIME

1972 Honorary Membership from the Spindletop Section of the Society of Petroleum Engineers of AIME

1973 Honorary Membership, American Institute of Mining, Metallurgical and Petroleum Engineers (AIME)

1975 Anthony F. Lucas Gold Medal, AIME

1975 Human Needs Award, The American Association of Petroleum Geologists (AAPG)

1977 Sidney Powers Memorial Medal Award, AAPG

1977 William T. Pecora Award, NASA

1977 Texas A&M University named its geoscience building The Michel T. Halbouty Geosciences Building

1978 Horatio Alger Award, American Schools and Colleges Association

1978 Spirit of Life Award, Oil Industry Council of the City of Hope

1979 Elected into membership of the National Academy of Engineering

1981 Breath of Life Award, Cystic-Fibrosis Foundation

1982 Best Symposium Paper Award, Institute of Electrical and Electronics Engineers, Inc. Geoscience and Remote Sensing Society for his paper, "Applications of Remote Sensing to Petroleum Exploration," which he presented at the 1981 International Geoscience and Remote Sensing Symposium in Washington, D.C.

1982 Medal of Merit for Distinguished and Outstanding Achievement from the Circum-Pacific Council for Energy and Mineral Resources

1982 Hoover Medal, American Association of Engineering Societies

1982 Honorary Membership, Gulf Coast Association of Geological Societies (GCAGS)

1983 Distinguished Service Award, Paul Carrington Chapter of the Sons of the American Revolution

1983 Texas Heritage Award, Angleton Chamber of Commerce

1983 Distinguished Texas Scientist of the Year, Texas Academy of Sciences

1983 Honorary Membership, Society of Exploration Geophysicists

1986 Honorary Membership, Geophysical Society of Houston

1988 Texas A&M University's Distinguished Alumni Award in Engineering

1988 Ben H. Parker Memorial Award from the American Institute of Professional Geologists (AIPG)

In addition to receiving the highest awards bestowed by AAPG, Halbouty has also received the highest honors conveyed by the American Institute of Mining, Metallurgical and Petroleum Engineers. He is the only earth scientist to have achieved the distinction of being so singularly honored by these two great scientific and professional societies.

In the Fall of 1964 and the Spring of 1965, he was a Distinguished Lecturer for the Society of Petroleum Engineers of AIME, and in the Fall of 1965 and the Spring of 1966, he was a Distinguished Lecturer for The American Association of Petroleum Geologists. In February, 1982, he was named the first Distinguished Lecturer Emeritus for the Society of Petroleum Engineers of AIME.

He served as president of the world's largest organization of earth scientists, The American Association of Petroleum Geologists, for the 1966–67 term.

Halbouty has written and published over 280 papers, mainly on petroleum geology and petroleum engineering; one book entitled *Petrographic and Physical Characteristics of Sands from Seven Gulf Coast Producing Horizons*, and another entitled *Salt Domes—Gulf Region, United States and Mexico* (Gulf Publishing Co., 1st ed., 1967, revised and enlarged ed., 1979)—the only such single volume on this subject in the world's scientific literature. He co-authored the best seller *Spindletop* (Random House, 1952, reprinted by Gulf Publishing Co., 1980), one on the East Texas giant oil field entitled *The Last Boom* (Random House, 1972, Shearer, 1984), and *Grady Barr*, a fictionalized account of the oil industry in Venezuela (Arbor House, 1981).

He has edited or has been special editor of numerous scientific publications, including *Geology of Giant Petroleum Fields*, AAPG Memoir 14 (1970); *Giant Oil and Gas Fields of the Decade: 1968–1978*, AAPG Memoir 30 (1981), for which he received AAPG's President's Award for Best Publication; *Energy Resources of the Pacific Region*, AAPG Studies in Geology 12 (1981); *The Deliberate Search for the Subtle Trap*, AAPG Memoir 32 (1982); and *Proceedings of the Wallace E. Pratt Memorial Conference on Future Petroleum Provinces of the World*, AAPG Memoir 40 (1986). He was co-editor of AAPG Memoir 25, *Circum-Pacific Energy and Mineral Resources* (1976).

Halbouty has been the subject of two books, *Ahead of His Time: Michel T. Halbouty Speaks to the People*, edited by James A. Clark (Gulf Publishing Co., 1971), and *Wildcatter: The Story of Michel T. Halbouty and the Search for Oil*, by Jack Donahue (McGraw-Hill, 1979; reprinted by Gulf Publishing Co., 1984), as well as numerous interviews by leading newspaper, magazine, and television journalists.

He is a member of many worldwide professional and technical societies, including The American Association of Petroleum Geologists; the Geological Society of America; the

American Institute of Mining, Metallurgical and Petroleum Engineers; the Society of Petroleum Engineers of AIME; the American Association for the Advancement of Science; the Society of Economic Paleontologists and Mineralogists of America; the Society of Exploration Geophysicists; the Seismological Society of America; the Institute of Petroleum, London, England; International Association of Sedimentologists; and the Asociacion Mexicana de Geologos Petroleros. He has served on committees and as an officer of many of the societies.

He is also a past member of the National Energy Study Committee and of the Executive Committee of the Division of Earth Sciences, National Academy of Science, National Research Council. He currently serves on the Board of Earth Sciences of the National Research Council.

In addition to his oil and gas operations, Halbouty has owned banking interests in the state of Texas, and was chairman of the board of Bank of the West in San Angelo, Texas. He currently serves as a director of the Allied Bank of Texas, Houston, and in January 1985, he was appointed to a four-year term on the board of directors of the Federal Home Loan Bank of Dallas.

Halbouty takes an active part in community and civic leadership. He is chairman of the board of the Geosciences and Earth Resources Council of Texas A&M University. He is a member of the board of directors of the Houston Area Research Center (HARC). He is a member of the board of trustees of the Texas Heart Institute and the Texas Children's Hospital in Houston, Texas, and serves on many other civic projects. In 1964, he was appointed Civil Defense Director for Houston at $1.00 per year salary and served in that capacity until December 1973.

During the presidential campaign of 1980, he served as chairman of Governor Reagan's Energy Policy Advisory Task Force and later President Reagan appointed him leader of the Transition Team on Energy.

Halbouty was chairman of the board of the Halbouty Alaska Oil Company, known as Halasko. The company owned acreage in many of the basins in Alaska, where it discovered a gas field, the first independent company to do so. Currently, he is chairman of the board and chief executive officer of the Michel T. Halbouty Energy Co., in Houston, Texas, an active oil and gas exploration and production firm.

# Bibliography of Publications

**Abbreviations**

| | |
|---|---|
| AAPG Bull. | The American Association of Petroleum Geologists Bulletin |
| AIPG | American Institute of Professional Geologists |
| API | American Petroleum Institute |
| GCAGS | Gulf Coast Association of Geological Societies |
| HGS Bull. | Houston Geological Society Bulletin |
| Ind. Pet. Monthly | Independent Petroleum Monthly |
| JPT | Journal of Petroleum Technology |
| JSP | Journal of Sedimentary Petrology |
| NOGS LOG | Newsletter of the New Orleans Geological Society |
| OGJ | Oil and Gas Journal |
| Pet. Dev. & Tech. | Petroleum Development & Technology Transactions of the |
| Trans. of AIME | American Institute of Mining and Metallurgical Engineering |
| SPE | Society of Petroleum Engineers of AIME |

(1) 1931a. "Geology of Atascosa County, Texas," *Thesis*, Master's Degree, Texas A&M University Library.

(2) 1931b. "Petrographic Characteristics of Some Eocene Sands from Southwest Texas," (with John T. Lonsdale and M. S. Metz) *JSP*, v. 1, no. 2, November, pp. 73–81

(3) 1932a. "Vicksburg Formation in Deep Test, Acadia Parish, Louisiana," AAPG *Bull.*, v. 16, no. 6, pp. 609–610.

(4) 1932b. "High Island Dome, Galveston County, Texas," AAPG *Bull.*, v. 16, no. 7, pp. 701–702.

(5) 1935a. "Conservation of Colloidal Material in Native Drilling Muds," *Petroleum Engineer*, April, p. 60.

(6) 1935b. "Geology and Geophysics of Southeast Flank of Jennings Dome, Acadia Parish, Louisiana, with Special Reference to Overhang," AAPG *Bull.*, v. 19, no. 9, pp. 1308–1329.

| (7)  | 1936a. | "Unusual Boiler Feed Hook-up, Entire Unit May be Carried from One Location to Another Without Dismantling," *Oil Weekly*, February 3, pp. 33–34. |
|------|--------|---|
| (8)  | 1936b. | "Geology, Chemistry and Petroleum Engineering Play Important Parts in Drilling Mud Control," Part I, *Oil Weekly*, v. 80, no. 13, March 9, pp. 19–20. |
| (9)  | 1936c. | "Arrangement of Economical Circulating Mud System Essential to Proper Control," Part II, *Oil Weekly*, v. 81, no. 3, March 30, pp. 36–38. |
| (10) | 1936d. | "Economic Use of Mud Materials in Rotary Fluid Control," *Oil Weekly*, v. 81, no. 4, April 6, pp. 30–32. |
| (11) | 1936e. | "Geology and Geophysics Showing Cap Rock and Salt Overhang of High Island Dome, Galveston County, Texas," AAPG *Bull.*, v. 20, no. 5, pp. 560–611. |
| (12) | 1936f. | "Mud Treatment for Heaving Shales," *World Petroleum*, May, pp. 268–273. |
| (13) | 1936g. | "Petrographic and Physical Characteristics of Sands from Seven Gulf Coast Producing Horizons," *Oil Weekly*, Part I, November 23, Introduction, Part II, November 30, Laboratory Procedures, Part III, December 7, Texture Results, Part IV, December 14, Shape Results, Part V, December 21, Mineral Study Results, Part VI, December 28, Permeability Results. |
| (14) | 1937a. | *Petrographic and Physical Characteristics of Sands from Seven Gulf Coast Producing Horizons*, Gulf Publishing Company, Houston. |
| (15) | 1937b. | "Use of Viscosimeter in Determining Drilling Mud Viscosity and Gel Strength," *Oil Weekly*, February 15. |
| (16) | 1937c. | "Geology and Economic Significance of the Anahuac Oil Field, Texas," (with J. Brian Eby) *World Petroleum*, v. 8, no. 4, April, pp. 46–55. |
| (17) | 1937d. | "Spindletop Oil Field, Jefferson County, Texas," (with J. Brian Eby) AAPG *Bull.*, v. 21, no. 4, pp. 475–490. |
| (18) | 1937e. | "Geology and Economic Significance of Hastings Field, Brazoria County, Texas," *World Petroleum*, v. 8, no. 9, pp. 36–51. |
| (19) | 1938f. | "La Fitte—World's Deepest Major Field," *World Petroleum*, May, pp. 44–48. |
| (20) | 1938g. | "Probable Undiscovered Stratigraphic Traps of the Gulf Coast," *World Petroleum*, v. 9, no. 6, pp. 27–29. |
| (21) | 1938h. | "Characteristics, Methods of Combating and Economic Importance of Heaving Shales," (with Nicholas A. Kaldenbach) *Oil Weekly*, Part I, v. 9, no. 7, October 24, pp. 17–26, Part II, v. 9, no. 8, October 31, pp. 42–54. |

(22) 1938i. "Oil and Gas Development of South Texas During 1937," Pet. Dev. & Tech. *Trans.* of AIME, v. 127, February, pp. 552–579.
(23) 1939a. "Geology and Economic Significance of Barbers Hill," *World Petroleum*, v. 10, no. 1, pp. 40–55.
(24) 1939b. "Oil and Gas Development of South Texas During 1938," Pet. Dev. & Tech. *Trans.* of AIME, v. 132, February, pp. 453–493.
(25) 1939c. "Story of Texas Oil Industry Fascinating," book review of *Texas Oil and Gas Since 1543* by C. A. Warner, *Houston Post*, May.
(26) 1939d. "Temperatures as Affecting Oil Well Drilling and Production," *Oil Weekly*, Part I, "Temperature Effects on Oil Well Drilling," v. 96, no. 2, December 18, pp. 10–16. Part II, "Temperature Affecting Crude Oil Production," v. 96, no. 3, December 25, pp. 15–19.
(27) 1940a. "Temperatures as Affecting Oil Well Drilling and Production," Symposium on Temperatures, Institute of Physics, pp. 1039–1057.
(28) 1940b. "Oil and Gas Development of South Texas During 1939," Pet. Dev. & Tech. *Trans.* of AIME, v. 136, March, pp. 458–498.
(29) 1940c. "Sedimentation," (with Houston Geological Society Group) AAPG *Bull.*, v. 24, no. 2, pp. 374–376.
(30) 1941a. "Hawkins Field Valuable Addition to Nation's Reserves," *World Petroleum*, February, pp. 24–26.
(31) 1941b. "Oil and Gas Development of South Texas During 1940," Pet. Dev. & Tech. *Trans.* of AIME, v. 142, pp. 476–504.
(32) 1941c. "The Spindletop Oil Field, Jefferson County, Texas," (with J. Brian Eby) *OIL*, November, p. 24.
(33) 1941d. "Geology of the Hitchcock Field, Galveston County, Texas—Showing Stratigraphic Accumulation and Structure," (with Benjamin T. Simmons), Stratigraphic Type Oil Fields, a Symposium, AAPG, Tulsa, pp. 641–660.
(34) 1941e. "Oil and Gas Stratigraphic Reservoirs in the University Oil Field, East Baton Rouge Parish, Louisiana," Stratigraphic Type Oil Fields, a Symposium, AAPG, Tulsa, pp. 208–236.
(35) 1941f. "Progress in Oil Exploration Has Been Steady Since Discovery of Spindletop," *Houston Post*, December 20, Sec. 4, p. 2.
(36) 1941g. "U.S. Reserves Show Slight Increase in 1941," *World Petroleum*, January, pp. 36–37.
(37) 1941h. "Oil and Gas Development in South Texas During 1941," (with James J. Halbouty) Pet. Dev. & Tech. *Trans.* of AIME, v. 146, pp. 475–508.

NOTE: Entered military service in February, 1942. Separated from service in September, 1945.

(38) 1947a. "Unconformities to Play Major Role in Arkansas-North Louisiana Discoveries," (with George C. Hardin, Jr.) *Oil Weekly*, March 31, April 7, April 14 (in 3 parts).

(39) 1947b. "Trends in Petroleum Geology of the Gulf Coast," (with George C. Hardin, Jr.) *OGJ*, v. 46, no. 4, May 31, pp. 194-196.

(40) 1950. "Types of Hydrocarbon Accumulation and Geology of the South Liberty Salt Dome, Liberty County, Texas," (with George C. Hardin, Jr.) abs., *Transactions*, 1950 Annual Meeting of AAPG-SEPM-SEG, Chicago, April 24-27.

(41) 1951. "Types of Hydrocarbon Accumulation and Geology of the South Liberty Salt Dome, Liberty County, Texas," (with George C. Hardin, Jr.) AAPG *Bull.*, v. 35, no. 9, pp. 1939-1977.

(42) 1952. *Spindletop* (with James A. Clark), Random House, New York.

(43) 1953. "Spindletop's Second Fifty Years," (with James A. Clark) *Texas Preview*, January, pp. 26-28.

(44) 1954a. "New Exploration Possibilities on Piercement Type Salt Domes Established by Thrust Fault at Boling Salt Dome, Wharton County, Texas," (with George C. Hardin, Jr.) AAPG *Bull.*, v. 38, no. 8, pp. 1725-1740.

(45) 1954b. "Thrust Faults on Salt Domes," (with George C. Hardin, Jr.) a reply to Theodore A. Link's discussion, AAPG *Bull.*, v. 38, no. 12, pp. 2566-2567.

(46) 1954c. "Salt Dome Geology May Enter New Phase," (with George C. Hardin, Jr.) *OGJ*, v. 53, no. 26, November 1, pp. 93-98.

(47) 1955a. "Factors Affecting the Quantity of Oil Accumulation Around Some Texas Gulf Coast Piercement Type Salt Domes," (with George C. Hardin, Jr.) AAPG *Bull.*, v. 39, no. 5, pp. 697-711.

(48) 1955b. "Significance of Salt Dome Geology in Past and Future Oil Exploration," (with George C. Hardin, Jr.) *The Oil Forum*, Special Oil Finders Issue, April, pp. 129-131, 152.

(49) 1955c. "New Geological Studies Result in Discoveries of Large Gas and Oil Reserves from Salt Dome Structures in the Texas-Louisiana Gulf Coast," (with George C. Hardin, Jr.) *Papers*, Fourth World Petroleum Congress, Rome, Italy, Sec. 1, pp. 83-101.

(50) 1955d. "Sixty-four Chances to Find New Gulf Coast Oil," (with George C. Hardin, Jr.) *OGJ*, v. 54, no. 23, October 10, pp. 321-324.

(51) 1956a. "Why Some Geologists and Geophysicists Don't Mix," *OGJ*, v. 54, no. 31, January 9, pp. 148-150.

(52) 1956b. "Genesis of the Salt Domes of the Gulf Coastal Plain," (with George C. Hardin, Jr.) AAPG *Bull.*, v. 40, no. 4, pp. 737-746.

(53) 1957. "Geological and Engineering Thinking in the Gulf Coast of Texas and Louisiana—Past, Present and Future," (1) *Texas Oil Journal*, May, pp. 18-19, 26, (2) *The Ind. Pet. Monthly*, May, pp. 30-32, 39, (3) *JPT*, May, pp. 19-20.

(54) 1958a. A Statement in Reply to W. L. Clayton's "What Price Oil?" (1) *The Ind. Pet. Monthly*, April, (2) *OIL*, April, pp. 9, 11.

(55) 1958b. "Geological Prospects for Discoveries Brighter than Ever," *World Oil*, Gulf Coast Issue, v. 146, no. 7, pp. 102-103, 127-128.

(56) 1958c. "Alaska—Its Oil Potentialities," *Petroleum Week*, v. 7, no. 12, September 19, pp. 24-26.

(57) 1958d. "An Independent's Blueprint for Survival," (1) *World Oil*, November, pp. 103-106, (2) *The Ind. Pet. Monthly*, v. XXIX, no. 8, December, pp. 26-27, 58-60.

(58) 1959a. "Why—Alaska?" ("Why Independents Should Tackle Alaska") *OGJ*, v. 57, no. 12, March 16, pp. 116-119.

(59) 1959b. "A Geological Appraisal of Present and Future Exploration Techniques on Salt Domes of the Gulf Region of the United States," (with George C. Hardin, Jr.) (1) Presented at the Fifth World Petroleum Congress, New York, Sec. 1, pp. 1-13.

(60) 1959c. "Exploration Techniques on Salt Domes of the Gulf Region of the United States," (with George C. Hardin, Jr.) *OGJ*, v. 57, no. 24, June, pp. 134-137.

(61) 1959d. "A Review of Geological Concepts and Economic Significance of Salt Domes in the Gulf Coast Region," abs., HGS *Bull.*, v. 2, no. 2, October.

(62) 1959e. "Mandatory Pooling Advocated," *OIL*, December, p. 6.

(63) 1960a. "Petroleum Conservation—Total or Partial?" *Houston Post*, Sec. 3, April 24, p. 3.

(64) 1960b. "You Can't Bury Your Head in the Sand," *Drilling*, April, pp. 66-67.

(65) 1960c. "Need for Strengthening Conservation Program," Rocky Mountain Oil & Gas Association *Program*, Denver, Colorado, October 21.

(66) 1960d. "The Effects of Excessive Foreign Imports on Domestic Exploration as Related to the Independent Producers," *Program*, Joint AAPG, SEPM & SEG Meeting, Los Angeles, California, November 3.

(67) 1960e. "Prepare Now to Drill 92,000 Wells a Year," *Drilling*, December, pp. 75–96.

(68) 1961a. "One Step Toward Survival," (1) Independent Oil of the Oklahoma Independent Petroleum Association, *Convention Report Issue*, v. 6, no. 2, February, (2) *OIL*, v. XI, no. 2, February, p. 7.

(69) 1961b. "History and Forecast of Academic and Employment Relationships in the Geological Profession," abs., HGS *Bull.*, v. 4, no. 2, October.

(70) 1961c. "Gulf Coast Salt Domes Show Arctic Island Possibilities," (with George C. Hardin, Jr.) *Oilweek*, October 2, pp. 31–41.

(71) 1961d. "Port Acres and Port Arthur Fields, Jefferson County, Texas," (with Thos. D. Barber) GCAGS *Transactions*, San Antonio meeting, v. XI, October, pp. 225–234.

(72) 1962a. "Port Acres and Port Arthur Fields, Jefferson County, Texas," (with Thos. D. Barber) *Typical Oil and Gas Fields of Southeast Texas*, Houston Geological Society, pp. 169–173.

(73) 1962b. "If They Had No Fear, Why Should We?" *JPT*, v. 14, no. 8, August, pp. 821–824.

(74) 1962c. "Independents to Survive Stronger, Wiser. . .," *Ind. Pet. Monthly*, December.

(75) 1962d. "South Liberty Field, Liberty County, Texas," *Typical Oil and Gas Fields in Southeast Texas*, Houston Geological Society, pp. 200–206.

(76) 1962e. "Nash Salt Dome, Fort Bend and Brazoria Counties, Texas," (with George C. Hardin, Jr.) *Typical Oil and Gas Fields of Southeast Texas*, Houston Geological Society, pp. 134–137.

(77) 1962f. "Present Trends in Well Spacing and Possible Effects of Normanna and Port Acres Decisions," *Annual Report 1962*, National Institute for Petroleum Landmen, Southwestern Legal Foundation, Dallas, Texas, pp. 117–141; also in same volume "Seminar on Well Spacing and Compulsory Unitization," pp. 401–437.

(78) 1963a. "How Unnecessary Wells Are Hurting the Oil Industry, the People of Texas, and the Reasons and Benefits for Pooling Legislation," *TIPRO Reporter*, v. 15, no. 1, February–March, pp. 17–24.

(79) 1963b. "The Industry's Stake in Proper Well Spacing," *Bulletin of the Rocky Mountain Petroleum Economics Institute*, Boulder, Colorado, June 17–21.

(80) 1963c. "The Petroleum Professional's Obligation in Public Affairs," International Oil Scouts Association *Annual*, v. 4, no. 9, September, pp. 13–15.

| | | |
|---|---|---|
| (81) | 1964a. | "The Responsibility of Geologists and Petroleum Engineers in Meeting Exploration Demands in the Future," (with Thos. D. Barber) *OIL*, January, pp. 15–19. |
| (82) | 1964b. | "Responsibility of Petro-Professionals," *The Landman*, v. IX, no. 3, February, pp. 4–7, 64–70. |
| (83) | 1964c. | "New Uses to Widen Petroleum's Value; the Petroleum Industry in the Year 2000 A.D.," *Houston Post*, Special Edition, February 9, Part 1, p. 12. |
| (84) | 1964d. | "The Responsibility of Geologists and Petroleum Engineers in Meeting Exploration Demands in the Future," (with Thos. D. Barber) *JPT*, March, pp. 239–243. |
| (85) | 1964e. | "Independents Holding Key to Oil in Twenty-First Century," *Ind. Pet. Monthly*, April, pp. 150–151. |
| (86) | 1964f. | "Responsibility of the Petroleum Professional to Participate in Public Affairs," AAPG *Bull.*, v. 48, no. 5, pp. 723–726. |
| (87) | 1964g. | "Can't Count Out Independents," *Ind. Pet. Monthly*, October, p. 16. |
| (88) | 1964h. | "A Forecast of Domestic Petroleum Demands for the Next Two Decades," (1) Preprint for 35th Annual California Regional Fall Meeting of SPE of AIME, Los Angeles, California, November 6, (2) *OIL*, December, pp. 10, 24. |
| (89) | 1965a. | "Possibilities Along One Edge of a Basin: Stratigraphic Discoveries Highly Probable on Basin Flank of the San Marcos Arch," abs., *Program*, Southwestern Federation of Geological Societies, January 27–29, pp. 11–12. |
| (90) | 1965b. | "Can We Meet U.S. Demands of the Next Twenty Years?" *Drilling*, v. 26, no. 4, February, pp. 39–42. |
| (91) | 1965c. | "Bold Thinking is Key to Giant Reserves," *OGJ*, August 16, p. 88. |
| (92) | 1965d. | "Geology—For Human Needs," Proceedings, 1st Annual Meeting of the Texas Section of the AIPG, San Antonio, Texas, September 17–18, pp. 4–12. |
| (93) | 1965e. | "If They Had No Fear, Why Should We?" SPE *Student Journal*, Fall, p. 4. |
| (94) | 1965f. | "By Year 2000: 'Find or Import' a Lot," *Standard-Times*, San Angelo, Texas, Oil Edition, October 10. |
| (95) | 1965g. | "Economics—the New Dimension in Geological Thinking," abs., Shreveport Geological Society *Newsletter*, v. 4, no. 2, October. |
| (96) | 1965h. | "Maximum Brain Power: New Exploration Breakthrough," AAPG *Bull.*, v. 49, no. 10, pp. 1597–1600. |
| (97) | 1965i. | "Petroleum Geologists Must See the Big Picture," *OGJ*, November, pp. 147–148. |
| (98) | 1965j. | "Economics—the New Dimension in Geological Thinking," abs., *NOGS LOG*, v. 6, no. 1, November. |

(99)   1965k.  "Geology—For Human Needs," *Geotimes*, v. 10, no. 4, November, pp. 14–17.
(100)  1965l.  "Economics—The New Dimension in Geological Thinking," abs., HGS *Bulletin*, v. 8, no. 4, December, p. 19.
(101)  1966a.  "Geological and Engineering Concepts and Economic Significance of Salt Domes in the Gulf Coast Region," *Transactions*, New York Academy of Sciences, Series II, v. 28, no. 3, January, pp. 378–386.
(102)  1966b.  "Stratigraphic-Trap Possibilities in Upper Jurassic Rocks, San Marcos Arch, Texas," AAPG *Bull.*, v. 50, no. 1, pp. 3–24.
(103)  1966c.  "The Role of the Independent in Modern Exploration," *Exploration and Economics of the Petroleum Industry*, Southwest Legal Foundation, v. 4, March, pp. 163–175.
(104)  1966d.  "Alaska, America's New Oil Frontier," *Areas of Promise, Petroleum Management*, v. 38, no. 5, May, pp. 95–97.
(105)  1966e.  "Economics—The New Dimensions in Geological Thinking," AAPG *Bull.*, v. 50, no. 5, pp. 830–845.
(106)  1966f.  "Geology—For Human Needs," *OGJ*, Extra for IPE Meeting, May 16, pp. 20–23.
(107)  1966g.  "The Independent: His Role in Modern and Future Exploration," *Ind. Pet. Monthly*, "Independent Oilman Is Not Vanishing Breed," v. 37, no. 2, June, p. 11.
(108)  1966h.  "Geology—For Human Needs," *Town Hall*, Los Angeles, v. 28, no. 32, August.
(109)  1966i.  "Needed: Exploration Ingenuity," (1) *Nickle's Daily Oil Bulletin*, September 15, (2) Abs., *Program*, 16th Annual Meeting, Rocky Mountain Section of AAPG, October 23–27.
(110)  1966j.  "The Independent: His Role in Modern and Future Exploration," Proceedings, Second Annual Meeting of the Texas Section of AIPG, Abilene, Texas, September 9–10.
(111)  1966k.  "Conservation and the Public Interest," abs., Program and Transactions, Economics and the Petroleum Geologists, West Texas Geological Society, Midland, Texas, Publication No. 65-53, October 10–15.
(112)  1966l.  "The Independent: His Role in Modern and Future Exploration," *Shale Shaker*, Oklahoma City Geological Society, v. 17, no. 3, November, pp. 46–49.
(113)  1966m.  "Needed: Exploration Ingenuity," *OGJ*, v. 64, no. 46, November 14, pp. 232–237.
(114)  1966n.  "Needed: Exploration Ingenuity," *The Journal of the Canadian Society of Exploration Geophysicists*, v. 2, no. 1, December.
(115)  1966o.  "Our Profession's Challenge and Responsibility," AAPG *Bull.*, v. 51, no. 1, pp. 124–125.

(116) 1966p. "Needed: Exploration Ingenuity in Geological and Geophysical Coordination," *Geophysics*, v. XXXII, no. 1, February, pp. 12–16.

(117) 1966q. "Economics—The Essential Requirement in Exploration," abs., *Program*, Southwestern Federation of Geological Societies and Regional AAPG Meeting, Hobbs, New Mexico, February 1–2.

(118) 1966r. "Creativity—The Basic Need in Future Exploration," abs., *Bulletin*, Corpus Christi Geological Society, v. VII, no. 7, March.

(119) 1966s. "The Heritage of Petroleum Explorers," *Explorer's Journal*, v. XLV, no. 1, March, pp. 59–62.

(120) 1967a. "Drought of Geologists Bringing Serious Consequences," *OGJ*, v. 65, no. 15, April 10, pp. 116–118.

(121) 1967b. 'Geology—For Human Needs," *Journal of Geological Education*, v. XV, no. 2, April, pp. 80–82.

(122) 1967c. "The Middle East Crisis," (1) *Western Oil Reporter*, v. 24, no. 7, July, (2) *OIL*, July, pp. 12–13.

(123) 1967d. "Heritage of the Petroleum Geologist," AAPG *Bull.*, v. 51, no. 7, pp. 1179–1184.

(124) 1967e. "The Recent Crude Oil Price Adjustments," *Tulsa World*, Sec. 3, August 6, p. 4.

(125) 1967f. "The Middle East Oil," (1) *Newsletter*, Rocky Mountain Association of Geologists, Denver, August, (2) *OGJ*, v. 65, no. 35, August 28, pp. 12, 15.

(126) 1967g. *Salt Domes—Gulf Region, United States and Mexico*, Gulf Publishing Company, Houston, 424 pp.

(127) 1967h. "Needed—Greater Teamwork Between Disciplines," (1) Abs., *JPT*, September, p. 1164, (2) SPE paper no. 1875, Preprint, 42nd Annual Fall Meeting of the Society of Petroleum Engineers of AIME, Houston, October 1–4.

(128) 1967i. "Shape Up or Get Shipped Out," (1) Abs., *Program*, 2nd Bi-Annual AAPG-Mid-Continent Regional Meeting, Wichita, Kansas, September 27–29, (2) Abs., AAPG *Bull.*, Association Roundtable, v. 51, no. 10, p. 2173.

(129) 1967j. "Oil Need Next 20 Years Tops Production to Date," *San Angelo Standard Times*, Oil Edition, October 8.

(130) 1967k. "Hidden Trends and Features," Transactions, 17th Annual Meeting of GCAGS, San Antonio, v. XVII, October.

(131) 1967l. "The Urgent Need of Effective Communication Between the Oil Industry and the Public," *Oil Daily*, November 15, pp. 17, 20.

(132) 1967m. "New Exploration Ideas Needed to Locate the 'Unfound' Traps," *Oil Daily*, December 11, pp. 7, 8.

(133) 1967n. "Heritage and Challenge of the Petroleum Geologist," (1) The Institute of Petroleum (London) *Review*, v. 21, no. 252, December, pp. 397–402, (2) Abs., *Journal of the Institute of Petroleum*, v. 54, no. 532, April.

(134) 1967o. "Our Responsibility in Public Affairs," *The Journal of Geological Education,* v. XV, no. 5, December, pp. 205–208.

(135) 1968a. "Economic and Geologic Aspects of Search for Gas in Texas Gulf Coast," Natural Gases of North America, a symposium, AAPG Memoir 9, v. 1, pp. 271–283.

(136) 1968b. "Old Ocean Field, Brazoria and Matagorda Counties, Texas," Natural Gases of North America, a symposium, AAPG Memoir 9, v. 1, pp. 295–305.

(137) 1968c. "Port Acres and Port Arthur Gas-Condensate Fields, Jefferson County, Texas," (with George C. Hardin, Jr. and Thos. D. Barber), Natural Gases of North America, a symposium, AAPG Memoir 9, v. 1, pp. 368–375.

(138) 1968d. "El Petroleo De Oriente Medio Es El Producto Mas Caro De EE. UU.," Petroleo, Petrolquimica y Gas, *OILGAS*, no. 3, March, pp. 17, 18.

(139) 1968e. "Our Responsibility in Public Affairs," *Bulletin*, Corpus Christi Geological Society, v. VIII, no. 8, April, pp. 6–16.

(140) 1968f. "The Supply and Demand of Geologists," *Geoscience News*, v. 1, no. 4, March-April, pp. 12–14.

(141) 1968g. "Petroleum and the People," *The Town Hall Journal*, Los Angeles, v. 30, no. 7, April 23, pp. 109–111.

(142) 1968h. "Needed: Greater Teamwork Between Disciplines," *JPT*, June, pp. 555–558.

(143) 1968i. "Petroleum," *American Educator Encyclopedia*, Tangley Oaks Educational Center, Lake Bluff, Ill., v. 12, P-Q-R, pp. 156–169.

(144) 1968j. "Rock Structures: Diapirism and Diapirs," a book review, *Science*, v. 160, no. 3833, June 14, p. 1217.

(145) 1968k. "Giant Oil and Gas Fields in the United States," AAPG *Bull.*, v. 52, no. 7, July, pp. 1102–1151.

(146) 1968l. "Shape Up or Get Shipped Out," AAPG *Bull.*, v. 52, no. 9, September, pp. 1633–1637.

(147) 1968m. "Petroleum—Civilization's Life Blood," *Bulletin*, South Texas Geological Society, San Antonio, Texas, v. IX, no. 2, October.

(148) 1968n. "The Future of the Domestic Oil and Gas Industry," Symposium, Petroleum Economics and Valuation, Dallas Section, SPE of AIME, March 5, pp. 61–64.

(149) 1968o. "The Influence of International Factors on Domestic Exploration," Proceedings, Southwestern Legal Foundation's Ex-

| | | |
|---|---|---|
| | | ploration and Economics of the Petroleum Industry, Dallas, March 6, v. 6, pp. 25–44. |
| (150) | 1968p. | "The Impact of Natural Resources on Society," Proceedings, 4th Annual Meeting of the Texas Section of APIG, Austin, Texas, September 12–13, pp. 7–15. |
| (151) | 1968q. | "Shale Oil—Will It Ever Be a Reality?" Fifth Symposium on Oil Shale, Quarterly of the Colorado School of Mines, v. 63, no. 4, October, pp. 127–134. |
| (152) | 1968r. | "What Now—Geologists, Geophysicists?" abs., HGS*Bull.*, v. 11, no. 4, December, p. 10. |
| (153) | 1969a. | "Hidden Trends and Subtle Traps in Gulf Coast," AAPG *Bull.*, v. 53, no. 1, pp. 3–29. |
| (154) | 1969b. | "The Future of the Domestic Oil and Gas Industry," (1) *JPT*, February, pp. 149–152, (2) *The TIPRO Reporter*, "Viewpoints," Spring, pp. 13, 35. |
| (155) | 1969c. | "Needed: Greater Teamwork Between Disciplines," Institute of Petroleum (London) *Abstracts*, March. |
| (156) | 1969d. | "Needed: More Wildcatting to Increase Reserves," *World Oil*, v. 168, no. 5, April. |
| (156a) | 1969e. | "The Environment: The Earth and Beyond," Proceedings, 5th Annual Convention, Texas Section of AIPG, Midland, Texas, August 14–15, pp. 31–37. |
| (157) | 1969f. | "What Are We Going to Do About Petroleum Image?" *Oil Daily*, no. 4588, September 26, pp. 5, 6. |
| (158) | 1969g. | "What Are We Going to Do About It?" (1) *Drilling Contractor*, v. XXV, no. 6, September–October, pp. 41–44, 46, (2) *California World Oil*, v. 62, no. 19, October 15, pp. 1–3, (3) *OIL*, November–December, pp. 7–8, 33–34. |
| (159) | 1970a. | "Import Controls: How Drastic Changes Would Affect the Explorationists," (1) HGS *Bull.*, v. 12, no. 7, March, pp. 4–6, (2) HGS *Bull.*, v. 12, no. 8, April, pp. 6–7. |
| (160) | 1970b. | "Mr. Scripps Said It," (1)*Congressional Record*, no. S9816, June 25, (2) *The Landman*, v. XV, no. 8, July, pp. 26–36, (3) *Vital Speeches of the Day*, v. XXXVL, no. 22, September 1, pp. 688–692, (4) *Shale Shaker*, v. 21, no. 5, January, 1971, pp. 111–115. |
| (161) | 1970c. | "World War III—Is Under Way,"*Drilling-DCW*, October, pp. 35–37. |
| (162) | 1970d. | "The Exploration Geologist in the Seventies," Transactions, 20th Annual Meeting, GCAGS, Shreveport, Louisiana, v. XX, October. |
| (163) | 1970e. | "How Washington Can Solve the Energy Crisis,"*Oil Daily*, no. 4874, November 16, pp. 1, 2. |
| (164) | 1970f. | *Geology of Giant Petroleum Fields*, Special Edition, Memoir 14, AAPG. |

(165) 1970g. Foreword to *Geology of Giant Petroleum Fields*, Memoir 14, AAPG, pp. vii–viii.

(166) 1970h. Introduction to *Geology of Giant Petroleum Fields*, Memoir 14, AAPG, pp. 1–7.

(167) 1970i. "Giant Oil and Gas Fields in United States," *Geology of Giant Petroleum Fields*, Memoir 14, AAPG, pp. 91–127.

(168) 1970j. "World's Giant Oil and Gas Fields, Geologic Factors Affecting Their Formation, and Basin Classification," *Geology of Giant Petroleum Fields*, Memoir 14, AAPG, pp. 502–528, Part I: "Giant Oil and Gas Fields," pp. 502–528 (with A. A. Meyerhoff, Robert E. King, Robert H. Dott, Sr., H. Douglas Klemme and Theodore Shabad), Part II: "Factors Affecting Formation of Giant Oil and Gas Fields, and Basin Classification," pp. 528–555 (with Robert E. King, H. Douglas Klemme, Robert H. Dott, Sr. and A. A. Meyerhoff).

(169) 1971a. "Economics Without Which. . .!" abs., *Program*, Southwest Section of AAPG, Thirteenth Annual Meeting, Abilene, Texas, February 7–9.

(170) 1971b. "Rationale for Deliberate Pursuit of Stratigraphic and Paleogeomorphic Traps," (1) Abs., AAPG *Bull.*, v. 55, no. 2, p. 341, (2) Abs., *Program*, AAPG 56th Annual Meeting, Houston, Texas, March 28–31.

(171) 1971c. "Geology and Environmental Factors Affecting Giant Fields," (with A. A. Meyerhoff and Robert H. Dott, Sr.) (1) Abs., AAPG *Bull.*, v. 55, no. 2, p. 341, (2) Abs., *Program*, AAPG 56th Annual Meeting, Houston, Texas, March 28–31.

(172) 1971d. "Natural Gas," *McGraw-Hill Encyclopedia of Science and Technology*, 3rd ed., pp. 6–8.

(173) 1971e. "A Commentary on and a Review of the National Petroleum Council Report *Future Petroleum Provinces of the United States*," (1) Preprint, Division of Production, American Petroleum Institute, paper #360-1-F, presented to the First Annual Meeting of the Division of Production, American Petroleum Institute, Los Angeles, California, May 5, (2) *Annual Meeting Papers*, Division of Production, API, pp. 187–209.

(174) 1971f. "Mineral Economics Symposium: Introduction," AAPG *Bull.*, v. 55, no. 6, p. 771.

(175) 1971g. Preface to *Potential Technological Advances and Their Impact on Anticipated Water Requirements*, a report to the National Water Commission by the National Academy of Science, Committee on Technologies and Water, June, pp. v–vii. (Michel T. Halbouty, Committee Chairman).

(176) 1971h. "Petroleum Geology of the United States," a book review, *American Scientist*, v. 59, no. 3, May–June, p. 369.

(177) 1972a. "Rationale for Deliberate Pursuit of Stratigraphic, Unconformity, and Paleogeomorphic Traps," AAPG *Bull.*, v. 56, no. 3, pp. 537–541.

(178) 1972b. *Ahead of His Time: Michel T. Halbouty Speaks to the People*, James A. Clark, ed., Gulf Publishing Co., Houston, April.

(179) 1972c. "Port Acres and Port Arthur Fields, Jefferson County, Texas: Stratigraphic and Structural Traps in a Middle Tertiary Delta," (with Thos. D. Barber) AAPG Memoir 16, pp. 329–341.

(180) 1972d. "Geologic Framework and Petroleum Potential of Atlantic Coastal Plain and Continental Shelf," a book review, AAPG *Bull.*, v. 56, no. 4, pp. 824–825.

(181) 1972e. "Energy—The Gut Issue in America," Preprint. Presented before the general session of the Midyear Meeting of the Interstate Oil Compact Commission, Hot Springs, Arkansas, June 13.

(182) 1972f. "How Long Are We to Remain as Sitting Ducks?" *The Landman*, v. XVII, no. 5, May–June, p. 60.

(183) 1972g. "Salt Deposits, Their Origin and Composition," a book review, *Journal of Geological Education*, v. XX, no. 3, p. 166.

(184) 1972h. "Mr. De: A Biography of Everett Lee DeGolyer," a book review, *American Scientist*, v. 60, no. 4, July–August, p. 498.

(185) 1972i. "An Economic and Geologic Survey of Deep Exploratory Drilling," Preprint. Presented before the 1972 Deep Drilling and Production Symposium sponsored by the Amarillo Section, Society of Petroleum Engineers of AIME, September 11.

(186) 1972j. "Oil is Found in the Minds of Men,"*Transactions*, GCAGS, v. 22, Corpus Christi, pp. 33–38.

(187) 1972k. "The Energy Crisis," *The Time Break*, v. 10, no. 54, Fall, pp. 6–9.

(188) 1972l. *The Last Boom* (with James A. Clark) Random House, New York.

(189) 1973a. "It is Too Late for Herpicide," (1) *Drilling*, v. 34, no. 6, April, pp. 26–27, (2) *Congressional Record*, v. 119, no. 41, March, p. E1558, (3) *Well Servicing*, v. 13, no. 2, March–April, pp. 11–12, 26–27, (4) *American Oil and Gas Reporter*, May, pp. 32–33.

(190) 1973b. "The Influence of International Factors on Domestic Petroleum Exploration," *Congressional Record*, v. 119, no. 43, March 20, pp. 1–4.

(191) 1973c. "The World Petroleum Market," a book review, *Chemical Engineering*, September 3, p. 9.
(192) 1973d. "Power Play—Oil in the Middle East," a book review, *Geotimes*, October, p. 48.
(193) 1973e. "What This Nation Needs is More Dry Holes,"*International Oil Scouts Association*, v. 14, no. 9, September, pp. 18–23.
(194) 1973f. "Proposal for Leasing Federal Offshore," AAPG *Bull.*, v. 57, no. 9, pp. 1765–1766.
(195) 1974a. "United States Mineral Resources," a book review, AAPG *Bull.*, v. 58, no. 1, pp. 158–159.
(196) 1974b. "Oil is Found in the Minds of Men," *The Landman*, v. XIX, no. 3, March, pp. 8–17.
(197) 1974c. "Crisis by Consent," (1) *Fortnightly*, v. 4, no. 6, March 22, pp. 3–8, (2) *Shale Shaker*, v. 24, no. 10, June, pp. 180–184.
(198) 1974d. "The Western Pacific Island Arcs, Marginal Seas, Geochemistry," a book review, *Geotimes*, June, pp. 32–33.
(199) 1974e. "Oilfields of the World," a book review,*Geology*, v. 2, no. 10, October, p. 486.
(200) 1974f. Introductory remarks, *Methods of Estimating the Volume of Undiscovered Oil and Gas Resources*, (1) AAPG Research Symposium, Department of Applied Earth Sciences, Stanford University, Stanford, California, August 21, pp. 17–25, (2) AAPG *Studies in Geology*, no. 1, pp. 8–10.
(201) 1974g. "Demagoguery: Its Abuse and Effect on the Petroleum Industry," Ontario Petroleum Institute, Thirteenth Annual Conference, Toronto, Ontario, Canada, October 27–29, pp. 1–18.
(202) 1975a. "Energy '75," *Vital Speeches of the Day*, v. XXXXI, no. 11, March 15, pp. 335–339.
(203) 1975b. "Who Ripped Off the Public?"*National Energy Forum III*, Washington, D.C., May 15–16, pp. 101–113.
(204) 1975c. "The Energy Boat—Where Is It Heading and How Do We Keep Afloat Until We Get There?" *Exploration and Economics of the Petroleum Industry*, Southwest Legal Foundation, no. 13, pp. 51–62.
(205) 1975d. "It Could Have Been Different,"*AGA Monthly*, December, pp. 29–33.
(206) 1976a. "The Energy Dilemma—Needed: Exploration Without Political Interference," *Vital Speeches of the Day*, v. XXXXII, no. 12, April 1, pp. 370–374.
(207) 1976b. "Application of Landsat Imagery to Petroleum and Mineral Exploration," AAPG *Bull.*, v. 60, no. 5, pp. 745–793.
(208) 1976c. "Needed: More Cooperation Between Earth Scientists and Petroleum Engineers," SPE Paper #6107, Preprint, 51st

|       |        | Annual Fall Meeting of the Society of Petroleum Engineers of AIME, New Orleans, Louisiana, October 3-6. |
| ----- | ------ | ---- |
| (209) | 1977a. | "Divestiture—Competition or Nationalization?" (1) *Vital Speeches of the Day*, v. XXXXIII, no. 12, April 1, pp. 379-382, (2) *Proceedings*, GPA 56th Annual Convention, March 21-23, pp. 67-71. |
| (210) | 1977b. | "It Was the Best of Times—It Was the Worst of Times," *American Oil & Gas Reporter*, v. 20, no. 1, April, pp. 100-B-103. |
| (211) | 1977c. | "Teamwork Needed to Find Reserves," *Petroleum/2000*, August, pp. 146-149. |
| (212) | 1977d. | "Tomorrow's Energy: Where Will it Come From?" *Shale Shaker*, v. 28, no. 1, pp. 4-9. |
| (213) | 1977e. | "Response to Sidney Powers Award," AAPG *Bull.*, v. 61, no. 11, pp. 2038-2040. |
| (214) | 1978a. | "Future Trends in Exploration to Discover New Hydrocarbon Reserves Throughout the World and the Role to be Played by OPEC Member Countries' National Oil Companies," *Proceedings*, OPEC Seminar, 1977, pp. 14-47. |
| (215) | 1978b. | "The Impact of Natural Resources on Society," HGS *Bull.*, v. 20, no. 6, February, p. 4. |
| (216) | 1978c. | "Acceleration in Global Exploration: Requirement for Survival," AAPG *Bull.*, v. 62, no. 5, pp. 739-751. |
| (217) | 1978d. | "The Impact of Landsat Imagery on Scientific and Technical Orientation," *OPEC Review*, v. II, no. 3, June, pp. 22-30. |
| (218) | 1978e. | "Elimination of Controls: Key to Future Exploration," *The Landman*, August, pp. 56-65. |
| (219) | 1979a. | "Future Programs and Prospects for Resource Exploration from Space by the Year 2000," *The Future United States Space Program, Advances in the Astronautical Sciences*, American Astronautical Society, v. 38, pp. 721-740. |
| (220) | 1979b. | "A Viable National Energy Policy: Will It Ever be a Reality?" *Harvard Journal of Law and Public Policy*, v. 2, pp. 57-72. |
| (221) | 1979c. | *Salt Domes—Gulf Region, United States and Mexico*, 2nd edition, Gulf Publishing Co., Houston, December, 561 pp. |
| (222) | 1979d. | "Geologic Significance of LANDSAT Data on Some Known Giant Fields," abs., AAPG *Bull.*, v. 63, no. 4, p. 698. |
| (223) | 1979e. | "The U.S. Is Not 'Drilled Out'," (1) *Wall Street Journal*, December 27, p. 8, (2) *Congressional Record*, February 20, 1980, p. E693-694, February 27, 1980, p. E868-869, (3) *Drilling*, March, 1980, pp. 31, 96. |
| (224) | 1980a. | "Geologic Significance of Landsat Data for 15 Giant Oil and Gas Fields," AAPG *Bull.*, v. 64, no. 1, pp. 8-36. |

(225) 1980b. "Prospects for 'Giant' Oil/Gas Fields," *Pipeline Industry Magazine*, January, pp. 31–33.

(226) 1980c. "Texas A&M University Commencement Address," *Fortnightly*, v. 10, no. 1, January 18.

(227) 1980d. "Outlook Promising for Future Discoveries," *Petroleum Independent*, February, pp. 12–18.

(228) 1980e. "Global Giant Discoveries Generate Giant Pipe Lines," (1) *The Pipeline Industries Guild*, London, Spring, pp. 5–16, (2) *3R International*, May, pp. 228–295, (3) *Brunnenbau-Bau Von Wasserwerken-Rohrleitungsbau*, December, pp. 526–530.

(229) 1980f. "The Future of Giant Fields," *Offshore*, June 20, pp. 51–54.

(230) 1980g. "World Ultimate Reserves of Crude Oil," (with John D. Moody) in *Proceedings, 10th World Petroleum Congress*, v. 2, pp. 291–301.

(231) 1980h. "Methods Used, and Experience Gained, in Exploration for New Oil and Gas Fields in Highly Explored (Mature) Areas," AAPG *Bull.*, v. 64, no. 8, pp. 1210–1222.

(232) 1980i. "The East Texas Field," (with James J. Halbouty), abs., *Geology of the Woodbine and Tuscaloosa Formations*, Program and Abstracts of the First Annual Research Conference, Gulf Coast Section of SEPM, Houston, November 30–December 3.

(233) 1980j. "Some Requirements and Concepts for Obtaining New Remote Sensing Data to Explore for Petroleum and Mineral Resources," *OPEC Review*, v. IV, no. 3, Autumn, pp. 13–18.

(234) 1980k. "The Present Need to Hire Might Result in the Future Need to Fire," (1) *South Texas Geological Society Bulletin*, v. XXI, no. 1, September, pp. 11–14, (2) *Shale Shaker*, v. 31, no. 2, October, pp. 31–33, (3) *Lafayette Geological Society Bulletin*, v. XXVI, no. 2, November, pp. 8–9, (4) HGS *Bull.*, v. 23, no. 3, November, pp. 3–4, (5) *Corpus Christi Geological Society Bulletin*, January, pp. 12–13.

(235) 1981a. "Some of Tomorrow's Needs for a Vital Energy Policy," *Vital Speeches of the Day*, v. XLVII, no. 8, February 1, pp. 252–255.

(236) 1981b. "Centennial Decade: Its Meaning and Significance to Geology," *GSA News & Information*, v. 3, no. 5, May, pp. 71–74.

(237) 1981c. "The Time is Now for All Explorationists to Purposefully Search for the Subtle Trap," abs., AAPG *Bull.*, v. 65, no. 5, p. 933.

(238) 1981d. "In the Beginning," (with Jack Donahue), *Offshore*, v. 41, no. 5, May, pp. 298–311.

(239) 1981e. "Future Prospects for Worldwide Drilling," Proceedings, Minerals and Chemicals in Drilling Muds, Industrial Minerals Symposium, pp. 11–14.

(240) 1981f. *Giant Oil and Gas Fields of the Decade: 1968–1978*, edited by Michel T. Halbouty, AAPG Memoir 30, (1) Introduction, pp. viii–ix, (2) "Geologic Significance of Landsat Data for 15 Giant Oil and Gas Fields," pp. 7–38.

(241) 1981g. *Energy Resources of the Pacific Region*, edited by Michel T. Halbouty, AAPG Studies in Geology No. 12, (1) Foreword, p. vii, (2) Introduction, p. xi.

(242) 1981h. "Methods Used and Experience Gained in the Exploration for New Oil and Gas Fields in Highly Explored (Mature) Areas," Petroleum Geology in China, United Nations, pp. 132–141.

(243) 1981i. "Requirements for a Strong Domestic Energy Policy," *58th Annual Meeting*, International Oil Scouts Association, Houston, June 24–26, pp. 28–30, 101–102.

(244) 1981j. *Grady Barr*, (with Jack Donahue) Arbor House, New York.

(245) 1982a. "World Petroleum Reserves and Resources with Special Reference to Developing Countries," *Petroleum Exploration Strategies in Developing Countries*, Proceedings of a United Nations Meeting Held in the Hague 16–20, March 1981, Graham & Trotman, Ltd., London, pp. 3–16.

(246) 1982b. "Basins and New Frontiers," abs., HGS *Bull.*, v. 24, no. 7, March, p. 2.

(247) 1982c. "Natural Gas," *McGraw-Hill Encyclopedia of Science and Technology*, 5th ed., April, pp. 15–16.

(248) 1982d. "A New Philosophy for Petroleum Exploration," abs., AAPG *Bull.*, v. 66, no. 5, p. 575.

(249) 1982e. "Petroleum Still Leader in Energy Race," *Offshore*, v. 42, no. 7, June 20, pp. 49–52.

(250) 1982f. "Basins of the World and New Frontiers," abs., AAPG *Bull.*, v. 66, no. 7, p. 970.

(251) 1982g. *The Deliberate Search for the Subtle Trap*, Special Editor, Michel T. Halbouty, AAPG Memoir 32, (1) Foreword (2) "The Time is Now for All Explorationists to Purposefully Search for the Subtle Trap," pp. 1–10.

(252) 1982h. "Relationships Between East Texas Field Region and Sabine Uplift in Texas," (with James J. Halbouty), AAPG *Bull.*, v. 66, no. 8, pp. 1042–1054.

(253) 1982i. "Remote Sensing: A Significant Exploration Tool for the Geoscientist," *Remote Sensing of Arid and Semi-Arid Lands*, University of Michigan Press, pp. 313–318.

(254) 1983a. "Application of Landsat Imagery to Petroleum and Mineral Exploration," *Remote Sensing*, SEG Geophysics Reprint Series #3, pp. 93–141.

(255) 1983b. "Que Podemos Esperar De Los Viejos Yacimentos," *Energia 2001*, Ano 2, no. 9, Enero de 1983, pp. 38–47.

(256) 1983c. "Energy in the Reindustrialization of America," *Energy Progress*, v. 3, no. 2, June, pp. 66–69.

(257) 1983d. "Geologists Ponder Billion Bbl Question," *Offshore*, v. 43, no. 7, June 20, pp. 39–40.

(258) 1983e. "Geology's Heritage and Promise," *Texas Journal of Science*, v. XXXV, no. 3, September, pp. 181–187.

(259) 1983f. "Our Abundant Natural Resources," *Strategies for Recovery in the Eighties*, Oil Daily, November, pp. 65–76.

(260) 1984a. "Reserves of Natural Gas Outside the Communist Block Countries," in *Proceedings*, 11th World Petroleum Congress, v. 2, John Wiley & Sons, London, April, pp. 281-291.

(261) 1984b. "Energy in the Reindustrialization of America," abs., AAPG *Bull.*, v. 68, no. 4, p. 482.

(262) 1984c. "Basins of the World and New Frontiers," Transactions, Third Circum-Pacific Energy and Minerals Conference, AAPG, Tulsa, pp. 23–39.

(263) 1984d. "New and Potential Oil and Gas Regions and Fields of the World," in *Proceedings*, 27th International Geological Congress, VNU Science Pr., Utrecht, v. 13, pp. 1–20.

(264) 1984e. "The Mediterranean Sea: Its Origin and Evolution," (with Farouk El-Baz) abs., AAPG *Bull.*, v. 68, no. 6, p. 794.

(265) 1984f. "Administration's Policies Make DOE Worth Keeping," (1) *Oil Daily*, July 10, p. 4, (2) *DOE THIS MONTH*, July, pp. 42–43.

(266) 1984g. "Energy in the Reindustrialization of America," *The Leading Edge*, v. 3, no. 8, pp. 62–64.

(267) 1984h. "World's Petroleum Potential Has Barely Been Tapped," *Oil Daily*, no. 8217, pp. 73–74.

(268) 1984i. "Basins and New Frontiers: an Overview," abs., AAPG *Bull.*, v. 68, no. 9, p. 1203.

(269) 1984j. "Reagan Has Made a Profound Impression on the People," *Houston Chronicle*, September 6, Sec. 1, p. 27.

(270) 1984k. "Why Ronald Reagan Must be Re-Elected," *Human Events*, October 10, v. XLIV, no. 4, pp. 12–13.

(271) 1985a. "The Role of Engineers in America's Energy Future," *Texas Professional Engineer*, January/February, pp. 10–12, (1) Reprinted in *Engineering Times*, May, p. 4.

(272) 1985b. "Needed: Exploration Ingenuity," *The Practice of the Professions of Geology and Geophysics*, ed. by The Associ-

(273) 1985c. ation of Professional Engineers, Geologists, and Geophysicists of Alberta (APEGGA), April, Edmonton, pp. 102–110.
"Look What Corporate Raiders are Doing to Life in Houston," *Houston Chronicle*, April 24, Sec. 1, p. 27.

(274) 1985d. "Pratt Memorial Session Views World Oil Scene," *Geotimes*, April, p. 15.

(275) 1985e. "Circum-Mediterranean Has Potential," (with Farouk El-Baz) AAPG *Explorer*, June, pp. 28–29.

(276) 1985f. "The Hostile Takeover of Free Enterprise," abs., HGS *Bull.*, June, p. 2.

(277) 1985g. "What Happened to Morality in Business," an editorial printed under several different titles in the following publications: (1) "Free Enterprise Not a License to Raid," *Journal of Commerce*, June 18, p. 17A, (2) "Lure of Instant Gratification," *OGJ*, June 24, p. 12, (3) "Whither Business Morality?" *Dallas Morning News*, July 2, p. 13A, (4) "Hostile Takeover Bids: The New Carpetbaggers," Paul Harvey column (carried via Los Angeles Times Syndicate) *Abilene Reporter-News*, July 15, np, (5) "Is Free Enterprise Turning into Frightened Enterprise?" Texas A&M *Battalion*, July 17, p. 2, (6) "Are Hostile Takeovers Immoral?" *Amoco Torch*, September/October, pp. 2–3, (7) Letter to the Editor, *Geophysics: The Leading Edge*, October, p. 10, (8) "What Happened to Morality in Business?" *Texas A&M Business Forum*, Fall.

(278) 1985h. "The Hostile Takeover of Free Enterprise: Respect for Human Dignity," *Vital Speeches of the Day*, v. LI, no. 20, August 1, pp. 613–616.

(279) 1985i. "Energy in the Reindustrialization of America," *Economics and the Explorer*, ed. by Robert E. Megill, AAPG Studies in Geology #19, AAPG, Tulsa, pp. 1–3.

(280) 1985j. "New Data Spurs Interest in Bahamas," AAPG *Explorer*, December, pp. 34–36.

(281) 1986a. "Mergers and Hostile Takeovers: Effects on R&D Programs in the Petroleum Industry," *Issues in Science and Technology*, Winter, pp. 15–16.

(282) 1986b. "Basins and New Frontiers: an Overview," Proceedings of the Wallace E. Pratt Memorial Conference on Future Petroleum Provinces of the World, Tulsa, AAPG, pp. 1–10.

(283) 1986c. "A Far Worse Crisis," *Houston Chronicle*, March 30, Sec. 6, p. 1.

(284) 1986d. "Ruining the Future for the Sake of the Present," *Houston Post*, May 4, p. 3B.

(285) 1986e. "Exploration's Most Vital Need: A Resurgence of the Human Element," abs., AAPG *Bull.*, May, p. 598.

(286) 1986f. "Petroleum and Petrochemical Technology," *One Hundred Years of Science and Technology in Texas*, Houston, Rice University Press, pp. 172–186.

(287) 1986g. "Deterioration+Dependence=Disaster," *Houston Chronicle*, October 26, Sec. 6, pp. 1, 5.

(288) 1987a. "The Petroleum Industry at Its Crossroads," *Vital Speeches of the Day*, v. LIII, no. 12, pp. 381–384.

(289) 1987b. "Oil Industry Has Hit Bottom of Barrel," *Houston Post*, March 29, p. 3B.

(290) 1987c. "Deterioration+Dependence=Disaster," abs., AAPG *Bull.*, v. 71, no. 5, May, p. 563.

(291) 1987d. "Give the People Light," *Vital Speeches of the Day*, v. LIII, no. 21, August 15, pp. 653–655.

(292) 1987e. "Why Our Energy Plans Never Work," *Houston Chronicle*, September 6, Sec. 6, pp. 1, 4.

(293) 1988a. "Evaluating Mature Basins," abs., AAPG *Bull.*, v. 72, no. 2, February, p. 192.

(294) 1988b. "Exploration: The Highest Imperative," abs., Houston Geological Society *Bulletin*, v. 30, no. 7, March, p. 8.

(295) 1988c. "Exploration is the Last Salvation of Domestic Oil," *Houston Chronicle*, March 20, Sec. 6, pp. 1, 4.

(296) 1988d. "Energy Exploration: The Highest Imperative," *Vital Speeches of the Day*, v. LIV, no. 14, May, pp. 431–434.

(297) 1988e. "America Can't Compete Without Energy," *Houston Chronicle*, June 27, Sec. 1, p. 9.

(298) 1988f. "Evaluating Mature Basins," *Geophysics: The Leading Edge*, v. 7, no. 8, August, pp. 20–21.

(299) 1988g. "Circum-Mediterranean Region: Its Petroleum Potential," abs., AAPG *Bull.*, v. 72, no. 8, August, pp. 1004–1005.

(300) 1988h. "World's Offshore Petroleum Potential," Transactions of the Fourth Circum-Pacific Energy and Mineral Resources Conference, August 17–22, 1986, Singapore, Tulsa: AAPG, pp. 7–21. Also Foreword, p. iv.

(301) 1988i. "Basins of the World and New Frontiers," 27th International Geological Congress General Proceedings, Moscow 4–14 August, 1984, pp. 53–61.

(302) 1988j. (a) "Opening Ceremony Remarks," pp. 7–8; (b) "Frontiers in Hydrocarbon Exploration," pp. 501–511; *Deep Drilling in Crystalline Bedrock*, v. 2: Review of Deep Drilling Projects, Technology, Sciences and Prospects for the Future, (Proceedings of the International Symposium held in Mora and Orsa, Sweden, September 7–10, 1987.)

(303) 1988k. "Exploration: The Highest Imperative," Corpus Christi Geological Society *Bull.*, September, pp. 37–45.

(304)   1988l.   "The Role of Energy in the Reindustrialization of America," *GSA News and Information*, October.
(305)   1989a.   "The Role of Energy in the Reindustrialization of America," *The Professional Geologist*, March, pp. 1–2.
(306)   1989b.   "Oil May be Important to Houston, but Water's Our Lifeblood," *Houston Chronicle*, May 14, p. 5H.

# INDEX

Adickes, David, 162
Alberta Association of Petroleum Landmen, 29
American Association of Petroleum Geologists (AAPG), 1–3, 6, 27, 37, 53, 94–98, 103, 116, 159, 161–162, 173
American Institute of Mining, Metallurgical & Petroleum Engineers (AIME), 27, 37
American Petroleum Institute (API), 144
AMOCO, 52
Anderson, Martin, 54, 75
ARCO, 7
Army-Navy Petroleum Board, 26
Ashland Field, 26
Atkin, James, 75, 78, 84
Baghdad, 2
Baker, Warren, 150
Beaumont, 7–8, 37
Beckman, Petr, 55
Benedum, Mike, 166
Bentsen, Lloyd, 130, 143–144, 171
Berg, Robert, 149
Beteta, Mario Ramon, 132
Bintz, Marsa, 78–79
Bird, Kenneth, 97
Bogdanov, Nikita A., 159
Boggs, Danny, 76
Bookout, John, 55
Bowen, W. J., 55
Brand, Howard, 98
Brown, William W., 159, 172
Buchanan, Anne, 78
Buckley, William, 131
Bueno, Rafael, 159
Bush, George, 48, 153, 169, 181–182
Busterud, John, 76
Butler, C. M. III, 77–78
Byrd, D. H., 21
Calgary Chamber of Commerce, 29
Canadian Society of Petroleum Geologists, 29
Canas P., Maria Teresa, 159
Carter, Jimmy, 47, 50–52, 55–56, 74, 79, 85, 95
Chalmers, Dave, 82
Chang Weng-Ping, 94–95
Chen Sizhong, 96, 103
China National Oil & Gas Exploration & Development Corp., 94–96
Chou En-Lai, 94
Circum-Pacific Council for Energy and Mineral Resources, 28–29, 94, 109, 159, 181
Cities Service, 122
Clark, James A., 151, 156
Commission on Fiscal Accountability of Nation's Energy Resources, 108–112
Connan, Dr. J., 97
Council on Energy Resource Tribes (CERT), 105, 109, 112
Croneis, Carey, 151
Culvert, Judge Frank, 6
D'Arcy, William K., 163–164
Davis, Randall, 76
Davis, W. K., 55
DeMares, Roberto, 165

del Solar, Carlos, 159
Department of Energy (DOE), 52–53, 79–80, 82, 84, 105
Department of Interior, 105, 107, 112
Diamond Shamrock, 129
Dingell, John, 171–172
Drake, Edwin Laurentine, 9
Duncan, Charles, 79
Eckes, Charles, 165
Edwards, James B., 81
Edwards, Mickey, 81
Eggers, Paul, 49
Eisenhower, Dwight, 46
Emma, Miss, 156–157
Energy Policy Advisory Group Report, 56–74
Energy Policy Task Force Advisory Group, 83
Engineers Council of Houston, 27
Fairbanks, Richard, 75
Fielding, Fred, 81
Folk, Robert L., 97
Ford, Gerald, 47, 50
Forrer, Martin, 97
Friedman, Dean Mel, 150
Fuel Use Act, 50, 52, 87
Galey, John, 21
Gardner, Dr. Herman, 147
Goodin, Phyllis, 90, 91
Goodin, Robert, 90, 91
*Grady Barr,* 151
Gramm, Phil, 143, 171
Gryc, George, 159
Gudao Oilfield, 96
Gulf Oil Corp., 122
Haas, Merrill, 159
Haig, Alexander, 83
Halbouty Alaska Oil Company (Halasko), 7
Halbouty, Billye Stevens (see Stevens, Billye)
Halbouty, Fay Renfro Kelly, 80
"Halbouty's scholars," 43
Halbouty, Michel T.
   awards, 188–192
      AAES Hoover Medal, 167

AAPG Distinguished Lecturer, 161
AAPG Distinguished Service Award, 27
AAPG Honorary Lifetime Membership, 27
AAPG President's Award, 150
AAPG Sidney Powers Memorial Medal, 37
American Association of Engineering Societies' Hoover Medal, 150
American Institute of Mining, Metallurgical, and Petroleum Engineers Honorary Membership, 27
Engineer of the Year (Texas Society of Professional Engineers), 27
Engineers Council of Houston, 27
Houston Geological Society Honorary Life Membership, 27
NASA/Department of the Interior William T. Pecora Award, 37
SEG Honorary Membership, 167
SPE (AIME) DeGolyer Distinguished Service Medal, 27
SPE Anthony F. Lucas Gold Medal, 37
SPE Distinguished Lecturer, 161
SPE Spindletop Section, 27
Texas A&M University Distinguished Alumnus Award, 27
Texas Academy of Sciences Distinguished Texas Scientist, 167
Texas Society of Professional Engineers Engineer of the Year Award, 27
born, 7
China, 93–104

community involvement, 147–150
considered as secretary of energy, 81
Council of Energy Resource Tribes, 105–114
in Czechoslovakia, 160–162
during World War II, 26
early years, 4, 7–9
editorial in *Houston Post* (1987), 144
future plans, 181–182
import tax and, 130–146
Indian affairs, 105–114
marriage to Billye Stevens, 89–91
in Moscow, 92–93
oil embargo, first warning, 1–2, 25
oil exploration in Alaska, 6–7
people who influenced, 156–158
politics and, 46–74
predicts Arab oil embargo, 18–19
publications, 193–231
sculpture of at Texas A&M, 162
speeches
  AAPG (1987), 173–180
  corporate raiders, 122–128
  "Don't Make the Same Mistakes We Did," 29–36
  environmentalists, 22–25
  import tax, 134–142
  Independent Petroleum Association of Canada, 29–36
  National Strategy Public Hearing, 182–187
  oil embargo, first warning (1960), 1–2, 25
  OPEC (1977), 43–45
  "Petroleum—Its Meaning to America," 8–19
  "Retrenchment" (AAPG, 1986), 116–120
  Texas A&M commencement address (1979), 38
  "What this Nation Needs is More Dry Holes," 20–22
at Texas A&M, 4
Texas A&M donor, 148

warnings of fuel crisis, 3
as writer, 150–152
Hallam, A., 97
Harrison, Sam, 22
Hartley, Fred, 159
Haynes, H. J., 55
Hedberg, Dr. Hollis, 55, 97
Hermitage, 93
Herrington, John, 88, 143–145, 169–170
Hewitt, Linda Fay Halbouty, 90, 147
Higgins, Patillo, 10
High Island, Texas oilfield, 4
Hodel, Donald, 106, 108, 142–143, 169
Hoover Institution, 54
Houston Geological Society, 27, 123
Hu Wenhai, 96
Hugo, Victor, 21
Hutchison, William W., 159
Ickes, Harold L., 22
Independent Petroleum Association of Canada, 29
International Oil Scouts Assoc., 20
Iran, 2
Iraq, 2
Jaidah, Ali, 43
Jefferson, Edward, 55
Johnson, Lyndon, 48, 167
Joiner, Columbis Marion (Dad), 11
Jones, Mary-Gardiner, 109
Kang Shi'en, 101, 104
Kear, David, 159
Kearney, Joseph, 76
Kellam, Dad, 158
Kenai, 7
Kittrel, Charles, 126
Klemme, H. Douglas, 97
Kuwait, 2
Kyser, Paul, 13
Lake End Field, 26
*Last Boom, The,* 151
Leningrad, 93
Lester, A. David, 112–113
Li Jian He, 102
Lian, Harold M., 129
Liang Shengzheng, 96

Linowes, David F., 108
Lof, George, 55
Lonsdale, John L., 157
Love, Ben F., 129
Lucas, Anthony F., 10, 37
MacDonald, Peter, 109, 113
Mallory, C. King, 76, 78
Mankin, Charles J., 109
Markey, Edward J., 171–172
McKetta, John J., 55
McLean, Marrs, 158
Meese, Edward, 75, 83
Mesa Petroleum, 122
Messick, Richard, 76
Meyerhoff, A. A., 151
Michel T. Halbouty Chair (Texas A&M University), 149
Michel T. Halbouty Energy Co., 115
Michel T. Halbouty Geosciences Building, 149
Mitchell, Edward J., 55
Mitchell, George P., 130–131, 159, 170
Moore, Thomas G., 55
NASA, 37
Natchitoches Parish, La., 26
National Academy of Sciences, 27
New Deal, 22
Nixon, Richard, 46
North Slope, 7
Nozawa, Tamotsu, 159
O'Donnell, Peter, 47–49
O'Keefe, Bernard, 55
O'Scannlain, Diarmuid, 77
Onnie, Janet, 78
Organization of Petroleum Exporting Countries (OPEC), 2, 3, 43–45, 50, 85, 115–116, 130, 132, 135, 137, 146, 159
Pan American Petroleum Corp., 4
Peacock, Thomas, 77
Pecora, William T., 37
Peng Zuoming, 102
Phillips Petroleum, 122, 128
Pickens, T. Boone, 122–123, 128–129, 171
Poh-Hsi Pan, 97
Port Acres, 4–6
Prudhoe Bay, 7
Quenon, Robert, 55
Rains, Jack M., 149
Reagan, Ronald, 47, 50, 52–55, 74, 79–80, 82, 84–85, 89, 97, 104–105, 130, 132, 143, 153, 166, 169
Reinemund, John, 159
Renqui Field, 98
Rensch, Joseph, 55
Richfield Oil Co., 7
Robertson Research Co., 159
Rome, Italy, 91
Rule 37, 4
Russell, Fred, 55
Rutland, Roye W. R., 159
Ryckman Field, 52
Rymer, Father Michael, 90
Rymer, Marina, 90
Sabine Pass, 22
Salas, Guillermo P., 159
Saldivar-Sali, Arthur, 159
*Salt Domes,* 151
Saudi Arabia, 2
Schlesinger, James, 50
Schliesher, Max, 158
Shengli oilfield, 96
Silcox, John H., 159
Smith, Preston, 48
Snyder, Bruce, 83
Society of Petroleum Engineers, 27, 37
Spindletop, 7, 37
*Spindletop,* 151, 156
St. Luke's Episcopal Hospital, 147
Staats, Elmer B., 109
Stevens, Billye, 80, 83–84, 89–93, 99–102, 153, 160–161, 181
Stevens, Joy, 90
Stevens, Shyrrel, 90
Stewart, Mary, 82, 95, 114, 148, 154, 161, 163, 167
Student Conference on National Affairs (SCONA), 161–162
Suez Crisis, 1, 85
Sununu, John, 81

Swain, Frederick, 97
Swanson River, 7
Swindon, V. G., 159
Texas A&M University, 3, 26, 27, 46, 148, 149, 157, 161
Texas Mid-Continent Oil & Gas Association, 27
Texas Railroad Commission, 4, 5, 6, 22
Tissot, Dr. B., 97
*The Last Boom,* 151, 156
Thompson, Ernest O., 22
Thurmon, Strom, 81
Tower, John, 47, 48
Trabandt, Charles, 77
Union Oil Co. of California (UNOCAL), 7, 122
U.S. Geological Survey, 27, 37
Vatican School of Mosaics, 153–154
Venezuela, 2
Verleger, Philip, 55, 56

Vlcek, Jan, 77
Walker, Robert, 150
Walton, T. O., 149, 157
Wang Jinxia, 96
Wang Ping, 96
Wang Tao, 96, 103
Watkins, James, 182, 187
Watt, James G., 106, 108–110
West Fork, 7
White House Fellows, President's Commission on, 166
Willson, Sam & Betty, 82
Windfall Profits Tax, 51–52, 63, 87, 138
Wyatt, Oscar, 130
Yount-Lee Oil Co., 157
Yount, Miles Frank, 157–158
Zarb, Frank, 81
Zhai Guangming, 94–96, 159
Zhang Yancai, 101